Praise for John Feinstein's

The First Major

"[Feinstein] keeps up the quick pace even while fleshing out the stories of individual players, and offers insights on just what motivates and challenges the world's best to find another level on a stage unlike any other. . . . By the time Feinstein gets to the blow-by-blow of the matches, we're feeling that fire, too. And loving it." —*Golf Tips*

"Golf fans love Feinstein's books because he's trusted by the pros and thus can give inside information no other journalist can capture; plus he has a flair for telling a great story." —*Kirkus Reviews*

"A colorful story . . . that even non-golfers will enjoy. . . . Feinstein digs deep into the event's illustrious history, peppering his prose with astute observations and witty lines. . . . This [book] ranks among his best." —*Publishers Weekly*

"Feinstein compellingly re-creates the excitement, sometimes shot by shot. . . . A great moment in golf history, vividly captured." —*Booklist* (starred review)

"A rich and rousing account. . . . [Feinstein] does a magnificent job of creating drama. . . . An outstanding book that tells a compelling story for golfers and non-golfers alike." —Bookreporter.com

John Feinstein

The First Major

John Feinstein is the #1 *New York Times* bestselling author of the classic sports books *A Season on the Brink* and *A Good Walk Spoiled*, along with many other bestsellers, including *The Legends Club* and *Where Nobody Knows Your Name*. He currently writes for *The Washington Post* and *Golf Digest* and is a regular contributor to the Golf Channel and Comcast Sports Regional Networks; in addition, he hosts a college basketball show and a golf show on SiriusXM Radio. Feinstein lives in Potomac, Maryland, with his wife, Christine, and is the father of three children: Danny, Brigid, and Jane.

jfeinsteinbooks.com

NONFICTION BY JOHN FEINSTEIN

The Legends Club
Where Nobody Knows Your Name
The Classic Palmer
One on One
Moment of Glory
Are You Kidding Me?
Living on the Black
Tales from Q School
Last Dance
Next Man Up
Let Me Tell You a Story
Caddy for Life
The Punch
Open
The Last Amateurs
The Majors
A March to Madness
The First Coming
A Civil War
Winter Games
A Good Walk Spoiled
Play Ball
Running Mates
Hard Courts
Forever's Team
A Season Inside
A Season on the Brink

The First Major

THE INSIDE STORY OF THE 2016 RYDER CUP

John Feinstein

ANCHOR BOOKS

A Division of Penguin Random House LLC

New York

The Library of Congress has cataloged the Doubleday edition as follows:
Names: Feinstein, John, author.
Title: The first major : the inside story of the 2016 Ryder Cup / John Feinstein.
Description: New York : Doubleday, 2017.
Identifiers: LCCN 2017021758 (print) | LCCN 2017036666 (ebook)
Subjects: LCSH: Ryder Cup (Golf tournament) (41st : 2016 : Chaska, Minnesota) |
Ryder Cup—History. | Golf—Tournaments—Minnesota—Chaska. | BISAC: SPORTS
& RECREATION / Golf. | SPORTS & RECREATION / History. |
BIOGRAPHY & AUTOBIOGRAPHY / Sports.
Classification: LCC GV970.3.R93 F45 2017 (print) | LCC GV970.3.R93 (ebook) |
DDC 796.352/66—dc23
LC record available at https://lccn.loc.gov/2017021758

Anchor Books Trade Paperback ISBN: 978-1-101-97109-3
eBook ISBN: 978-0-385-54110-7

Author photograph © Christine Bauch Feinstein
Book design by Michael Collica

www.anchorbooks.com

Printed in the United States of America
10 9 8 7 6 5 4 3 2 1

This is for Dave Kindred, who has been a friend, a mentor, and an inspiration to me for forty years . . .

Introduction

PEOPLE FREQUENTLY ASK me where I get book ideas. The answer is there is no process, no rhyme, reason, or rhythm. It is totally random. In the case of the Ryder Cup, though, I can pinpoint the exact moment when I knew with absolute certainty that I wanted to chronicle what I believe is golf's most dramatic event.

It began shortly after six o'clock on a cool, cloudy September Sunday in the English Midlands. That was almost exactly what I wrote on the first page of *A Good Walk Spoiled,* my first golf book. The 1993 Ryder Cup had, for all intents and purposes, come down to one match: Davis Love III against Costantino Rocca.

Rocca, a stocky Italian with an appealing smile, had held a one-up lead standing on the 17th tee. He'd had a 15-foot birdie putt on that green that would have won the match and almost certainly given the Cup to Europe. But he'd gotten a little too bold with it and then missed a four-footer coming back as the crowd groaned in horror.

The match was tied.

In those days, before the Ryder Cup completely exploded in popularity and media coverage, having the privilege to walk inside the ropes as a member of the media was an absolute joy. As long as you didn't try to walk right down the middle of the fairway, no one bothered you.

As the players trudged up the hill to the 18th tee at the Belfry (a truly ordinary golf course, but one the British PGA owned, making it a Ryder Cup cash cow every four years), I fell into step with Bruce Edwards.

—

Bruce was Tom Watson's caddie and closest friend. Watson was the U.S. captain and had brought Bruce to the Belfry as an unofficial assistant captain since he was as respected by the players as by the caddies. There were people shouting encouragement at both players as we walked onto the tee, and I saw Watson, arms folded, standing next to Love, a few yards from where Bruce and I were standing.

Fifteen minutes earlier, Watson had arrived on the 17th tee with a grim look on his face. As Love departed the 16th green and walked to where Watson stood, the captain had said, "Davis, we really need this match."

Love is one of the truly nice people in sports. I've always said if there were a picture in the dictionary of a "gentle man" (or a gentleman), it would be of Love. He was a Ryder Cup rookie, fighting Rocca, the crowd, and his nerves every step of the way.

But when Watson told him that the U.S. really needed this match, Love almost burst out laughing.

"I almost said, 'No shit, Tom.'" Love said later. "But I kept it to myself."

The 18th hole at the Belfry is one of the great match-play finishing holes in golf—a truly wonderful par-4 that comes after sixteen holes that run together in one's mind (and one other excellent hole, the short par-4 10th, a terrific risk/reward hole).

The 18th also had plenty of risk and reward, with water running down the left side of the fairway. In 1989, with the Cup at stake on Sunday, no fewer than four Americans had found that water, leading to a 14–14 tie—with Europe retaining the Cup since it had won the matches in the U.S. in 1987.

Love was one of the longest hitters on tour, so if he crushed a driver it would run through the fairway and into the right rough—perhaps into the large bunker in the landing area. The question was three-wood or one-iron.

"Might be a one-iron," Watson said.

Love disagreed. He had the tee and wanted to give Rocca something to think about. So he took out the three-wood and smashed it down the fairway to a perfect spot. As the ball landed, I felt Bruce's hand on my arm.

"Thank God," he said in a barely audible voice.

He leaned over and began taking deep breaths. "I've never been this nervous," he said. "Never."

Bruce had caddied for Watson for twenty years and had been by his side when he chipped in on the 17th hole at Pebble Beach in 1982 to beat Jack Nicklaus in the U.S. Open. He had been in a lot of pressurized situations. To put it mildly.

"Never?" I asked. "Pebble Beach?"

Bruce shook his head. "This is different. This is bigger than that."

I looked around the tee—packed with players and caddies from both teams whose matches were over—and saw European captain Bernard Gallacher whispering in Rocca's ear before Rocca pulled a club from his bag.

A sudden chill went through me. This *was* a big deal—it was also remarkable fun to watch and to *feel*. I remembered something Bud Collins had said to me years earlier during an extraordinarily intense U.S. Open tennis semifinal between Chris Evert and Tracy Austin. "Some things in sports have to be *felt*. Seeing and hearing isn't enough."

The Ryder Cup is one of those events. As everyone walked down the fairway—Rocca had missed right and was in deep rough—I looked around and thought, "Someday, I want to write about all *this*."

It took me only twenty-three years to get around to it. I was at the Belfry for those matches as part of my research for *A Good Walk Spoiled*.

As it turned out, Love and Rocca gave me the perfect opening for that book, especially after Love later told me that he had stood in the middle of the 18th fairway feeling as if he might get sick in front of millions of people. Nerves are one thing; feeling physically ill about hitting a golf shot is another.

That's the way the Ryder Cup is though—for everyone involved. Every player who has ever teed it up in one has a story about walking onto the 1st tee to play his first match. Keegan Bradley, who played superbly for the U.S. in 2012 at Medinah in his Ryder Cup debut, can remember that first morning almost minute by minute.

"It started when I was driving to the golf course," he said. "It was five thirty in the morning—still dark outside. But as I drove in, I went past the grandstand behind the 17th green. It was *full*—at five thirty in the morning. It occurred to me that no one would come anywhere close to that green for more than five hours—at least. And it was already packed.

"I thought, 'My God, what have I gotten myself into?'

"It kept getting worse. Phil [Mickelson] and I were playing the second match against Luke [Donald] and Sergio [García]. I was standing on the putting green when Jim Furyk and Brandt Snedeker left to walk across the bridge to the 1st tee for the first match. I saw them heading across the bridge and I thought, 'Oh God, we're next.'

"I walked over to Phil. I felt like I was hyperventilating. I said, 'Phil, I'm not sure I can go through with this.' I was wondering if there was any way at all I could get out of it. He just looked at me, smiled, and said, 'Don't worry, Keegan. Luke and Sergio have never lost a foursomes (alternate shot) match. Nothing to be nervous about.'

"By the time I got onto the bridge, I wasn't sure I could put one foot in front of the other."

Bradley's story is like a lot of others. He was one of the lucky ones. On pure adrenaline, he hit his first drive well over 300 yards, and Mickelson put a wedge so close he left Bradley with a tap-in birdie.

"After that I was all right," he said.

He and Mickelson went on to win, 4 and 3.

Snedeker was also a rookie that day. Furyk—who was playing in his eighth straight Ryder Cup—had the tee for the Americans. He hit a snap hook.

"I should have been thinking, 'Oh God, do I have a shot from over there?'" Snedeker said. "Instead I was thinking, 'Hey, if Jim Furyk can be nervous enough to hit a snap hook, then it's okay for me to be scared to death too.'"

Padraig Harrington, who has played on five European teams and was a vice captain at Hazeltine in 2016, may have explained it best for all of them: "I remember standing over the ball and standing over the ball and standing over the ball," he said. "At some point the thought occurred to me that 'none of these people are leaving until I swing the club.' It was a terrifying thought."

Terror is a very real emotion in the Ryder Cup. So is absolute joy and absolute despair. When the U.S. team blew a 10–6 lead on Sunday in those 2012 matches at Medinah, every single person in the American team room—players, vice captains, caddies—cried. That night, the unofficial tradition of the two teams getting together to toast one another and have a few—or more—drinks together was broken.

Most of the time, the losing team goes to the winning team's wrap-up party to congratulate the winners and toast them. When the Americans didn't show up, the Europeans sent word wondering if they were coming—or if they'd prefer that the Europeans come to them.

The answer was neither. "We were told, 'No thanks, we're just not up to it,'" said Ian Poulter, a huge part of that European win. "I remember Davis [Love] coming in to represent them, but that was about it."

"We just thought—we *knew*—they were too devastated to spend time with us that night," Rory McIlroy said. "The best thing we could do for them was leave them alone."

Major championships bring out major emotions—especially when there is a dramatic finish. When Phil Mickelson played superbly in 2016 at Royal Troon but lost the Open Championship to Henrik Stenson because Stenson played historically well, there was consolation in knowing he had played great golf and that there was no shame in finishing second to Stenson that day.

There is no second place at the Ryder Cup—no consolation prize. Playing well on a losing team does almost nothing to make the defeat more bearable. At the Ryder Cup, one team wins and one team loses. No one finishes second.

That may explain why Bubba Watson, who was the thirteenth man on a twelve-man American team in 2016, wept after the U.S. won the matches at Hazeltine. Watson had played on losing American teams in 2010, 2012, and 2014. Early in 2016 he had talked about how much he wanted to be part of a winning team *once* before he retired.

But he had lost out to Ryan Moore for the final spot on Love's team and went to Hazeltine as a last-second vice captain because he wanted to be part of the team—in any way possible. He had surprised even his would-be teammates by throwing body and soul into the week.

As fate would have it, Moore scored the clinching point for the U.S. on Sunday afternoon. In the midst of the celebration next to the 18th green, Watson found Moore, hugged him, and then leaned down (Watson is six-three, Moore five-nine) and kissed him firmly on the cheek.

"I love you, man," Watson said. "I love you."

Then he wept. And he hadn't hit a single shot.

—

Ian Poulter didn't play at Hazeltine either. Like Bubba Watson, he was a vice captain, only on the losing side. It was a feeling Poulter was unaccustomed to, having played in five Ryder Cups for Europe, winning four times. Poulter has never won a major title, but he is considered one of the great Ryder Cup players of all time, with a record of 12-4-1.

In 2012, when Europe pulled off the "Miracle at Medinah" (better known in the U.S. as the "Meltdown at Medinah"), it was Poulter leading the way as Europe rallied from what had been a 10–4 deficit on Saturday afternoon to what became a 14½–13½ win on Sunday evening.

Poulter started the rally in Saturday's final four-ball match when he birdied the last five holes to give him and Rory McIlroy a come-from-behind one-up victory over Jason Dufner and Zach Johnson. Since Sergio García and Luke Donald had pulled out a one-up victory over Tiger Woods and Steve Stricker a few minutes earlier, the 10–4 lead the U.S. had enjoyed suddenly became 10–6—and Europe had all the momentum.

"I remember looking at the board at some point and thinking to myself, 'This is a blowout, we're getting embarrassed,'" McIlroy remembered. "Then Ian went on that run and it was like a jolt of electricity went through all of us. We charged into the team room that night feeling like we were *leading* 10–6. We were convinced we were going to win."

McIlroy likes to jokingly point out to people that he started the rally by birdieing the 13th hole, but he's the first to admit that Poulter was the hero that weekend.

The Americans were fully aware of how remarkably Poulter had played. "When we shook hands on 18 after he'd made the fifth birdie, I said, 'Great playing, man, just unbelievable,'" Dufner said. "Then I turned to Rory and said, 'Glad to play with you today.'"

McIlroy understood. He *had* birdied 13, but Poulter had won the match.

"You cannot—*cannot*—describe what that feels like," Poulter said. "I've had good moments in my career, very good ones. I've been in contention on Sunday at majors. But there is nothing like the feeling in that cauldron. It's not just electrifying, it's someplace out there beyond electrifying."

The next night, after Europe had rallied to win, Lee Westwood, who is the third leading scorer in European Ryder Cup history (behind only Nick Faldo and Colin Montgomerie), made an announcement during the Euros' raucous post-victory press conference.

"We have a new system for picking the team going forward," he said. "It'll be eight guys on points, three captain's picks, and Poults—regardless of how he's playing."

That scenario had almost come into play in 2016. Poulter was struggling with his game in the spring, but still holding out hope he would come around enough to allow Captain Darren Clarke to pick him for the "Poults" slot. Just when he felt his game starting to improve, he began to experience severe pain in his right foot in mid-May. Cortisone shots didn't help. It turned out he had an arthritic joint that doctors said required at least four months of rest and rehab. It meant he couldn't possibly play at Hazeltine.

"Hard to take," Poulter said. "I'll still be in the room [Clarke named him a vice captain almost instantly], but it won't be the same. Can't be the same. I'll miss it terribly."

The European team, as it turned out, would miss him more. When it was over, Poulter wasn't sure if that was the case.

"Painful to have to watch," Poulter said. "Helpless feeling. You miss a major, it's disappointing. You miss the Ryder Cup, it's heartbreaking."

Or, as American Jimmy Walker put it early in 2016 when it appeared he might not make the team, "I don't think I can watch if I'm not playing. I've played in it once. I don't ever want to not play in it again."

Walker won the PGA Championship later that summer—his first major title. One of the first things he said after hoisting the Wanamaker Trophy was "Winning this is absolutely great. And now I'm on the Ryder Cup team."

In truth, it might have been Rafael Cabrera-Bello, one of the six rookies on the European team at Hazeltine, who spoke most eloquently for all twenty-four players.

"The only problem with this weekend," he said, "is that now I feel as if playing in any other tournament is ruined for me because this was so good."

Cabrera-Bello was on the losing team.

The Ryder Cup, as Tom Watson pointed out to his players before those

1993 matches at the Belfry, is the only event in golf where your legs will shake on the 1st tee. For the players, it is the most cherished moment of terror in golf. For the rest of us, it's just a moment to be cherished.

It has become golf's most intense and emotional weekend, which is why I have come to think of it as golf's first—and best—major.

One

REMARKABLY, THE ENDING was almost quiet. After arguably the three most raucous days in golf history, the final meaningful stroke was a 20-foot birdie putt on the 18th green at Hazeltine National Golf Club that Ryan Moore cozied to within a foot of the cup.

From there he had *two* putts to clinch the Ryder Cup for the United States. Lee Westwood wasn't going to make him bother with a tap-in. He conceded the putt—and their match—and, for the first time in eight years, the U.S. had won the Ryder Cup.

It was 4:11 p.m. Central time on a bright, breezy, early fall afternoon in the southwestern corner of Minnesota, and an American quest—one that had, at times, felt like Don Quixote tilting at the windmill—was finally over.

Moore was thirty-six, arguably the quietest member of the American team, an eleven-year PGA Tour veteran who, a week earlier, had been the last player selected by U.S. captain Davis Love III. Given that he had been 2 down with three holes to play and had rallied to win his match *and* clinch the Cup, he might have been expected to leap into someone's arms.

Instead, he took his cap off and shook hands with Westwood. The crowd applauded and some broke into what felt like the millionth "USA!" chant of the weekend. Love, who had been given a second chance to captain a Ryder Cup team, gave Moore a heartfelt hug. Others lined up to do the same.

There were hugs all around for the American players, caddies, and wives. But there was no singing—as there always is when Europe wins the Cup—and no splashing of champagne. That would come later. Although Moore's win had given the Americans the point that clinched the Cup, there were still three uncompleted matches on the golf course, and, since Ryder Cup tradition holds that all matches are played to completion, the six players involved kept on playing.

Watching the quiet American celebration, Rory McIlroy was a little bit surprised.

"It was almost weird," McIlroy said later. "They waited so long, worked so hard, and played so well. I expected more." He paused. "Maybe they were just relieved."

Love noticed it too. "Honestly, for a second I thought, 'Hang on, am I wrong, did we *not* just win? Is it possible that it's *not* over? But then I looked around, and everyone—I mean everyone—had tears in their eyes. Some guys were just sobbing. Everyone had worked so hard for almost two years to get to that moment that the reaction was actually beyond joy or elation—it was more than that. It was like seeing your child graduate from college when you just well up with so much pride and relief and memories that you don't cheer, you break down and cry."

Relief. Joy. Catharsis. Every emotion was understandable. No American Ryder Cup team had ever been under the kind of pressure that Love's team faced at Hazeltine. It wasn't just three straight losses; six out of seven or eight out of ten—dating to 1995. It wasn't just playing on home ground, after an extraordinary meltdown the last time the matches had been played in the U.S., or the fact that Europe was playing six Ryder Cup rookies—on the road.

There was more—much more. There was the infamous "task force," which the PGA of America had formed in the wake of an embarrassing and acrimonious—among the Americans—loss in Scotland in 2014. There was Phil Mickelson's feud with Tom Watson, the American captain in Scotland. There was Love's labeling of his team as "maybe the best team ever assembled," the week before everyone made the trip north to Minnesota.

And finally, there was Mickelson's baffling decision to publicly take down 2004 U.S. captain Hal Sutton two days before the 2016 matches began.

"It's almost as if they're *trying* to figure out a way to help Europe win," said Chubby Chandler, agent and best friend of European captain Darren Clarke. "I have no idea what they're thinking over there."

Love had brought up New England Patriots coach Bill Belichick, whom he had spent a little time with during one of the thousands (or so it seemed) of public appearances he had made as U.S. captain. Normally one of the most open and honest people in golf, Love had actually been a little bit cagey when answering questions leading up to Hazeltine.

"I'm channeling Coach Belichick," he had said, smiling, on several occasions.

In truth, he *was* channeling Belichick—and many other successful coaches—but not by being circumspect with the media. It was all about creating an us-against-them mentality in his team room. There were twelve players, one captain, five vice captains, and—to a lesser extent— wives and partners, caddies and past Ryder Cup captains, who had been invited for the week. That was *us*. Everyone else was *them*. Even the fans, because Love knew they would turn on his players in a heartbeat if they didn't play well—especially after all the prematch rhetoric and the past failures.

There was no better example of that us-against-them mentality than Love's reaction to an on-air argument between Golf Channel analysts Brandel Chamblee and David Duval, on Tuesday night before Friday's start to the Ryder Cup.

Duval had played on two Ryder Cup teams—the one that came from 10–6 down at Brookline in 1999 to win and the one that lost at the Belfry in 2002. He was a former number-one player in the world and a major champion—having won the Open Championship at Royal Lytham & St. Annes in 2001. In short, he'd been a star.

Chamblee was a solid tour player, who won once in his PGA Tour career—at the 1998 Greater Vancouver Open. He got his degree from Texas in speech communications and has used his ability to communicate, along with a remarkable work ethic, to become *the* star on Golf Channel since going to work there in 2003.

Because he's never afraid to express an opinion, Chamblee isn't terribly popular among the current players, most of whom believe that former players should never be critical of current players. Like Chamblee, Duval has his college degree—most tour players don't graduate from college—and is one of the few ex-players who can stand toe to toe with Chamblee intellectually.

The questions asked most often on-air on the first full day of practice rounds leading to Friday morning's start of the matches were: Who's to blame for the U.S.'s past failures in the Ryder Cup? And was it lack of leadership?

Chamblee, as usual, was direct and prepared. He blamed the failures of the American team on the two men who had been the leaders of those losing teams—Tiger Woods and Phil Mickelson.

"A team takes on the personality of its leadership," Chamblee said. "If there's apathetic leadership, there will be apathetic play."

Duval adamantly disagreed. "You can't assign losses to certain players," he said. "It's not about leadership, it's about execution."

The two argued vehemently for almost ten minutes—with Frank Nobilo stuck in the middle, literally and figuratively. When Nobilo finally did get a chance to speak, he sided with Duval. At one point, Duval said to Chamblee, "I realize you're never wrong, I understand that."

The anger was genuine—not staged for TV. By the time Golf Channel's re-air of the evening show came on, word had spread—largely on the Internet and social media—about the Duval-Chamblee dustup. Several of the American players were watching the show in the team room on the lobby level of the Sheraton Bloomington Hotel—where both teams were staying. The hotel had been a Sofitel until Sheraton had bought it in 2013 and put $18 million in renovations into the property, in part because they were hoping to host the Ryder Cup teams. There were two large-screen TVs in the team room, and most of the U.S. players gathered around them, squeezing onto comfortable couches directly in front of the televisions to watch the entire nine-minute-and-fifty-four-second segment.

Love was sitting on the other side of the room, grabbing a late dinner, when he saw his players suddenly crowding around the TV.

"What's going on over there?" he asked.

"Something you have to see," several players responded.

Love could see that the Golf Channel was on and that the usual evening foursome of Rich Lerner, Chamblee, Nobilo, and Duval was on the screen.

"I slammed my hand on the table and I said, 'Hey, fellas, what did we say about tuning out the noise this week?'" Love remembered. "They all just looked at me and said, 'Okay, okay, but you gotta see *this*.'"

So Love put his dinner aside and walked over to where the sound was turned up and he could hear the argument unfold. Brandt Snedeker, who had heard the debate the first time it aired, had attached a microphone to one of the TVs to make sure the sound could be heard in the entire room.

Jordan Spieth had also seen it and sat on the arm of a couch where Mickelson was feeling concerned.

"We'd done everything right until then," he said. "I was thinking, 'Oh boy, this is going to upset Phil and set us back.' I was watching him closely. By the time it was over, he had this big grin on his face and I knew it was okay."

Love's players were practically cheering Duval on by the time the segment finished.

Love suddenly had an idea. He turned to Mac Barnhardt, who has been his agent forever, and had also represented Duval in his TV negotiations.

"You have any idea where Duval's staying?" he asked.

"Sure," Barnhardt said. "Right here."

Love was a bit baffled. The PGA of America controlled all 244 rooms in the hotel for the week, and no one from the media was supposed to be staying there. Duval was a past major champion and a two-time Ryder Cupper, but he was in town as a member of the media.

"I got him in," Barnhardt admitted. "Used your name. He just wanted to see the guys as the week went on."

Love wasn't the least bit upset. He looked up Duval's number in his phone and texted him.

"Where are you right now?" he wrote.

"Pulling up to the hotel," Duval answered.

"I'll meet you in the lobby," Love wrote back.

He walked quickly from the big room at the back of the skylit lobby to the entrance of the hotel without saying anything to anyone. "It would be great if you came into the room right now," Love told Duval. "Everybody was watching. They're all fired up about it."

Duval agreed and walked across the lobby with Love. He waited around a corner and out of sight while Love went back into the room. "Hey, fellas," he said. "There's someone outside who wants to say hello to you guys."

He signaled Jim Furyk, one of his vice captains, whom he had stationed in the doorway, and Furyk waved Duval inside. When Duval walked in the door, the room exploded.

"It was perfect," Love said. "It was totally unscripted, not part of any of the planning for the week."

Love asked Duval to say a few words. Duval did—talking about the difference between statistics and passion. "You can't explain the Ryder Cup with statistics," he said. "That's what I was trying to tell Brandel. You have to experience the Ryder Cup as a player to understand what it really means. I will always think of myself as a Ryder Cupper—even though I haven't played in one since 2002."

The players loved this. To them, Duval was one of their own, one of *us* because he had played in the Ryder Cup, knew the pressures that came with it, and was *on their side.* Chamblee had been a very solid tour player and was then probably the most insightful golf commentator on TV. But he was, most definitely, one of *them.*

The passion that filled the room that night—almost sixty hours before the first shot was going to be struck on Friday morning—may explain why, in their moment of victory, the Americans seemed almost subdued. Later, several of them would stand on the bridge that had been built across the walkway that would normally lead from the clubhouse to the range (built there so players could make that walk without having to push through throngs) and spray cheering fans with champagne. But they weren't about to go all out with TV cameras rolling; with the media around; even with adoring fans chanting their names and their country's initials repeatedly.

"Wow, it was crowded up there," Zach Johnson said later. "My wife [Kim] is a little claustrophobic. She was definitely not comfortable."

The real celebration would come later, back at the hotel, inside the team room, where even player agents and swing coaches would eventually be asked to leave the American party. No one who wasn't *us* belonged in the room. No exceptions.

Because even in their moment of ultimate victory, there was still a good deal of scar tissue in the room. For some—like Mickelson and Love—it dated back more than twenty years. For others—Spieth, Patrick Reed, Jimmy Walker—it went back only a couple of years. But they all felt it—perhaps even more than their joy.

Amid all the hugging and sobbing that afternoon, Love had been struck most by the reaction of Bubba Watson—the last man left off the team, who had volunteered to be a vice captain after Love gave him the news he wouldn't be playing.

"Bubba came over and was just sobbing on my shoulder," Love said. "My son, Dru, was standing there waiting to get his hug. After a while, he realized this was going to go on for a while and he went to find someone else to hug.

"That was the moment it all really hit me and *I* broke down. Bubba hadn't even *played* and it meant that much to him. We were all just too emotional to storm the green and jump on one another."

And too exhausted. It had been a long week. And a long two years.

The process that led to the moment when Westwood conceded the final putt to Moore had actually begun four years earlier, at the 2012 Ryder Cup at Medinah Country Club, outside Chicago, a little more than four hundred miles south and east of Hazeltine.

It started when Martin Kaymer rolled in a seven-foot par putt on Medinah's 18th hole to beat Steve Stricker one up in the eleventh of Sunday's twelve singles matches. Kaymer's win gave Europe a 14–13 lead, meaning that the best the Americans could do was a 14–14 tie. Since Europe had won the Cup in 2010, a tie meant they retained it. When Tiger Woods and Francesco Molinari halved the final match, Europe won by a score of 14½–13½.

Kaymer ending up as the hero was a complete surprise—to him, to his teammates, to everyone involved. He had played poorly for most of 2012—dropping from number four in the world rankings at the end of 2011 to number thirty-two—and had just squeezed onto the team as the tenth of the ten players who automatically qualified, largely on the basis of the points he had accumulated in 2011.

Captain José-María Olazábal had played him only once the first two days, in the Friday afternoon four-ball matches, and he and Justin Rose had lost comfortably to Matt Kuchar and Dustin Johnson—Kaymer failing to make a single birdie.

"The only reason I played at all was because José wanted everyone to play at least one match before Sunday," he said. "I felt sorry for Justin having to play with me. No one wanted to play with me at that point, and I didn't blame them."

By Sunday, though, Kaymer was feeling a little bit better about himself and his game. A lot of it stemmed from a conversation he'd had after his loss on Friday with Bernhard Langer—the greatest German player in history and Kaymer's boyhood hero.

"He's still my hero," Kaymer said with a grin. "He sat me down and said, 'Where do you see yourself within this team? Do you understand how good these players are and how good you have to be to be one of them?' Knowing what a massive role he'd played in the Ryder Cup in the past—with good results and bad results—I knew he knew what he was talking about. It made me think how fortunate I was to be there, not how much pressure there was on me because I was there.

"A lot of people thought I played badly that year because of my swing change. That really wasn't it. I changed my swing in 2011 and won with the new swing at the end of that year. I just didn't deal with everything that came with being number one in the world very well.

"At the time, I was the second-youngest player [Tiger Woods being the youngest] to ever be number one. When Rory [McIlroy] and Jordan [Spieth] got there after I did, they handled it better than I did. That simple. I questioned a lot of it and a lot of my feelings about it. I still remember sitting with my father the night I became number one [after the World Match Play tournament in February 2011] and thinking, 'Is this it?' All the years I'd worked to get to this and it felt good, I was proud, but I didn't feel like I was a different person. I think I expected something more. When I didn't get it, something went out of me a little. I didn't appreciate the whole thing the way I probably should have.

"But talking to Langer made me realize again that I was truly lucky to be where I was."

Somehow, Kaymer had kept that thought in his head during the last few holes of his match against Stricker, knowing their match might decide the outcome.

"That last hour, I've never felt anything like that in my life," he said. "I knew exactly where the matches stood and the importance of my match. There wasn't any doubt, because we were off 11th and you could see the scores of the other matches going up one by one.

"I kept thinking to myself, 'How brilliant is it that your teammates have given you this opportunity, this chance to be a part of history?' That doesn't mean I wasn't nervous or that I hit every shot just as I wanted to. But I was never scared, never felt as if I couldn't handle it all."

On the 18th hole, Kaymer found the back of the green from a fairway bunker, but his birdie putt slid about seven feet past the hole. Twenty-one years earlier, Langer had faced a six-footer on the 18th hole at Kiawah Island that would have retained the Cup for Europe—and missed.

Now Kaymer faced an almost identical situation, only with a slightly longer putt.

"I never doubted I would make the putt," he said. "I wasn't upset with the first putt, because I wasn't hesitant, I didn't leave it short. I left myself an uphill putt that if I could just get on line—I knew the speed would be right.

"It all felt good and when the putt went in, I was thrilled in a way I had never been thrilled before and doubt I will ever be thrilled again. Winning majors [Kaymer has won two] is a great thing. But that's just about you; it's for yourself. This was about the team; it was about my country and it was about knowing how much [Captain José-María] Olazábal wanted to win. The look on his face when we hugged is something I'll never forget."

Even as the Europeans celebrated on the 18th green—with Woods and Molinari waiting in the fairway to complete the final match—the questions had started for the Americans. It was Europe's seventh win in nine Ryder Cups and was, by far, the most stunning loss the U.S. had ever endured.

They had led 10–4 midway through the afternoon on Saturday, only to lose the last two matches of the day and then get outscored 8½–3½ in the singles on Sunday. Only once before had a team come from 10–6 down on Sunday—the U.S. at Brookline in 1999—but that had been on home ground. To win from 10–6 down on the road was almost unthinkable.

People questioned aspects of Captain Davis Love's strategy, most notably his decision to sit Phil Mickelson and Keegan Bradley on Saturday afternoon when the two of them had dominated three matches. When Mickelson defended Love by saying it was *his* idea to not play, the doubters said, "Aha, Love's too much of a players' captain—he let Mickelson talk him into a mistake."

Maybe Love, one of golf's nicest men, hadn't been tough enough on his team—although for most of two days his approach had apparently been letter-perfect. A change was needed. Einstein's oft-repeated saying, "Insanity is doing the same thing over and over again and expecting different results," was raised by many.

One person who had thought that was someone who had been up close with the U.S. team at Medinah, even though few who watched the matches knew who he was. His name was Ted Bishop. And he was about to change Ryder Cup history.

Ted Bishop was at Medinah as the vice president of the PGA of America—meaning he was the incoming president, his two-year term scheduled to begin in November. He watched from inside the ropes as the U.S. raced to a big lead only to collapse on the final day.

Perhaps the most important task that awaited Bishop was picking the next American Ryder Cup captain. That was both a burden and a privilege handed to each PGA president. All had advisers—the other two PGA officers, the vice president, and the secretary—and the PGA staff, most notably the CEO and those who worked on the Ryder Cup year after year. The most important of those was probably Julius Mason, who was the vice president of communications and had worked on every Ryder Cup since 1993. That was the last year the U.S. had won the Cup on European soil. The captain had been Tom Watson.

Years earlier, Mason had written down a list of potential U.S. captains on a piece of paper he kept in his desk drawer. Ryder Cup captains were almost always men who had won a major championship—preferably the PGA Championship—and were somewhere between forty-five and fifty-five, meaning their playing careers (the Senior tour aside) were either winding down or over.

The name on Mason's list for 2014 was David Toms—who fit all the basic criteria. Like Love, he was a past PGA champion, someone who was highly respected by his fellow pros. Toms would be forty-seven when the 2014 Ryder Cup was contested at Gleneagles in Scotland. Love had been forty-eight at Medinah. Corey Pavin had been fifty during the matches in Wales in 2010, and Paul Azinger, the last American captain to win, had been forty-eight when the U.S. had won at Valhalla in Kentucky in 2008.

Certainly no one would have objected to Toms as captain. There were only two players in the previous thirty years who clearly should have been captains and had been overlooked. The first was Larry Nelson—a three-time major champion (including two PGAs) who had fought in Vietnam. Nelson was an ideal person to lead a team representing his country. The other oversight was Hale Irwin, a three-time U.S. Open champion.

Irwin never understood why he was overlooked, although the fact that he was still very competitive as a player into his late forties may have hurt him. The fact that his major wins were all U.S. Opens and not PGAs might also have been a factor.

"I have no idea why I didn't ever get picked," Irwin said at Hazeltine during the 2016 Cup. "It would have been my greatest honor."

Nelson feels the same way. A year younger than Irwin, his time also should have come in the 1990s—he turned fifty in 1997. But Dave Stockton got the nod in 1991; Watson in 1993; Lanny Wadkins in 1995; Tom Kite in 1997; and Ben Crenshaw in 1999. Even though only Watson, with eight, had won more majors than Nelson, the others were all considered bigger names than the soft-spoken Nelson.

One might have thought that having a big name as captain wouldn't matter to the PGA of America. Azinger found out that wasn't the case when he met with PGA officials in 2014, after the U.S. had lost the Cup for a third straight time. Azinger, as the only winning American captain of the twenty-first century, had been asked to drive from his home in Bradenton, Florida, to PGA headquarters in Palm Beach as an unofficial consultant before the PGA decided what to do next.

"Do you want a captain who can win the Ryder Cup for you or sell the Ryder Cup for you?" Azinger asked.

"Both" was the answer.

"I gave them points for honesty," Azinger said.

Ted Bishop wasn't all that concerned with selling the Ryder Cup that would take place during his presidency. For one thing, it would be held in Scotland. That meant it was the responsibility of the European Tour to sell it. His job was to try to win it.

He was convinced that the best man to do that job for him was Tom Watson.

In many ways, Watson being the captain in 2014 made perfect sense. Five of his eight major championship wins had been at the British Open—or, as it is known in Europe, "The Open Championship." He was beloved throughout Great Britain, but especially in Scotland, where he had won four of his five Opens.

He was also the last American captain to win the Cup on European soil—in 1993. And he was about as respected as anyone in golf; not an iconic figure on the same level as Arnold Palmer or Jack Nicklaus, but one short step below them.

Bishop didn't know Watson—had never even met him. But he was able to get his phone number and called to ask if he would be interested in being captain again.

"Ted, I've been waiting for this call for a long time," Watson told him—once he'd figured out who Bishop was.

"I'd been hoping to get another shot at being captain for years," Watson said later. "I sat and watched us lose time after time, and it was torture. I honestly believed I could help. I think the PGA of America had known that for a while, but the tradition had become that you captained once and that was it. I understood that. But with each loss, I wanted another crack at it even more."

In all, six men had captained more than one American Ryder Cup team (Walter Hagen had captained the first six), but the last to do so had been Nicklaus in 1987. That was a special circumstance, since the matches were being held at Muirfield Village Golf Club in Dublin, Ohio, the club that Nicklaus had founded, built, designed, and owned. It didn't make sense for anyone else to captain.

As it turned out, Europe won the Cup that year, the first time since 1951—and the second time in history—that the U.S. had lost the matches on home ground. The European players were so thrilled with their 15–13 victory that they danced on the 18th green.

"I hated to lose, but if an American captain had to lose in the U.S. I was glad it was me," Nicklaus said years later. "I wouldn't have wished it on anyone, but I just thought I could take what came with the loss because, being honest, of my place in the game."

That didn't mean Nicklaus wasn't furious with the outcome. The American team arrived late at the closing ceremony because they were all at Nicklaus's house a couple of hundred yards away from the 18th green getting a tongue-lashing from their captain.

"I just couldn't believe how many of our guys hit it in the water at eighteen that day with matches on the line," Nicklaus said, able to laugh at the now-distant memory. "Honestly, I couldn't understand it. I felt badly later that I climbed all over them the way I did. It wasn't as if they weren't trying. Part of it was frustration, part of it was me wanting them to get the message that you have to be mentally prepared in match play for everything to be on the line on the 18th hole. For whatever reason, that day, our guys didn't handle the pressure of the 18th hole."

Those matches set a tone that changed only on occasion over most of the next thirty years. Beginning with Europe's 1985 win at the Belfry, through Kaymer's clinching putt at Medinah, Europe was 9-4-1 in a competition the U.S. had once dominated—Europe retaining the Cup in 1989 when the teams tied.

"It seemed like whenever Europe had to make a putt or win a hole, they did," Watson said. "It was heartbreaking to watch."

Bishop believed that he needed a captain who would *not* be one of the players' peers. They needed a true authority figure, someone they would look up to and respect. With Watson as captain, there wouldn't be any scenes like Saturday morning at Medinah when Mickelson had convinced Love to "stick to the plan" and sit him and Bradley out in the afternoon.

"Honestly, I would have said to Phil, 'Take a hot shower, get something to eat, and relax for a while,'" Watson said. "You guys are our best team. We need you out there."

In a twist, Watson would be involved in another crucial Saturday morning conversation with Mickelson, this time at Gleneagles. The outcome was different than at Medinah: Mickelson didn't convince his captain to change his mind. As it turned out, that was a history-changing moment.

Two

I T BEGAN AS a friendly get-together between players from the United States and Great Britain. The PGA of America, at the urging of a writer from *Golf Illustrated* magazine named James D. Harnett, had raised money to send a dozen American golfers to compete in the 1921 Open Championship at St. Andrews. Harnett's reasoning was that no American had won the Open—which had first been contested at Prestwick in 1860—in large part because so few American players could afford to make the trip.

A pre-Open match was arranged between ten Americans and ten players from Great Britain. According to newspaper reports of the day, it was referred to as "The Glasgow Herald Tournament," and was held at Gleneagles on June 6—exactly twenty-three years before the D-Day invasion of Normandy. The British side won 9-3-3 (winning nine matches, losing three, and halving three): there were five foursome matches—alternate shot—held in the morning, and ten singles matches were played in the afternoon.

Although the Americans lost the Glasgow Herald event, Harnett's goal was achieved weeks later when Jock Hutchison became the first American to win the Open Championship.

The notion of "U.S. versus Great Britain" matches lay dormant for five years, until Walter Hagen, by far the best known and most successful American pro of that era (he won eleven major titles), was asked to organize another U.S. team prior to the 1926 Open. By then, Samuel Ryder and his brother James had come forward to say they would commission a trophy to be awarded to the winning team.

Ryder was a seed salesman, who had made his fortune by creating "penny packs" of seeds—which were exactly that, small bags of seeds that people could buy to use in their gardens without having to buy massive amounts that they didn't need.

To this day, no one appears to be exactly sure why Ryder's new cup wasn't presented to the winning team—again Great Britain, this time in a 13-1-1 rout. There had been a general strike in May of that year, British coal miners protesting a cut in wages by the government. That apparently led to some doubt about how many Americans would make the trip. There are also histories that report that the Cup hadn't yet been made.

By 1927, the confusion had been cleared up. The Ryder Cup had been made for a reported cost of $400. It was a gold statue—with a golfer on top—and was (and still is) seventeen inches tall, nine inches wide, and weighed four pounds. A Ryder Cup "Deed of Trust" had been drawn up establishing the rules and logistics of the matches.

The first official Ryder Cup matches were held at Worcester (Massachusetts) Country Club with 12 points at stake. There were four foursome matches and eight singles matches—each of them thirty-six holes. It wasn't until after World War II that the format was changed to make each match eighteen holes.

The home team won the first five Ryder Cup matches—1927, 1929, 1931, 1933, and 1935. In 1937, the U.S. became the first road team to win the Cup, when it won 8–4 at Southport and Ainsdale Golf Club. For the next ten years, the matches weren't played because of World War II. They resumed in 1947, and the U.S. began to dominate, not only winning fourteen of the next sixteen matches—with one tie in 1969 in which the Americans retained the Cup—but often winning easily.

In 1961, the format was changed from a 12-point competition to 24. Two years later, a 32-point format was adopted. In truth, it didn't really matter how many points were at stake; Great Britain and Ireland (as the British team was called by then) simply couldn't compete with the U.S.

In 1973, the matches were played at Muirfield, considered by many to be the greatest of the Scottish golf courses. St. Andrews is the most historic; Turnberry the most scenic. Muirfield is the one most respected by the players.

Tom Weiskopf was a Ryder Cup rookie that year and struggled the first day for the American team, losing both matches in which he played. Jack Nicklaus went to the captain, Jack Burke Jr., and said, "Give me Weiskopf, I'll get him straightened out."

He did: Nicklaus and Weiskopf paired to win twice the next day. During their afternoon four-ball victory over Clive Clark and Eddie Polland, Weiskopf had a 15-foot birdie putt on one of the holes on the back nine and Nicklaus had a 20-foot birdie putt.

"Pick it up," Nicklaus told Weiskopf. "I'll make mine."

He made the putt, but regretted the gesture later.

"I disrespected the matches and the game when I did that," he said. "I almost made it into hit-and-giggle golf. That was wrong. But at the time, I didn't think anything about it. That's what the matches had become."

The U.S. went on to win, 19–13, even though Peter Oosterhuis heroically pulled out a half with Lee Trevino in the morning singles and then beat Arnold Palmer in the afternoon. It was a brilliant performance but didn't come close to making the Americans feel pressured.

Two years later the matches produced another American rout—21–11 at Laurel Valley Golf Club in Pennsylvania—with Arnold Palmer as the American captain in his hometown. In those days, there were still sixteen singles matches on Sunday—eight in the morning and eight in the afternoon. Some players teed it up twice. On that singles Sunday, Brian Barnes beat Nicklaus *twice*.

"And it didn't matter at all," Nicklaus said. "I didn't like losing, but Brian played very well, deserved to win, and I knew we were going to win easily anyway, so I wasn't at all worried about it. That was the problem: we all wanted to make the team, but actually playing in the matches wasn't that much fun because we *knew* we were going to win."

Years later, Barnes, who had battled a drinking problem for years, told Nicklaus he'd been drunk on the golf course that day. "Brian was a functional alcoholic," Nicklaus said. "In fact, he told me the first sober round of golf he played in eighteen years came on the European Tour, and one of the people who he was paired with that day was my son Gary. He told me he was dead drunk the day he beat me twice."

That year, Ken Schofield succeeded John Jacobs as the executive director of the European Tour. Schofield was only twenty-nine and had big dreams for the European Tour, plans to make it more than just a Triple-A affiliate of the PGA Tour, a place where those who couldn't make it to the U.S. Tour went to play.

Short and handsome, with a deep Scottish brogue and charm to match, Schofield knew that the European Tour was never going to earn any respect if it got waxed by the U.S. in the Ryder Cup every two years. His first idea was to limit the number of matches being played.

"I was hoping if there were fewer matches that our lack of depth wouldn't be quite so glaring," Schofield said. "At Laurel Valley, the outcome had been decided before the last eight singles matches. As it turned out, it didn't make any difference. They were just too good for us. Shame on me for suggesting it; shame on everyone else for going along."

Playing at Royal Lytham & St. Annes in 1977, the U.S. won 12½–7½. Weiskopf, who had been so nervous as a rookie in 1973, didn't even show up to play. He went hunting instead.

"No one blamed him," Nicklaus said. "He knew we'd win without him. That was the problem. We all loved representing our country; we loved hearing the anthems played at the opening ceremony; we loved all the folderol that came with the Ryder Cup. But the matches weren't fun because they weren't really challenging us."

By the time the 1977 matches were played, Nicklaus had decided something needed to be done because the Ryder Cup was dying a slow death.

"As long as we were winning and winning easily every time, no one was going to care about it," Nicklaus said. "The matches had to be more competitive. No one really cares about winning something until you know how it feels to lose it."

Nicklaus had been part of one of the few truly dramatic Ryder Cup moments of the previous thirty years. In 1969, with the matches being held at Royal Birkdale in England, a young British and Irish team rose up to seriously challenge the Americans. Nicklaus was actually a Ryder Cup rookie that year—one of ten on the American team—because of an archaic PGA of America rule that required that a player be a PGA member for five years before he could compete in the Ryder Cup.

As a result, Nicklaus hadn't been eligible to even make the team until 1967, when, after actually taking classes on how to run a pro shop that were required to become a PGA member, he earned the right to be on the team—too late to qualify for the matches that year.

"That was a wasted week in my life," Nicklaus said of his PGA training class. "And even after I did it, I only had six months to make the team. Everyone else had two years."

That meant that Nicklaus, who was a *seven*-time major champion, was playing in his first Ryder Cup in 1969. Then, no doubt to remind him of that, U.S. captain Sam Snead sat Nicklaus out of the morning matches on Friday.

By the time the eight afternoon singles matches began on Sunday, Great Britain and Ireland had a 13–11 lead. The outcome wasn't decided until the final hole of the final match. With the score tied 15½–15½, Nicklaus and Tony Jacklin, the twenty-five-year-old Brit with matinee-idol looks who had won the Open Championship that summer, stood on the 18th tee all square.

Both missed long birdie putts, Jacklin leaving himself about two and a half feet; Nicklaus five feet. When Nicklaus made his par putt, the U.S. could do no worse than tie, meaning it would retain the Cup. "The pressure on that putt was incredible," Nicklaus said. "I felt if I missed it, I would be letting my whole country down."

Even though, back then, almost no one in the country was paying attention. The matches weren't on TV, so only golf geeks would be aware of the outcome. Still, Nicklaus didn't want to lose to Jacklin twice that day (he'd lost to him in the morning) and cost the U.S. the Cup. Once he'd made his putt, meaning the Cup would return to the U.S., Nicklaus conceded Jacklin's short putt.

As they walked off the green, Nicklaus said to Jacklin, "I knew you'd make the putt, but I wasn't going to give you the chance to miss it."

That gesture, which went largely unnoticed at the time—except by an angry Sam Snead—has become symbolic of what the Ryder Cup is supposed to be about.

Snead was upset that Nicklaus conceded the putt, saying later: "When it happened, all the boys thought it was ridiculous to give that putt. We went over there to win, not be good ol' boys."

Snead's 1969 captaincy was at least as controversial as Tom Watson's was in 2014—it just came at a time when the Ryder Cup was an event even golf fans more or less ignored. Snead sat Nicklaus out for two of the six sessions, and most players were unhappy with Snead's demeanor throughout the week.

But there was no TV, no Internet, no Twitter. The term "viral" didn't exist. As the years went by, Nicklaus's gesture became an iconic moment because, in truth, it would never happen in today's world.

"Probably right," Nicklaus said. "The stakes have become so high. But I've never regretted doing it for one second. If the putt had been for them to win the Ryder Cup, I probably wouldn't have picked it up. I don't think people would have been happy with me if I'd just given the Ryder Cup away.

"But I didn't. We still took the Cup home, and Tony and I became lifelong friends. Golf is supposed to be a gentleman's game. I still believe in that, which is why there are times when I haven't liked the tension that's surrounded the Ryder Cup in recent years. In the end, it's a golf match—period."

Years later, Nicklaus and Jacklin codesigned a golf course in Bradenton, Florida, called "The Concession." During the opening ceremony at Hazeltine, the PGA of America brought Nicklaus and Jacklin back to remind people of their moment in the sun—not literally, though, since the 1969 matches *were* played in England.

It was a sweet idea, and when Nicklaus and Jacklin were introduced, the thirty thousand people who had jammed the back of Hazeltine's driving range for the ceremony stood and applauded. But the moment was lost when Nicklaus and Jacklin began reading lines written for them from a teleprompter.

Not surprisingly, the whole thing fell flat. Apparently there was concern that Jacklin, who doesn't hear well at the age of seventy-two, might not hear Nicklaus clearly enough to respond to him at the right moments.

It is impossible to overstate Nicklaus's role in the growth of the Ryder Cup. Like Ken Schofield, he was very concerned about how one-sided the matches had become. Which is why he approached Lord John Derby (pronounced *Darby*), who was then the president of the British PGA. Nicklaus and Derby had become friends through the years—by then Nicklaus had played in five Ryder Cups and sixteen Open Championships—and Nicklaus believed that it didn't really matter whether there were thirty-two, twenty, or twelve matches—Great Britain and Ireland simply couldn't compete with the United States anymore.

"Something had to be done," Nicklaus said. "I understood the tradition had been U.S. versus Great Britain, but that had been in the past when European golf was British golf—period. That had changed."

By then, continental Europe was starting to produce very good players—among them Seve Ballesteros, the swashbuckling Spaniard, who, a year earlier at the age of nineteen, had finished second at the British Open.

Derby and Nicklaus met over tea late one afternoon at the Clifton Arms Hotel, which was the headquarters hotel for the 1977 matches. Nicklaus brought Henry Poe, then the president of the PGA of America, with him to the meeting. Nicklaus pointed out to Derby that what had once been a British tour was now a European tour and that the Ryder Cup needed *something* to pump some life into it.

Derby listened—and agreed.

"To be honest, a lot of it had to do with Seve," Nicklaus said. "He was clearly going to be a star, and I guessed there would be more coming behind him. That's what I told John."

"Leave it to Henry and me," Derby said. "We'll get it done."

The next spring, when the golf world gathered at Augusta for the Masters, it was done. The Ryder Cup matches would be the United States versus Europe.

The Ryder Cup—and golf—would never be the same.

"The funny thing is, I came up with the idea to include Europe in the Ryder Cup because I wanted to be part of a competition that was more competitive—more fun—and then I didn't make the team in 1979."

Jack Nicklaus was sitting in the clubhouse at the golf club he had built outside his hometown of Columbus, Ohio. It was the week of the 2016 Memorial, the event Nicklaus had launched in 1976 with dreams of having it someday be considered a major championship.

In many ways, the Memorial and the club—Muirfield Village Golf Club—were modeled to have the look and feel of Augusta National Golf Club and the Masters.

There *were* differences, the most important one being that Nicklaus made certain that minorities—notably African Americans and women, who were excluded from Augusta until 1990 and 2012 respectively—were part of the club from the start.

Like Augusta National, Muirfield Village is a par-72, and, like Augusta National, its finishing stretch includes a reachable par-5; a difficult par-3 with water left; a not-too-long par-4; and a difficult par-4. That's not coincidence. The members wear gray jackets during tournament week that are as identifiable in their own way as the green ones the members at Augusta wear.

The Memorial never did become a major, but it is an important stop on the PGA Tour every year—one of a small handful of tournaments that don't always have a corporate name slapped on them. There is a presenting sponsor, but not a title sponsor. Nicklaus's event will never be called "The Waste Management Open" or anything like that.

Two days before the start of the 2016 tournament, Nicklaus sat at a corner table in the players' dining area, wearing his gray jacket, talking about the past while today's players almost formed a receiving line to stop and pay their respects to him. Some of the older players called him Jack; most called him Mr. Nicklaus. At the age of seventy-seven, there's no doubting Nicklaus's place in the golf pantheon.

"You know it was here that the Ryder Cup first made money," Nicklaus said proudly. "It had never made a dime before it came here in 1987. In a lot of ways, we showed the PGA how to do it, and it's been a huge cash cow for both sides ever since."

By the time those matches were played in 1987, the tone of the Ryder Cup had changed considerably. It had taken a while for the presence of continental Europe to make a difference, but it had kicked in during the 1983 matches at PGA National in Palm Beach—when Nicklaus had captained for the first time.

The U.S. had won easily at the Greenbrier in 1979 with only two continentals—Seve Ballesteros and Antonio Garrido—playing. The size of the event at the time is best summed up by Ken Schofield's description of the opening ceremony:

"It rained that day, so they decided to move the ceremony indoors," he said. "The only space available was the indoor tennis center, which only had a few courts. Getting everyone—fans included—in there wasn't a problem at all."

That was the first time the 28-point system that is still in effect today was used: eight four-ball (better-ball) and eight foursomes (alternate shot) matches the first two days and twelve singles matches the final day, guaranteeing all twelve team members played on Sunday. The U.S. won 17–11.

Two years later, there were three continentals on the team—but none of them was Ballesteros. He had become embroiled in a battle with the European Tour over appearance fees—he wanted more of them than he was receiving—and was left off the team as a result. The U.S. won 18½–9½.

It was in 1983 that the matches changed forever. It began when Schofield asked Tony Jacklin to captain the European team. Jacklin was a
huge star in Great Britain, having won both the British Open (1969)
and the U.S. Open (1970). He was respected and looked up to by all the
younger players in Europe. There was just one problem: he wasn't 100
percent willing to take the job.

"We met at the Sand Moor golf course in Leeds," Schofield said. I
offered him the job and he said, 'Ken, it's first-class or not at all,'" Schofield remembered. "He looked me right in the eye and said, 'I'll only do
it if everything's first-class. No first-class, no deal.'"

Schofield still smiles when he recalls his answer: "Well, they told me
to ask you to take the job, not tell you how to do it."

Jacklin said, "I'll take that as a yes."

And so, the deal was done.

"He meant that the team wasn't going to travel to Florida that fall
commercial—he wanted Concorde [the British Airways supersonic jet],"
Schofield said. "First-class hotel; first-class locker room; first-class *towels*.
I mean, everything.

"I realized he was right. How were we going to consistently compete
with the Americans if the playing field wasn't level? At that point in time,
we weren't even close."

With Jacklin as captain and Ballesteros back on the team and beginning to take on the role of spiritual leader, the Europeans almost won in
1983. The score was actually tied 13–13 with two singles matches still on
the golf course. Fortunately for Captain Nicklaus, the two Americans
still out there were Tom Watson and Lanny Wadkins. Watson pulled
out his match with Bernard Gallacher on the 17th hole, and Wadkins
hit a wedge to inside three feet for a birdie at 18 to halve his match with
José María Cañizares. Nicklaus ran over after Wadkins's shot landed and
kissed the divot. The unsung hero for the U.S. was Fuzzy Zoeller, who
came from 3 down at the turn to halve his match with Ballesteros.

Years later, Schofield and many of the European players remembered
Ballesteros's passionate talk to his teammates that afternoon in the team
room.

"He kept saying, 'This proves we can beat these guys,'" Schofield said.
"We were on their home ground and we were *so* close to winning. Two
years from now, it's our turn."

Ballesteros was right. Two years later, in 1985 at the Belfry, Europe won the Cup for the first time since Great Britain and Ireland had won it in 1957. They won in dominant fashion, the final score of 16½–11½ not reflecting how easily they had won. Sam Torrance, who would go on to captain Europe in 2002, scored the clinching point with a long birdie putt on the 18th hole to beat Andy North, one up. At that moment, Europe led 14½–8½. The U.S. never really had a chance.

Two years later, with the Europeans winning all five singles matches decided on the final hole (leading to Nicklaus's blunt assessment, "We couldn't friggin' finish"), the Europeans won for the first time on American soil, danced on Nicklaus's green, and took the Cup home on the Concorde.

"I certainly didn't like losing," Nicklaus said. "But that kind of competition was what I wanted the Ryder Cup to be when I went to talk to John Derby ten years before."

He smiled. "But I had no idea what it was going to become. No idea at all."

He wasn't alone.

Three

DAVIS LOVE GETS almost apopleptic when he hears people say the reason Europe has dominated the Ryder Cup for most of the last two decades is American apathy.

"If anything, our problem has been we've wanted to win *too* much," he said. "At times, we've tried too hard."

Love's right—up to a point.

There is no doubt that the loss at Muirfield Village in 1987 left a bad taste in the mouths of the American players. It also focused real attention on the Ryder Cup in the media and with fans for the first time.

The matches at the Belfry in 1985 hadn't been on American television at all. Two years earlier, in Palm Beach, ABC had televised the last four holes of the singles matches, and while there was certainly some drama, the result was the same as always: a U.S. victory. With the five-hour time difference between Great Britain and the U.S., no one bothered to televise the '85 matches live or on tape. Europe's victory might as well have happened in an empty forest as far as most of the American public was concerned.

In 1987, the matches were televised late in the afternoon on both Saturday and Sunday. For the first time, American golf fans not only saw the matches, they saw the U.S. lose. And they saw the joy of the Europeans when it was over.

That was when people began to care. Two years later, when U.S. captain Raymond Floyd introduced his team, he did so by saying, "Ladies and gentlemen, the twelve greatest players in the world."

Floyd was mimicking Ben Hogan, who had introduced his team in 1967 as "the U.S. Ryder Cup team—the finest players in the world."

The Americans backed Hogan up with a 23½–8½ victory. But that was 1967 in the Great Britain and Ireland era, and the venue was Houston, Texas. This was 1989 in the British Midlands with the U.S. facing a European team that included five major champions who would win sixteen majors in all—including a rookie named José-María Olazábal, who paired with Seve Ballesteros to go 3-0-1 in the debut of arguably the greatest Ryder Cup pairing of them all.

The U.S. team *was* stacked—with nine men who had or would win majors. But once again they were doomed by not being able to "friggin' finish."

After Paul Azinger had started the singles by stunning Ballesteros with a one-up victory, the Americans lost four straight matches decided on the final hole. When José-María Cañizares beat Ken Green in the last of those matches, Europe had a 14–10 lead. Even though the Americans won the last four matches, all that did was give them a tie—meaning Europe retained the Cup. That was the first time American players cried in defeat—because, score notwithstanding, it was a defeat.

Fred Couples, one of the 18th-hole losers, wept uncontrollably on Floyd's shoulder.

Having won the Cup twice and retained it once, Jacklin decided it was time to hand the mantle of the European team's captaincy to someone else. Bernard Gallacher, who had first made the European team as a twenty-year-old in 1969, was chosen to captain for the matches to be played in 1991 at a brand-new golf course on Kiawah Island in South Carolina.

Those matches have been glorified in both books and documentaries as "The War by the Shore." There's no doubting that the tension on the final day was as great as anything ever seen in golf, but the tone of the matches was far from what Samuel Ryder—or Jack Nicklaus—had in mind.

It began when a number of American players showed up dressed in camouflage outfits, the message being they were ready to "go to war" to get the Cup back. That opened the door to some boorish crowd behavior and some hard feelings among the players, notably Azinger and Ballesteros.

The two men had scuffled at the Belfry two years earlier when Ballesteros had tried to take a ball he said was scuffed out of play and Azinger objected. This time, it was an American ball that caused a ruckus. On the 7th hole Friday morning, Ballesteros complained that the American team of Azinger and Chip Beck had been using golf balls with different compressions—which is against the rules in four-somes play—and Azinger angrily denied the charge, then admitted later he'd made a mistake.

There was also the case of Steve Pate. He had injured his ribs in a car accident on Wednesday while being driven to the gala banquet. There was talk of replacing him on the U.S. team before the matches started, but Captain Dave Stockton stuck with him and paired him with Corey Pavin on Saturday afternoon in a match the Americans lost. The next morning, Stockton said Pate was unable to play. Under the rules, his singles match against David Gilford was declared a halve—each team getting a half point. The Europeans would insist later that Stockton had stolen a half point by holding Pate out on Sunday.

There was no doubt that the Ryder Cup had become a big-time event by then, although David Feherty, who played for Europe that year, *did* get a little bit confused about just how big when the Concorde carrying the Euros landed in Charleston.

"I looked out the window of the plane and there were people every-where," Feherty said. "I mean, there were thousands of them, hanging from the rafters, taking up every spot available to them.

"I was sitting next to Sam Torrance and I nudged him and said, 'Sam, look at this. I had no idea the Ryder Cup had become *this* big in the U.S.'

"He just looked at me and said, 'You idiot, they're here to see the fuck-ing plane.'"

Feherty loves and reveres the Ryder Cup, so much so that he wrote a slightly off-the-wall history of the matches. He was also, in spite of his insistence these days that he barely knew how to hold a club, a very good player before back problems ended his career prematurely. As it turned out, 1991 was the only Ryder Cup he played in. But he remembers it well.

"My most vivid memory of the week is Seve," he said. "Every night in the team room he would talk to us, reminding us that *we* were now the dominant team. He would tell stories about past matches—funny ones, poignant ones, inspirational ones. It was just unbelievable. He would walk around the room, giving guys shoulder rubs and telling us all how *good* we were, how he knew we could get the job done.

"I mean, for someone like me, it was unreal. I remember thinking, 'Wow, this is so cool, I'm actually Seve's teammate and his *friend*.' He was so warm, so giving. It was just great."

David Feherty paused. "Of course the next week the European Tour was in Stuttgart and I saw him in the locker room. I said, 'Seve!,' greeting my new mate. He looked up and said, 'Donald! great to see you.' Back to earth."

Feherty ended up beating Payne Stewart in an early singles match on Sunday. What he remembers—much like all the players—is the near chaos getting from hole to hole because of a lack of security and the wildness of the fans.

"I was trying to get from 16 green to 17 tee and I simply couldn't get through the crowds," he said. "I finally got up to the tee and a security guy *did* show up and said, 'Hey, pal, where do you think you're going?' For a second I thought he was kidding, but then he started to push me backward away from the tee.

"At that moment, Payne appeared, almost like magic. He put his arm on the guy and said, 'I completely understand your sentiment, pal, but I actually need him on the tee with me since I'm playing against him.'"

Feherty returned the favor by closing the match out on the 17th green.

When all the dust and bile and anger finally cleared, the entire weekend came down to match twenty-eight: Hale Irwin against Bernhard Langer. Each was a major champion and a future Hall of Famer. Neither had ever played in a match like this one.

Mark Rolfing, who is *the* expert on the Ryder Cup among TV commentators, was walking with that match. With about six holes to go, Tommy Roy, NBC's golf producer then as now, told Rolfing that he wanted him to leave the match to try to interview American Mark Calcavecchia.

Calcavecchia had blown a 4-up-with-four-holes-to-go lead against Colin Montgomerie and had been so beside himself after halving the match that he had to be dragged off the beach where he had gone looking for solitude and—perhaps—salvation. Calcavecchia was now willing to be interviewed, and Roy wanted Rolfing to hustle back to the clubhouse and talk to him.

"No," Rolfing told Roy. "I can't leave this match. It's going to decide the Ryder Cup and it's going to be unbelievably dramatic. Calc's interview can wait. This is too important for me to leave."

Roy decided to trust Rolfing's instincts. Rolfing knew what was going on. He could see Irwin, one of the calmest players in the game, bending over and taking deep breaths on each tee. At one point, Rolfing asked Irwin if he was okay.

"No," Irwin answered. "I've *never* felt like this on a golf course."

The match seesawed to the final hole. Irwin was 2 up through 14 but Langer made tough putts on 15, 16, and 17 to bring the match to all square on the final tee. By then, all the other matches had finished and all the players, wives, and caddies were walking inside the ropes trying to will their man to victory.

The U.S. led 14–13, meaning Irwin needed only to halve the match for the U.S. to take back the Cup. Langer had to win the 18th hole and the match to get Europe even at 14–14, meaning it would again retain the Cup as it had done two years earlier.

By then the late afternoon wind was howling and everyone understood that par would be a great score on that final hole. Langer managed to find the green with his second shot, leaving himself a 45-foot birdie putt. Irwin missed the green, chipped to 20 feet, and missed the par putt. Langer had two putts to win. His first putt—much like Martin Kaymer's putt twenty-one years later, slipped six feet past the hole. Kaymer was six years old on that afternoon and had never heard of the Ryder Cup.

As Langer and his caddie, Peter Coleman, stalked the putt, the green was completely surrounded by everyone involved in the matches. Feherty found himself lying on the ground right next to Lawrence Levy, an American photographer who had covered golf for years.

As Langer stepped to the putt, the silence was deafening, the only sound the howling wind. Suddenly, Feherty felt Levy poke him in the ribs.

"The last German who was under this kind of pressure committed suicide in a bunker," Levy cracked.

Given how tasteless the comment was, Feherty didn't want to laugh. But he had to clap his hand over his mouth to keep from doing so.

Years later, Langer said he and Coleman had read the putt with a slight left-to-right break but noticed two spike marks in that line. So he tried to putt the ball through the break, dead straight into the hole. The read had been correct; the ball broke inches to the right. The Americans had won.

They jumped on Irwin—who was too exhausted and drained to do much of anything except smile in relief—and on one another. They reminded the still-shaken Calcavecchia that his half point had been the difference.

The Ryder Cup had clearly gone to another level—as evidenced by the tone of the matches, the tension between the players, and the behavior of the fans. It was time to pull it back.

Tom Watson was the man chosen to do that. It wasn't because the PGA of America asked him to fix the problem when he was named the U.S. captain for 1993; it was because he believed it was his *job* to fix it.

Unlike Nicklaus, who says he watches the Ryder Cup in bits and pieces, Watson has always watched the Ryder Cup pretty much nonstop since it became a three-day TV marathon event. He had been thrilled to see the U.S. win the Cup back, but not so thrilled with the direction the event had taken.

"We needed to put civility back into the Ryder Cup," he said. "What happened at Kiawah, even though the golf was great, was not what Sam Ryder had in mind."

Which is why Watson spent a lot of time prior to the '93 matches at the Belfry talking to Europeans. He met with Bernard Gallacher, who had been named captain again for Europe, met with Nick Faldo, by then the best player in the world, and met with Ballesteros.

"It was actually brilliant of Tom," Faldo said after the matches were over. "He wasn't saying anyone should compete any less hard, he was saying we needed to play the matches in a good spirit. He thought the American fans had taken their cue from the players at Kiawah. He wanted us to send a different message to our fans at the Belfry."

The '93 matches still had their controversial moments. During the gala dinner, Sam Torrance asked Watson to sign his menu. It had become a tradition for the players on each team to sign menus for their counterparts after the dinner.

"Not now, Sam," Watson said, aware that there were two thousand people in the room—all with menus. "Let's do it later when it's just us."

Torrance was offended and said so. The next day the British tabloids ran wild. One headline read, "Menu-Gate!" Another screamed, "Fork You Tom Watson."

All that was just fuel for Watson and his team. Watson was already creating an us-versus-them mentality in his team room. Each morning, at the top of the schedule given to the players, was a "thought for the day." The one the players enjoyed the most was this one: "Remember, everything they invented, we perfected."

Just before the Americans flew to Europe, Ballesteros had been quoted as saying that the Concorde, as far as he was concerned, was just a taxi to bring the Ryder Cup back to Europe. Watson began a countdown from the minute the plane landed, tracking how many more hours the Cup would be on European soil.

"If I remember nothing else about that week, it's Tom giving us the hour countdown all week long," Paul Azinger said. "I can still hear his voice saying, 'Seventy-five hours until the Cup's back on the Concorde . . . fifty-two hours until the Cup's back on the Concorde . . .'"

When Davis Love made the clinching six-foot putt on the 18th hole Sunday that guaranteed the Cup was staying in the U.S., Lanny Wadkins's voice could be heard clearly as the Americans surrounded Love on the green.

"Cup's on the Concorde!" he said again and again. "Cup's on the Concorde!"

The next morning it was.

The tide, it seemed, had turned again: Europe had held the Cup from 1985 until 1991—two wins and a tie. The U.S. had now won two in a row, including the 15–13 win at the Belfry—the first U.S. win in Europe since Schofield had convinced Jacklin to take over the European team.

It swung back two years later on a Sunday afternoon at storied Oak Hill, outside Rochester, New York. The Americans had taken a 9–7 lead into the singles, and, given their dominance in singles through the years and the fact that they were playing at home, it was almost certain that they would be keeping the Cup for another two years.

Except Europe rallied, outscoring the Americans 7½–4½ in singles to win. The turning point was the match between Curtis Strange and Nick Faldo. With two holes to play, Strange was one up and it appeared the U.S. would—at worst—get a half point from the match. Instead, Faldo won the last two holes to win, changing the momentum of the afternoon.

That was Phil Mickelson's first Ryder Cup. He was twenty-five and had almost made the team two years earlier. In what might have been a harbinger, Mickelson sat out the morning foursomes on both Friday and Saturday—and wasn't at all pleased about it. He was even less pleased that he didn't find out he wouldn't be playing the first morning until the pairings were announced during the opening ceremony on Thursday afternoon.

"I just thought Lanny [Wadkins, the U.S. captain that year] should have told me himself," Mickelson said. "I think that's the way it should always be—captain tells a guy he's sitting out and why. But he didn't."

On Saturday, with the U.S. in the lead, Mickelson told Wadkins he'd like to play last in Sunday's singles. He had played very well in both his four-ball matches, winning easily with Corey Pavin and then with Jay Haas.

"If it came down to the last match, I wanted to be the guy playing," he said. "I just felt that confident. I told Lanny that and he agreed."

At the turn, Mickelson was 2 down to Per-Ulrik Johansson. Wadkins greeted him on the 10th tee.

"You asked for this," Wadkins said. "Get your butt in gear and beat this guy."

Mickelson did exactly that, turning the match around and winning 2 and 1. But as he came off the 17th green, he saw Davis Love waiting for him. Love had been another of the American winners that day, but he hardly looked like someone who had just won an important match.

"[Philip] Walton just closed Jay [Haas] out on 18," Love said. "We lost."

"It was a kick in the stomach," Mickelson remembered. "For about thirty seconds I got to enjoy the fact that I'd turned my match around and won. Then I felt awful. I remember saying to myself, 'I don't ever want to feel this way again.'"

Little did he know that it was a feeling he would become very familiar with over the next twenty years.

Four

T HE WIN AT Oak Hill for the European team was the start of an almost twenty-year stretch that became a biennial nightmare for American golfers and their fans. There was a pattern to the European victories: The Americans would be clear favorites going into the matches based on world ranking and the names of the players on the U.S. team—notably Tiger Woods and Phil Mickelson. But the Euros always seemed to find players like Philip Walton, David Gilford, and Paul McGinley—unknowns in the U.S.—who would be transformed into stars on Ryder Cup weekends.

Woods made his Ryder Cup debut in 1997, six months after winning the Masters by twelve shots and becoming *the* name in the game. "Tiger-mania" was the phrase, and it was a very real thing. It was as if everyone else in the sport ceased to matter.

"I've had players suggest to me we call it the TGA Tour—the Tiger Golf Association Tour," PGA Tour commissioner Tim Finchem joked—sort of—at the height of Tiger-mania.

To most, adding Woods to the American team that went to Valderrama in Spain (the first Ryder Cup held on the European continent) meant the U.S. was adding five almost automatic points. Except it wasn't that simple. There was really only one player on the American team comfortable playing with Woods—Mark O'Meara, his neighbor in Florida who had become his unofficial mentor on the Tour—and Woods was an almost silent presence in the team room, clearly not comfortable around his teammates.

"It wasn't that he didn't want to win, Tiger Woods always wants to win," said Mickelson, whose relationship with Woods in those days was famously unfriendly. "It was more about him being taught by his dad that his job was to go out and beat up on everyone. I think it was difficult for him to let go of that, to say, 'Okay, for one week we're all in this together, and I'll do whatever it takes to get *everyone* playing well.' That went against all his instincts."

O'Meara and Woods won their first match, but lost their next two. With the U.S. trailing 8–4 going into Saturday afternoon's foursomes, U.S. captain Tom Kite decided he needed to mix things up. He paired Woods with Justin Leonard, who had won the British Open two months earlier. They faced two European rookies: Ignacio Garrido and Jesper Parnevik, meaning all four players were first-time Ryder Cuppers. Two had won major championships that year—the Americans. And yet the match was halved, a big psychological boost for Europe, even if it didn't really need it.

Trailing 10½–5½, the Americans staged a mild rally on Sunday, but any real chance for a miracle turnaround evaporated when Costantino Rocca beat Woods, 4 and 2. The score was 14–10 with four matches to play before the U.S. rallied late—helped greatly by another rookie, Jim Furyk, shocking Nick Faldo—to make the final score 14½–13½.

As it turned out, that was Seve Ballesteros's last moment in the Ryder Cup spotlight. His game had faded badly in the years leading to Valderrama, and it was natural for him to be named captain for the matches in Spain. The joke among the players was that Seve not only picked the team and made the pairings, he selected every club, read every putt, and might have hit every shot had he been allowed to do so. Regardless, it was a triumphant and fitting climax for Ballesteros.

Two years later, in 1999, the Americans had their one real moment of glory, rallying from 10–6 down at the Country Club in Brookline, a Boston suburb. The win became a thing of legend, beginning with Captain Ben Crenshaw pointing his finger at the media during his Saturday evening press conference and saying, "I'm gonna leave y'all with this: I'm a big believer in fate. I have a feeling about this."

There were hundreds of stories later about everyone in the U.S. team room—wives included—getting up that night to deliver inspirational messages and former president George H. W. Bush and then–Texas governor George W. Bush speaking to the team. The younger Bush read a poem about the Alamo. Fortunately, few if any of the American players knew that every American who had been at the Alamo had died there.

Everyone spoke. It fell to Robin Love, Davis's wife, to speak last. Remembering how much Davis Love Jr.'s old friend and colleague Harvey Penick—who had taught Crenshaw, Tom Kite, and her husband—had meant to all of them, she quoted Penick's famous line on how to play golf: "Take dead aim."

The Americans won the first six matches the next day, aided greatly by the fact that European captain Mark James had opted to sit three players who hadn't been playing well coming into the matches throughout the first four sessions.

All three lost badly: Mickelson beating Jarmo Sandelin, 5 and 3; Love crushing Jean van de Velde, 6 and 5; and Woods, who had gone 1-3 on Friday and Saturday, beating Andrew Coltart, 3 and 2.

Mickelson and Sandelin was a true grudge match. They had played each other in the Dunhill Cup at St. Andrews three years earlier, in 1996. Sandelin had developed a routine where he would aim his putter at an opponent as if shooting him after making a key putt. Mickelson didn't like that in general and thought it especially tasteless given that St. Andrews was about sixty miles from Dunblane, which had been the site of a horrific school massacre earlier that year in which sixteen kindergartners had been shot and killed by a crazed gunman.

When Mickelson told Sandelin he needed to stop with the mock-shooting routine, Sandelin, by his own admission, told Mickelson to fuck off. That was the last time they spoke.

Waiting for Sandelin on the first tee that Sunday morning at Brookline, Mickelson was tempted to say to him, "Okay, I know you haven't played the golf course in a few days, so the first hole is a slight dogleg left . . ."

On the 2nd hole, after hitting his second shot to five feet, Sandelin reached into his pocket for the lucky coin he always carried. Apparently, it had dropped from his pocket. Neither he nor his caddie had another coin. Sandelin finally said, "Anyone have a coin?" and was promptly bombarded with coins tossed from the crowd. He missed the putt. The match was pretty much over after that.

Although the Americans' victory at Brookline was dramatic, the day wasn't without controversy. Both the crowd and many of the American players went over the top with their behavior, most notably in the final match between Colin Montgomerie and Payne Stewart.

Montgomerie had long been a target for American fans, and his play in the Ryder Cup—usually brilliant—made him an even larger target. Throughout the day he was subjected to brutally profane shouts and taunts. On a number of occasions, Stewart had security remove fans.

That, however, wasn't the worst moment of the day. Justin Leonard, playing the eleventh match, was 4 down to José-María Olazábal after eleven holes. Inexplicably, Olazábal went 5-6-5 on the next three holes (double bogey; bogey; bogey) to let Leonard back into the match. Given new life, Leonard holed a 35-foot birdie putt on 15 to draw even. Then, on 17, with the U.S. needing him to halve the match to clinch the Cup, Leonard rolled in a miraculous 45-footer for birdie. That meant Olazábal needed to make his putt from 25 feet to keep the match all square and give Europe a chance.

But before Olazábal could even think about putting, the Americans— players, wives, even a few fans—stormed the green, burying Leonard because they were so overjoyed that he had made the putt. Later, there were some claims that the Americans had stomped on Olazábal's putting line during their charge to Leonard. They hadn't, but their reaction was inexcusable—and they knew it.

Olazábal missed his putt and the Americans had the Ryder Cup back—if not their dignity.

A few minutes later, Stewart got some of it back. His match with Montgomerie had become meaningless, but was played out anyway. They were even on the 18th green, and Stewart had a short putt for par; Montgomerie had a long birdie putt. A halve seemed likely.

Instead, Stewart walked over to Montgomerie, gesturing with his hands. "Pick it up," he said. "It's good."

Stunned, Montgomerie clapped for his opponent as he walked up to him, hand extended, to congratulate him on winning the match.

"We'd won the Cup, which was all that mattered to me," Stewart said. "After what Colin had been through that day, no way was I going to make him putt that."

As it turned out, that was Stewart's final moment on an international golf stage. Four weeks later, he was killed in a plane crash.

—

Among those watching that day were a ten-year-old Irish golfing prodigy and a six-year-old Texan who was only just beginning to play golf.

Rory McIlroy was devastated when Leonard's putt went in.

"The funny thing was, I had kind of pulled for the U.S. in '97 at Valderrama because I was so taken by Tiger that year at the Masters," he said, many years and Ryder Cups later. "I think I watched every shot he hit there. So I was a little bit torn at Valderrama. I certainly wanted Tiger to win his matches, so I was probably leaning U.S. that weekend.

"Two years later, I was all about Europe. I understood what it meant for Europe to win. Darren Clarke [like McIlroy, a northern Irishman] was my hero by then. When Justin made that putt, I took it very hard. In fact, I kind of held a grudge against him for years. Whenever I watched him play, I wanted him to lose—to not play well."

McIlroy smiled. "Then, when I started playing on tour and met him, he was one of the nicest people in the world. I felt kind of guilty that I'd rooted against him all those years."

The six-year-old from Texas—Jordan Spieth—didn't completely understand what the Ryder Cup was about when he watched it with his parents that year. Two months earlier, he had turned six and was much more into baseball at that point in his life than golf.

But he knew who Justin Leonard was because, like the Spieths, Leonard was from Dallas.

"It was one of those things where we knew people who knew Justin and, needless to say, that putt became the stuff of legend," Spieth said. "In fact, after Justin made that putt I think *everyone* living in Dallas claimed to be a friend of Justin's. Even at six, I knew it was a very big deal."

It was a very big deal. Crenshaw's finger-pointing is still repeatedly relived on video to this day, and so is the 17th-green celebration. The one person who wasn't criticized for that moment was Leonard—he was almost as much of an innocent bystander as Olazábal.

The 2001 matches, scheduled for the Belfry, were postponed for a year because they were supposed to begin on September 28—seventeen days after the 9/11 attacks. Everyone agreed there was absolutely no way to go ahead with the matches.

A year later, at the Belfry in 2002, Europe won the Cup back, 15½–

12½. Again it was relative unknowns chipping in with key points: Paul McGinley was supposed to sit out all day Saturday, but when Thomas Bjørn struggled in the morning, Captain Sam Torrance inserted him into the afternoon lineup and he made several critical putts late to give him and Lee Westwood a halve with Scott Hoch and Jim Furyk.

That left the matches tied going into Sunday. On Sunday afternoon, Woods and Mickelson, the top two players in the world, combined for a half point: Mickelson lost one of the day's critical matches, 3 and 2, to another unknown, Phillip Price. Woods halved with Jesper Parnevik in a match that was rendered meaningless because Europe had already clinched the Cup when McGinley made a 10-foot par putt on 18 for the half point that put Europe over the top.

Two years later—2004 at Oakland Hills outside Detroit—Europe won in an embarrassing rout, 18½–9½. For the U.S. to lose on home ground was bad enough, but the score was stunning.

Captain Hal Sutton had decided that week that it was time for the world's top two players to form what should be an unbeatable team— regardless of whether they liked one another.

Nowadays, Woods and Mickelson play down the notion that they didn't get along, and they have become friendly—if not friends. Back then, though, everyone knew they were hardly friends.

"Exaggerated," Mickelson insisted. "Exaggerated by the media. I think we both kind of liked the idea of playing together. But we weren't given enough time to prepare. We found out two days out we were going to play together."

Mickelson made these comments in May 2016—more than four months before the matches at Hazeltine began and before he took Sutton down with similar comments in his pre–Ryder Cup press conference. Sitting in the champions' locker room at TPC Sawgrass on the Monday of the Players Championship, Mickelson had talked at length about his frustrations with various U.S. captains—starting with Lanny Wadkins in 1995.

"Everyone talked about the fact that I went and played a different golf course for two days before the matches in '04 and I was somehow not being a team guy," he said. "Not true. I needed to go off alone to play with Tiger's golf ball, so I could get used to how far I hit it as opposed to how far I hit my own ball."

In foursomes play—alternate shot—players must play each other's golf ball. Each player uses his own ball to tee off and the players alternate shots with that ball the rest of the hole.

Top players are so precise that they can literally feel the difference between brands of golf balls. Woods's Nike ball was notorious for not flying as far as most other golf balls—in fact, many players, including Mickelson, had expressed awe that he could be so dominant with both a ball and clubs (also Nike) that were considered inferior.

"When I played Tiger's ball, there was about an eight-yard difference for me between it and my own ball," Mickelson said. "That's a big adjustment. Even though I thought I knew the difference in how far my shots were going to fly, I just never felt as if I could trust it."

Even if you buy that explanation, it doesn't explain why Woods and Mickelson lost *twice* on the first day—losing the opening four-ball match on Friday morning. In four-ball (best ball), you play your own ball throughout. Woods and Mickelson lost 2 and 1 to Montgomerie and Padraig Harrington, setting the tone for the morning (Europe led 3½–½) and, as it turned out, for the weekend. The duo actually played a little better in the foursomes, losing on the 18th hole to Darren Clarke and Lee Westwood.

The fact that they barely spoke to each other for thirty-six holes that day probably wasn't terribly helpful.

"I thought we won the match because we played better," Westwood said with a laugh. "Didn't Phil choose to play with new clubs that week?"

Mickelson had signed a contract with Callaway earlier that year and unveiled his new clubs that weekend in Detroit. Much was made of that decision at the time—especially after he and Woods lost twice.

Even so, Sutton's decision to team Woods and Mickelson has been criticized for years. How could he possibly consider teaming two players who so disliked each other?

The best answer to that question comes from Poulter, the heart and soul of so many of Europe's wins in the twenty-first century.

"There's this myth out there that everyone on Europe's team have always been best friends," he said. "We're not. Some guys are close; other guys get along okay, other guys don't really like one another all that much.

"But when we get in that room for that one week every two years, any issues between us go away. We leave them outside the door, and they stay there until the week's over. Then we pick them up again on our way out. The captain doesn't have to worry about putting guys together who might not get along. That week we all get along."

Or, as another European player from past teams put it: "We'd all be pals all week long, then when it was over we'd go back to thinking Monty was a pain in the ass."

Monty is Colin Montgomerie, one of the greatest Ryder Cup players ever. Like Poulter, he never won a major title, but his Ryder Cup record was so good he was voted into the World Golf Hall of Fame in 2013.

Montgomerie was fully aware of his reputation. In fact, he often joked that the reason he and Nick Faldo were always paired together is that no one else really wanted to play with either one of them. Faldo won 25 Ryder Cup points, Montgomerie 23½—meaning they rank first and second on the all-time points list. They didn't have to sing Kumbaya together to make a great team.

That's what Sutton was thinking when he paired Woods and Mickelson. But unlike the Europeans, they couldn't put their personal differences aside.

"I'll probably get in trouble for saying this," Poulter said with a laugh many years later. "But you're the two best players in the world and you're asked to work together for four hours doing something that's important. It shouldn't be that hard to pull off."

They didn't pull it off though, and Sutton took the fall for it.

If Sutton can be faulted for anything that week, it was telling his players he didn't want them signing autographs during their practice rounds so they could stay focused on their preparation.

"When Bernhard heard about that he told us to sign *every* possible autograph," Poulter said, laughing. "By the time the matches started on Friday, it felt like we had as many fans as they did—on U.S. soil. It was brilliant."

Two years later, in 2006, at the K Club in Ireland, the result was just as one-sided, Europe winning by an identical score of 18½–9½. The Woods-Mickelson experiment had been abandoned—forever as it turned out—and American captain Tom Lehman teamed Woods with Jim Furyk. They split four matches.

Woods inadvertently revealed his approach to the Ryder Cup during a press conference early in that week. Someone asked him if he could explain why his Ryder Cup record was so poor compared to his dominance of the sport in all other events. At that moment, at the age of thirty, Woods had already won eleven majors and appeared well on his way to breaking Jack Nicklaus's record of eighteen major victories. But his Ryder Cup record was 7-11-1.

Woods almost snorted when the question was asked: "What was Jack's Ryder Cup record?" he said in response.

Nicklaus's record was 17-8-3, albeit in a different era. Nicklaus faced Europe only once (1981), playing against Great Britain and Ireland in his five other appearances. That wasn't the point Woods was making: *Everyone* knew that Nicklaus had won eighteen majors. Most people would have to look up his Ryder Cup record. According to Woods's thinking, that was because the majors mattered first, second, and always; the Ryder Cup was, more or less, just an event he was obligated to play in because he'd be attacked in the media if he didn't.

Most of the attention prior to the '06 matches in Wales wasn't focused on Woods, or on Woods and Mickelson, or on who was going to play with Monty since Faldo wasn't on the team.

The focus was on Darren Clarke. Six weeks earlier, after a five-year battle with breast cancer, his wife, Heather, had passed away, leaving Darren with two young sons. Everyone in golf had known what was going on, and Clarke had taken several long breaks from the Tour in 2004 and 2005 to be with his family.

Whether he would play was an open question until the week before the matches. He had missed so much playing time because of Heather's illness that he was nowhere close to making the team on points. But Captain Ian Woosnam had told him he wanted him on the team as a captain's pick. After a good deal of thought, Clarke decided to go.

"It felt like the right thing to do," he said. "I thought it would be good for the boys to be there; it would be good for me to be with my mates and focus on golf for a few days. There isn't any doubt that when you're dealing with something like that, your escape is when you get between the ropes."

During that year's opening ceremony, the players and their wives were asked to line up side by side, one player and wife from each side walking next to one another onto the stage: wife, player, player, wife. Clarke was assigned to walk in with Phil and Amy Mickelson. As the music started, signaling the teams to begin their entrance, Amy Mickelson walked around her husband, stood in between him and Clarke, and took both their hands. The three of them walked in that way.

"It was one of those moments you never forget," Clarke said ten years later, his voice very quiet. "Neither one of them ever said a word to me. It was quite unbelievable."

"It was completely spontaneous," Mickelson said. "Amy and I never discussed it. She just felt like it was the right thing to do for Darren— and clearly she was right."

Three years later, when Phil and Amy Mickelson made public the fact that Amy was dealing with breast cancer, the first player to call Phil to offer support and help was Darren Clarke.

The Europeans led from start to finish that weekend in 2006, and the only real question on Sunday was which European would score the clinching point. It turned out to be Henrik Stenson, then a Ryder Cup rookie, who beat American Vaughn Taylor to get Europe to 14½ points.

Clarke was 3-0 for the week. He paired with Westwood in foursomes on both Friday and Saturday, beating Mickelson and Chris DiMarco on Friday and Woods and Furyk on Saturday. Then he beat Zach Johnson, 3 and 2, in an emotion-filled singles match, one that was probably as wrenching for Johnson as for Clarke.

"If I wasn't playing against him, I'd have been pulling for him," Johnson said. "How could you not? I had very mixed emotions walking on the 1st tee, especially hearing all the cheers for him. I had to put it out of my mind, though, because I had a job to do and we needed every point we could get since we were down [10–6]. I would never say it affected my play, but I was totally drained when the match was over.

"When we hugged on the green, part of me wanted to just walk away and join in the cheering for him."

The final score was another embarrassment for the U.S.—a third straight Ryder Cup defeat and a fifth loss in six matches, dating to the Sunday collapse at Oak Hill in 1995. Only the comeback at the Country Club in 1999 had prevented Europe from a six-match clean sweep.

Maybe Governor Bush had known what he was doing when he read the Alamo poem seven years earlier, on that Saturday night in Boston not far from Bunker Hill. That famous battle had also been lost by the Americans. Maybe it was time to find a different battle to fight.

Five

PAUL AZINGER WAS the perfect choice to be the U.S. captain in 2008. He had been an excellent Ryder Cup player, as fiery in his own way as Seve Ballesteros had been on the European side. That had led to a couple of shouting matches between the two men in 1989 and 1991.

Azinger also knew something about real adversity, having beaten cancer in 1993—a diagnosis he received not long after finally winning his first major title, the 1993 PGA, and playing a key role in the U.S. victory that year at the Belfry.

Not long after he was named captain, Azinger—as he recounts in his book *Cracking the Code*—happened to watch a TV show about Navy SEALs. He quickly took note that SEALs were divided into pods of three or four men and that the small size of the groups seemed to bring them closer together.

The first person Azinger asked about the SEALs and their pods was Tiger Woods. He knew that Woods had become almost obsessed with the SEALs and had trained with them at times.

"He loved the idea of the pods," Azinger said. "He thought applying it to our team was a great idea."

As it turned out, Woods didn't play on Azinger's team. After winning the U.S. Open at Torrey Pines in June 2008 for his fourteenth major title, he underwent knee surgery that ended his year. It would be the first Ryder Cup team since 1997 that Woods wouldn't play on. Whether he was disappointed or relieved, no one knew for sure.

Azinger had another thing going for him at Valhalla, the golf course outside Louisville, Kentucky, that the PGA had chosen as the site of the matches. "Valhalla" is from the Old Norse for "heaven"—"a place of honor, glory or happiness," according to the dictionary.

The golf course named for honor, glory, and happiness was a fairly ordinary track, but it was owned by the PGA. Jim Awtrey, then the CEO, had decided to buy it in the early 1990s because he believed the PGA needed a backup golf course that would be quickly available in case of an emergency caused by catastrophic weather or an emergency like the one at Shoal Creek in 1990.

That had occurred when Hall Thompson, who had founded the club outside Birmingham, Alabama, was asked about the club inviting an African American to become a member. Thompson was quoted in the *Birmingham News* as saying, "That would never happen in Birmingham."

In the ensuing national uproar, the PGA initially wanted to move the championship to Muirfield Village. At first, Jack Nicklaus said yes but later changed his mind because, according to Awtrey, he didn't want to offend Thompson—who was also a member of (then) all-white Augusta National.

Hall, after first insisting he wouldn't apologize for the comment, capitulated and a local African American insurance executive named Louis J. Willie was invited to join the club. That calmed the waters enough to allow the tournament to be held at Shoal Creek.

Awtrey made the decision to buy Valhalla in the wake of Shoal Creek. The PGA then staged its championship there in 1996 and 2000. Both events had ended in playoffs: Mark Brooks beating local hero Kenny Perry in '96, and Tiger Woods dramatically holding off unknown Bob May four years later.

Playing at Valhalla was an advantage for the U.S. because the fans in Kentucky were thrilled to host the Ryder Cup and even more enthusiastic when Perry made the team, as did fellow good ole boys J. B. Holmes and Boo Weekley. They set a tone for the week quite different from the deadly serious approach previous U.S. teams had taken.

Azinger had one other thing going for him: Nick Faldo.

Arguably Europe's greatest Ryder Cup player—along with Ballesteros and Montgomerie—Faldo was Europe's captain in 2008, which made absolute sense. Montgomerie was warming up in the bullpen for 2010. This was Faldo's year.

Even before the Europeans arrived in Kentucky, there were signs of trouble. Faldo had named José-María Olazábal and Paul McGinley as his vice captains. Montgomerie wasn't on the team for the first time since 1991 and, even though the European "system" made him a logical choice as a vice captain since he was a lock future captain, his old playing partner didn't select him.

Then, a year out from the matches, McGinley resigned as vice captain. "I just didn't feel right about it" is all McGinley will say, even now, about the decision.

Faldo never named a replacement for McGinley and came to Louisville with only Olazábal assisting him. Azinger had three vice captains: Raymond Floyd (past U.S. captain), Dave Stockton (past U.S. captain), and Olin Browne.

When the Europeans arrived and went to pick up their golf bags, they all noticed that Søren Hansen's name had been misspelled. The bag said, "Soren Hanson." Then Faldo mispronounced Miguel Ángel Jiménez's name in his opening press conference.

"Neither one was a big deal in itself," David Feherty said later. "But to the players it was symptomatic. If there's one thing a Ryder Cup captain has to do, it's pay attention to detail. They didn't feel as if Nick did that."

Azinger did. He set up his team in four-man pods, sending them out to practice in those groups and telling them well in advance that they would be playing with those in their pods. He allowed the eight players who had made the team on points to help him choose the captain's pick—or picks—who would be part of their pods.

"We all felt included," Phil Mickelson said. "I told Paul that I wanted Hunter Mahan in our pod and we got Hunter in our pod. Basically he said, 'This is your team as much as it is mine.' We all felt invested after that."

Mickelson uses the word "invested" often when talking about the role he believes the captain should play. He used it when talking about his feud with Tom Watson during the 2014 Ryder Cup.

What's confusing about this is the notion that the captain somehow has to get his players to feel "invested" in winning the Ryder Cup.

"I think the Americans were a bit later to the party when it came to thinking of the Ryder Cup as a must-win event," said Chubby Chandler, the former European Tour player turned agent who has represented Darren Clarke, Lee Westwood, Danny Willett, and Rory McIlroy—among others. "The Europeans have been all in dating to Seve. I don't think the Americans really got it until they started to lose all the time."

Clearly, there's something to that notion. If Woods and Mickelson had been paired together in 2016 as the number-one and number-two players in the world, they would have put aside their differences to try to win.

In 2008, Azinger brought a new approach to being the captain—and it worked—at least if he's judged by the result, which is exactly how all captains are judged. Win, you're a genius; lose, you're a moron.

"That's what was unfair about Medinah," said Brandt Snedeker, referring to 2012. "Davis did everything right for two days, handed us a 10–6 lead going into the singles, and we couldn't finish. Somehow, that became his fault."

In 2008, the lead Azinger handed his team after two days at Valhalla was 9–7. The Americans dominated on Sunday, winning the singles 7½–4½. There were a few nervous moments early in the day for the U.S. After Justin Rose had beaten the "invested" Mickelson 3 and 2, the lead was down to 10½–9½. But the self-described "redneck" trio of Perry, J. B. Holmes, and Boo Weekley won the next three matches to regain control and the U.S. won easily, 16½–11½.

Azinger was a genius and all was well in U.S. Ryder Cup land again.

Until the Americans lost the next three Cups.

The loss in Wales in 2010 had a surreal quality to it. There was so much rain the first three days that the captains—Colin Montgomerie and Corey Pavin—agreed to two sessions in which six matches were played—meaning all twenty-four players were on the golf course at once. The singles were postponed until Monday in the hope that the sixteen foursome and four-ball matches could be completed by Sunday.

They were—barely.

The Keystone Kops feeling was added to when the U.S. broke out its rain gear on Friday. The gear had been selected by Pavin's wife, Lisa, who had been dubbed (and had embraced) the nickname "The Captainess" because she was so involved in everything her husband did leading to the matches.

There was just one problem with the Captainess-selected rain gear: it didn't stop the rain. The American players were almost comically soaked by the time the rain became so heavy that it forced a stoppage in play on

Friday, and PGA of America employees were sent on a buying spree for off-the-rack rain gear that wasn't as eye-catching as what the Captainess had selected but had the distinct advantage of keeping the players and caddies dry.

The sun finally came out on Monday, and Europe held off an American rally when Graeme McDowell, who had won the U.S. Open earlier in the year, scored the clinching point in the final match against Hunter Mahan.

"I think I had a one-footer to clinch the match, and my hands were shaking," McDowell said later.

There were a total of eleven Ryder Cup rookies involved that weekend—six on the European side and five on the American side. One of Europe's rookies was Rory McIlroy.

McIlroy had been a golf prodigy almost from the time he could walk. He had grown up in the tiny town of Holywood in Northern Ireland and had learned the game from his father, Gerry, who was a low-handicap player most of his adult life. Gerry was a bartender who worked two jobs—one at the golf club, the other at a local pub. Rosie, Rory's mother, worked a nightshift at the 3M plant. Their three salaries enabled them to have enough money so that young Rory could travel to junior golf tournaments in Great Britain and around the world.

At the age of ten, Rory won the nine-and-ten-year-old division of the World Junior Golf Championships at Doral Park Country Club in Miami. He was the number-one-ranked amateur in the world at seventeen and turned pro at eighteen after playing in the 2007 Walker Cup matches.

He won on the European Tour in February 2009 and made his American debut as a pro a couple of weeks later when he reached the quarterfinals of the World Match Play Championships. Then he tied for twentieth at the Masters—still a month shy of turning twenty.

What was noticeable about McIlroy, right from the beginning, was his comfort with the spotlight. Clearly his parents had raised him to respect *everyone* he met—not just those he might think important.

In 2010, a reporter walking through the hotel lobby at the PGA National Resort and Spa, the site of the Honda Classic, noticed McIlroy talking to an older man who was showing him something on his cell phone.

"She's absolutely beautiful," the reporter heard McIlroy say. "Is she your first?"

The next day, the reporter ran into McIlroy and asked him who he had been talking to in the lobby the night before. McIlroy looked at him blankly.

"The guy who was showing you pictures on his cell phone," the reporter said. "I've never seen him before."

"Oh, that guy," McIlroy said with a smile and a shrug. "I have no idea who he was. He just walked over and asked if we could take a picture together and then started showing me pictures of his granddaughter."

McIlroy also had—and has—a penchant for telling the truth. When he's asked a question in a press conference, he almost never answers the question quickly. He will think about it and then answer. Occasionally his answers get him into trouble.

One such occasion came in 2009 when it was becoming apparent he was going to make Europe's Ryder Cup team in 2010. Just before he was scheduled to play in the 2009 Irish Open with Montgomerie, he was asked how important it was to him to make Montgomerie's team the next year.

"It's not a huge goal of mine," he answered. "It's an exhibition. In the big scheme of things, it's not that important an event to me."

McIlroy went on to say he wouldn't change his schedule or add events in order to make the team. To his credit, Montgomerie answered very calmly—and smartly—when he was asked about McIlroy's comments.

"Rory will understand when—and that's not an if—he's a Ryder Cup player."

Montgomerie was right. From the moment he stepped inside the team room in Wales, McIlroy figured out that this was far more than an exhibition. He felt the tension and he felt the camaraderie. Seeing how much the matches meant to men like Clarke, Westwood, McDowell, and Poulter—all of whom he looked up to—he quickly came to understand what all the hype was about.

"I knew I'd been wrong pretty much right away," he said, smiling sheepishly at the memory. "Looking back, what I was said was pretty selfish. I had always thought of golf in terms of individual performance—winning majors, accomplishing things on your own. I suspect to some degree there was an only-child aspect to it too."

He paused and smiled. "Can you imagine that?" he said. "A golfer being selfish. Has to be a first, right?"

McIroy went 1-1-2 in Wales—paired with fellow Northern Irishman

Graeme McDowell in the first three sessions before halving his singles match with Stewart Cink on Monday. Because of the rain, no one played more than four times, so McIlroy played in every session.

The most frustrated man in Wales might have been Mickelson. He went 0-3 in the four-ball/foursomes sessions before winning his singles match against Peter Hanson. Mickelson had thought that Azinger's captaincy and the win at Valhalla would mean a change in the way captains approached the matches and in the outcomes. He got neither in Wales.

"I sat down with Corey after they named him captain and I said to him, 'Look, the pod system worked. We all felt prepared and ready even before we got to Louisville.' Corey just looked at me and said, 'We have a twelve-man pod.' I can't tell you how frustrating it was to hear that."

Mickelson had wanted Azinger to be named captain again after the victory in 2008. During the celebration at the Brown Hotel on Sunday night in Louisville, he had cornered Julius Mason—the PGA's keeper of the future-captains list—and told him the PGA should name Azinger right away as the 2010 captain. Although Mason was highly respected inside PGA headquarters, he technically had no say in naming captains. Back then, the decision was made solely by the president of the PGA, presumably with input from the executive board and the staff. Pavin was named captain on December 10 at a lavish press conference at Tavern on the Green in New York City.

It was a choice that made sense. Like Azinger, Pavin had been an excellent Ryder Cupper and had played a key role in 1993—the last U.S. win in Europe—at the Belfry. His nickname was "The Gutty [or Gritty] Little Bruin," a reference to his size, five-nine and 155 pounds, and his alma mater, UCLA.

The toughest part of Pavin's job in Wales in 2010—other than the rain gear debacle—may have been deciding what to do with Tiger Woods. In the wake of the Thanksgiving night accident (nine months earlier) that led to explosive revelations about his personal life, Woods had become something of a missing man on tour in 2010.

He had played in only eight tournaments that year prior to the PGA Championship and wasn't going to come close to making the team on points, even though he *had* finished tied for fourth at both the Masters and the U.S. Open. But there had been a number of un-Woods-like performances: a rare missed cut at Quail Hollow; a walk-off with an injury during the final round of the Players Championship—which turned out to be the beginning of what would become a familiar sight the next few years—and a tie for seventy-eighth place at the Bridgestone Championships, meaning he beat one player in an eighty-man field, on a golf course (Firestone Country Club) where he had won *seven* times in the past.

All that left Pavin with a dilemma: If Woods had been anyone but Woods, he wouldn't have even considered picking him. But Woods *was* Woods, which led many people to say, how can you *not* pick him?

The simmering controversy blew up during the week of the PGA when Golf Channel's Jim Gray reported on Tuesday that Pavin had told him he would definitely pick Woods—regardless of how Woods played that week. Pavin flatly denied saying that, and Gray confronted him as he left the podium following his pre-tournament press conference.

There was a good deal of shouting—some of it involving Lisa Pavin—and both men left angry. Gray has always had a reputation for very aggressive reporting—especially for a TV reporter—but no one had ever accused him before of making something up.

Bottom line: Pavin picked Woods.

And then the twelve-man pod went to Wales and lost. Woods actually played better than he had in any previous Ryder Cup, going 3-1. The U.S. still came up a point short. Four months later, Davis Love was named the American captain for the 2012 matches at Medinah.

That same week in January 2011, José-María Olazábal was named to captain Europe. Four months after that, Seve Ballesteros, Olazábal's partner in Ryder Cup brilliance (they were 11-2-1 as a team), his mentor, and the father of European Ryder Cup golf, died after a long battle with cancer.

All of which set the stage for 2012 and, arguably, the most emotional Ryder Cup matches ever played.

The two teams that arrived at Medinah Country Club, which is located about thirty miles north and west of downtown Chicago, were both on a mission: The U.S. team wanted to win the Ryder Cup back *and* wanted to make certain that Davis Love, as respected and well liked as any player in golf, did not lose the Cup on home ground.

Europe's players knew how much José-María Olazábal wanted to honor Seve Ballesteros's memory by following in his footsteps as a winning Ryder Cup captain.

"The notion that we wouldn't win for José, who wanted so much to win for Seve, was almost unthinkable," Ian Poulter said. "I think for a while, we were trying too hard."

The U.S. led 5–3 on Friday night after winning the afternoon four-ball session, 3–1. That night, Olazábal surprised his players by giving them a tongue-lashing. Since he was normally one of golf's truly gentle souls, it was completely out of character for him.

"What was important was that nobody doubted his sincerity," said Paul McGinley, who was a vice captain. "They knew it came from the heart and they knew he was right."

Even so, things got no better for Europe the next morning, the U.S. again winning the session 3–1 and extending the lead to 8–4. It was during that session, though, that the matches began to turn—slowly—in Europe's direction.

Love hadn't put together any pods à la Paul Azinger, but he had made a point of talking to each player he thought might be on the team about how often he wanted to play and whom he might want to play—or not play—with. He didn't want to "surprise" anyone the way Mickelson and Woods had been surprised in 2004.

He and Mickelson had talked at length about whom Mickelson would play with and, more important, how much he would play. Mickelson was forty-two, and the notion that he might play five times was pretty much out of the question, largely because both men agreed he might be tired on Sunday if he played thirty-six holes on both Friday and Saturday.

"We actually discussed the possibility of him playing only once on Friday and Saturday," Love said. "Eventually, though, we agreed he'd play the first three sessions and then rest Saturday afternoon to be ready for singles on Sunday."

Mickelson wanted to play with Keegan Bradley. He had taken Bradley under his wing, especially after Bradley won the PGA in 2011 and it became apparent that he was going to be part of the team a year later.

Mickelson loves to play Tuesday money matches, and often he does it with younger players he thinks need to be put under pressure—specifically match-play pressure—to give them some sense of what the Ryder Cup will feel like.

There is, of course, no gambling allowed on the PGA Tour. But if there *were* gambling, Mickelson's group would play for $1,000 a hole with automatic presses. That meant there were times when several thousand dollars might be at stake on the last hole, and, even though that was chump change to players on the PGA Tour, no one wanted to have to hand over cash—the games are cash-only; pay as soon as it's over—to anyone, especially Mickelson, who is one of the kings of tour trash talk.

Mickelson and Bradley had partnered often on Tuesdays, and Mickelson told Love he wanted to play with the energetic and talented Ryder Cup rookie.

They turned out to be a spectacular team. On Friday morning, once Bradley overcame the nerves that were so bad he had considered fleeing the premises, they beat the previously unbeaten foursomes team of Luke Donald and Sergio García. That afternoon, in four-balls, they beat McIlroy and McDowell.

Then, Saturday morning, they completely humiliated Donald and Lee Westwood, 7 and 6. It was during that match that Mickelson, seeing Love watching from his cart, went over to talk to the captain.

"I told him he shouldn't change the plan," Mickelson said later. "I knew the temptation would be there to send Keegan and I out in the afternoon because we were playing so well and I understood that. But I told him that Keegan and I probably wouldn't be mentally ready to play because that hadn't been the plan all week and that we wanted to be fresh for Sunday."

Love agreed. In hindsight, many have pointed to that moment as the turning point of the matches, even though both Love and Mickelson always bring up the fact that the team Love put out instead of Mickelson and Bradley—Webb Simpson and Bubba Watson—won their match.

But what those people don't know is that Love and his vice captains gave considerable thought to putting Bradley out with Tiger Woods—and benching Steve Stricker, who was struggling with his game. Bradley, who was only twenty-six, had enough energy to play ten matches if need be, and he was on fire, breathing energy into his partnership with Mickelson, into the crowd, and into the U.S. team.

It wasn't until later, after the matches were over, that Bradley found out that he had almost been paired with Woods on Saturday afternoon. "It was so disappointing to hear they almost did that but didn't," he said. "I wanted to play—period. I understood Phil needing to rest. To go out there with Tiger would have been amazing."

In the end, with what looked like a comfortable lead, not wanting to embarrass Stricker, and not sure how a Woods-Bradley partnership would play out, the leadership group decided to stick with Woods and Stricker. They lost to García and Donald.

"When you have a team down, you should step on them," McGinley said. "That's the way I look at it. We were all a little bit surprised they weren't back out there. We understood Davis's thinking, but we were surprised anyway."

That afternoon proved to be the turning point of the weekend. After the U.S. had upped its lead to 10–4 in the first two matches, the European rally began with García and Donald's win on the 18th hole and then the remarkable turnaround by Poulter and McIlroy to win their match from Zach Johnson and Jason Dufner.

"The funny thing is, I think Poulter fed off our crowd," Zach Johnson said. "He was enjoying every second of it."

McIlroy—as he points out—*did* birdie the 13th hole to start the rally. Poulter birdied the next five.

"I always tell Rory that *we* birdied six in a row," Poulter said. "And he got us started."

That win sent an absolute jolt through the European team room.

"It was more like we were up 10–6 than down 10–6," said Darren Clarke, also a vice captain that year. "We knew the U.S. had won from 10–6 down at Brookline, although that had been at home. But we didn't care. I think everyone in that room that night felt like we were going to win."

When the captains sat down right after the Saturday matches had ended, their first instinct was to put Poulter out in the first singles match: let the spiritual and emotional leader of the team lead things off and keep the momentum going. It was McGinley who first suggested *not* doing that.

"We were on the road," he said. "Poults would get the crowd wound up, especially playing Bubba, who we expected to be out there first," he said. "We didn't want that. We wanted to take the crowd out of it early as much as we could because that was when we needed to make our move.

"I suggested we put Luke [Donald] out there first. No one in Chicago was going to get all wound up about Luke. He's quiet and unassuming *and* he'd gone to Northwestern. He was one of their own—at least a little bit. They weren't going to cheer for him, but they weren't going to get all fired up to cheer *against* him either."

Ultimately, Olazábal agreed with McGinley. Donald led off, with

Poulter second, McIlroy third, and Justin Rose fourth. Love, expecting Olazábal to front-load with his team behind, countered with Watson, Simpson, Bradley, and Mickelson—the four players who'd had the most success the first two days. He back-loaded his other veterans, figuring they would handle the pressure best *if* the matches got close: Stricker went off eleventh against the struggling Martin Kaymer, and Woods was last, facing Francesco Molinari.

Saturday night has become a traditional night for the U.S. team to hand out gifts—notably from the players to the captain—with the captain, vice captains, players, and—sometimes—wives and caddies talking. This dates to the '99 rally at Brookline. In fact, both Presidents Bush were in the team room on Saturday night at Medinah in 2012, just as they had been at Brookline thirteen years earlier.

What happens in the European team room tends to vary from year to year, captain to captain. It was Olazábal who did most of the talking that night, and much of it was about how much he wanted to win for Ballesteros. He had been angry on Friday night. On Saturday, he was filled with emotion, almost pleading with his players to honor Ballesteros by finding a way to rally on Sunday.

"The ghost of Seve was in their team room that night," Azinger said. "Our guys were giving out gifts."

Love kept telling his players, "We'll all be in this room drinking champagne tomorrow night," almost as if he was trying to convince himself that was the truth.

As it turned out, Europe's biggest challenge the next day was getting McIlroy to the golf course. Casually watching Golf Channel in his room Saturday night, he noticed that his tee time was at 12:25. He woke up in the morning, had some breakfast, went to the gym for a brief workout, and then went back to his room to FaceTime with his fiancée, Caroline Wozniacki, who was playing in a tennis tournament in China.

He was just getting out of the shower when he heard someone pounding on his door. McIlroy normally gets to the golf course about an hour before his tee time. It was a little before eleven o'clock and he was planning to arrive at about 11:30, give or take five minutes.

There was just one problem: his tee time was at 12:25 *Eastern* time, which meant 11:25 *Central* time. He was due on the tee in less than thirty minutes.

At about 10:45, Olazábal had noticed that McIlroy hadn't arrived.

Concerned, he notified the PGA of America and they tracked him down. Two PGA of America officials arranged for a local police officer to pick McIlroy up at the hotel and drive him, lights and sirens blazing, to the golf course.

"It was terrifying," McIlroy said, years later, able to laugh about it. "I mean, he was taking side streets to make the route shorter, and a couple of times we were up on the sidewalk. He did an amazing job."

The officer, Patrick Rollins, who was the deputy police chief of the Lombard Police Department, told a local reporter later that he was "just doing my job" in getting McIlroy to Medinah.

McIlroy arrived at 11:15. By then, word had spread that he wasn't on the grounds. When Love told Keegan Bradley that the U.S. would win the match by forfeit if McIlroy was more than five minutes late for their tee time, Bradley objected.

"I said, 'No way, we're not doing that,'" Bradley said. "I told Davis that if he was late, we should go off fourth or fifth—whatever. I didn't want to win that way. Plus, I was dying to play him."

Whether Love and Olazábal would have gotten together and agreed to push the Bradley-McIlroy match back or if the rules would have been strictly adhered to became moot when McIlroy arrived. He had no time to warm up on the driving range, instead going to the putting green to hit a few putts before walking onto the tee at 11:22 with the entire crowd chanting, "Central Time Zone!" in his direction.

He laughed. They were right.

"My only thought was that I needed to be even after six holes, just not get blown away at the start when I wasn't warmed up," he said. "Fortunately, I managed to get a halve on number one and was 2 up after six. After that I felt pretty confident. Plus, by then, there was a lot of blue on the board [blue being Europe's color; red being the U.S. color]."

McIlroy pushed his tee shot on the first hole way right but managed to get it on the green and make par—matching Bradley. From that point on, most of the day belonged to Europe.

McGinley's theory about sending Donald off first proved to be correct. Plus, he beat Watson. Then Poulter beat Webb Simpson, McIlroy beat Bradley, and Rose beat Mickelson in what might have been the key match of the day.

Rose's win was remarkable. He was one down on the 15th hole and had to get up and down from a tough lie in a greenside bunker to halve the hole. He did. Then he made a 12-footer at 16 to also halve the hole.

"If I don't get up and down at 15 and make that putt at 16, the match could have been over," Rose said. "I was barely hanging on."

At 17, the difficult par-3, Mickelson just missed the green and had about a 50-foot chip. He almost holed it.

"I knew I'd made it," he said. "I was moving as I watched it track the hole. I knew it was going in."

Only it didn't, stopping two inches away. Still, at worst he was going to take his one-up lead to the 18th tee, since Rose had a 35-foot birdie putt and needed to make sure he didn't get overaggressive and three-putt. That would end the match.

Except that Rose, never known as a great putter, holed the putt. It was one of those European turnarounds where what looked great for the Americans turned out great for Europe. Standing behind the green, Mickelson shook his head for an instant, then gave Rose a thumbs-up and clapped for Rose as he walked off the green.

It was a great Ryder Cup moment—though not so much for the U.S.

Then, on 18, after missing the fairway left, Rose got his second shot on the green and made another putt, this one a 15-footer, to win the match. He had also beaten Mickelson in singles in 2008—but that hadn't mattered as much in the U.S. runaway at Valhalla.

As they shook hands, Rose, about as nice a person as there is in golf, said softly, "I'm not sure why, but you always seem to bring out the best in me."

Mickelson smiled. "Yeah, I know. I'm not sure I'm really happy about that."

Nine months later, Mickelson would finish second in the U.S. Open for the sixth time. The winner was Justin Rose.

By the time Rose beat Mickelson at Medinah, the score was tied and Europe was riding a wave of momentum. Dustin Johnson and Zach Johnson managed to slow things down with wins, as did Dufner. But Sergio García rallied to beat Jim Furyk one up and breathed new life into his team.

By late afternoon, it all came down to Kaymer and Stricker and Kaymer's unforgettable moment. Watching Kaymer line up his putt, a lot of people flashed back to Kiawah and Langer's putt twenty-one years earlier. It never crossed Kaymer's mind.

"I was just thankful to be there in that moment with the chance to make a putt I knew I'd be remembered for making forever," he said. "I knew I was going to make it."

When he did, the Europeans celebrated wildly. The first person to get to Olazábal, who was racing up the 18th fairway as Kaymer lined up his putt, was Poulter. As they hugged, Olazábal, with tears streaming down his face, said, "Thank you, thank you, thank you."

"I've had a lot of great moments in golf," Poulter said. "A lot of them in the Ryder Cup. That was the best one of all."

There were plenty of American tears that day too, most of them shed in the team room after the Woods-Molinari match had been halved to make the final score 14½–13½.

"Every single person was in tears," Brandt Snedeker said. "We all felt like we had let the country down and we'd let Davis down. There was just no getting around it. We felt like we should have won and we didn't and it was incredibly painful."

That night, after they had celebrated for several hours, the Europeans were ready to carry out the Sunday night tradition of joining their opponents for a toast and some bonding. As a courtesy, they sent word to the Americans that they wanted to come to their room to congratulate them on a great weekend of golf.

A little while later the word came back: "Please don't come."

Davis Love learned one lesson that day. "We focus so much on getting the pairings right the first four sessions," he said. "Sometimes we almost forget singles is 12 points—not just 4. Once, the singles were our strength. At Medinah, they killed us."

Six

O N JANUARY 18, 2013, Tom Watson was formally introduced as the American Ryder Cup captain for the matches at Gleneagles, Scotland, in 2014. The announcement came at a lavish press conference held in the Empire State Building—a perfect spot for two reasons.

First, it helped fulfill the PGA's continuing desire to both win the Ryder Cup and to sell the Ryder Cup. By making the announcement in the media hub of the U.S., the PGA guaranteed that Watson's appointment would receive massive publicity, which—even with the matches overseas—would help with promoting all things Ryder Cup for almost two years.

Second, staging the press conference in the 102-story Empire State Building was symbolic of the uphill climb the Americans faced in trying to end Europe's dominance, which had now stretched to seven wins in nine matches, dating to 1993 when Watson's team had won at the Belfry.

The U.S. hadn't won overseas since then, and Ted Bishop was hoping that having Watson—an adopted Scot—as his captain at Gleneagles might give the U.S. a small edge that could be the difference between a one-point win and the back-to-back one-point losses the Americans had suffered.

As much as he wanted the job, Watson was fully aware that captains received too much credit and too much blame, depending on the outcome of the matches.

Or, as Butch Harmon, who had taught numerous Ryder Cup players and captains through the years, put it: "If the good Lord jumped off the cross to become captain, it wouldn't make a bit of difference if the players didn't play well."

Publicly, the naming of Watson was greeted with great enthusiasm. To most, the choice made absolute sense, even though at sixty-five, he would be the oldest captain in Ryder Cup history—eight years older than Sam Snead had been when he had been the captain at Birkdale in 1969, the famous Nicklaus-Jacklin "concession" match.

Even Tiger Woods, whose relationship with Watson had been—at best—frosty through the years, put out a statement saying that Watson was a great choice. Asked about his past comments criticizing Woods, specifically saying that his on-course behavior showed a "lack of respect" for the game, Watson shrugged it off.

"Water under the bridge," he said. "Tiger and I will be just fine."

As it turned out, he was right about that—Woods was the least of his problems.

One person not happy with the choice was Phil Mickelson. To him, Watson's selection was another example of a PGA of America president who was out of touch with the players, picking someone *he* wanted rather than someone the players wanted.

"If he [Bishop] had asked the players likely to be on the team, I guarantee you very few of them would have been happy with the choice," Mickelson said, long after the 2014 matches were over. "Players are different now than in 1993. Back then, Tom was leading guys he knew; his peers in many ways. The sport was different; players were different. Tom is very authoritarian in his approach to leadership. That doesn't work with this generation of players."

Clearly, it wasn't likely to work with Mickelson, even though he and Jim Furyk—who were born six weeks apart—would be the oldest members of Watson's team. Mickelson was (correctly) fairly certain that if Watson had been the captain at Medinah, he wouldn't have gone along with Mickelson's plea to "stick with the plan" and sit him and Keegan Bradley out on Saturday afternoon.

Watson believed he had plenty of time to get to know his players. When he played at the Masters and the British Open, he made a point of playing practice rounds with those who were either going to be on the team or might be on the team. He showed up at other events—notably the U.S. Open—to observe how his future players handled pressure.

But Mickelson was right about another thing: he was never going to have the kind of relationship he had with the players on the 1993 team. That year, Watson had been forty-four, and three of his players were over forty: Tom Kite, forty-three; Lanny Wadkins, forty-three; and Raymond Floyd, fifty-one—who had captained in 1989 and was the oldest player in Ryder Cup history.

The two youngest players had been Lee Janzen and Davis Love—both twenty-nine. That meant the largest age gap between Watson and any of his players had been fifteen years. In 2014, the *smallest* gap was twenty-one years—Mickelson and Furyk were forty-four. The largest was forty-four years—Jordan Spieth had been born two months prior to the '93 Ryder Cup. As good as Spieth's memory is, he didn't remember those matches.

What's more, as Mickelson pointed out, Watson was no longer one of the guys. In the two years leading up to the '93 Ryder Cup, Watson played thirty-one PGA Tour events. That meant he was a regular in the locker room, a familiar face to everyone on the team. In 2015 and 2016 he played a total of four times—which was understandable given his age.

Beyond that, Mickelson was 100 percent correct about how players had changed. In '93, Watson brought Stan Thirsk, a pro at Kansas City Country Club when Watson was a kid, to England as his one and only vice captain.

Very few players brought teachers or sports psychologists with them. They brought their caddies and their wives—period. By 2014, many players referred to themselves as "we" when talking about their game—not the royal "we," but as a reference to their "team." Those teams usually consisted of a swing coach; a personal trainer; a masseuse; at least one agent—often more; a sports psychologist; equipment reps; a caddie; and a wife or girlfriend. Parents were sometimes involved too.

Once, when a player went to the range on practice days, he was accompanied by his caddie. Now, often as not, he has an entourage with him.

Those on the U.S. team saw their job—whatever it was—to make sure the players were happy at all times. There weren't a lot of people around giving a player orders. Love had been considered a "players'" captain because he saw to every player's needs, whether it was Zach Johnson needing an hour by himself each day to go through his practice routine, Bubba Watson wanting multiflavored smoothies, or Mickelson, if he so desired, going off by himself to another golf course.

Because the entourages were smaller than usual during a Ryder Cup week, vice captains—four on each side now—were expected to make sure the players' needs were attended to at all times. When Love had been a vice captain in 2010, Stewart Cink, one of the gentler souls on tour, had said to him, "I'm not sure I can get my head around the idea of sending *you* to get me a peanut-butter-and-jelly sandwich."

"It's my job," Love replied. "That and making sure you have all the towels you need."

Paul Goydos, who was also a vice captain that year, had one job each morning that was an absolute: make sure the players were all wearing the right clothes for the day. He would sit at the end of the hallway in a chair and check them all as they headed for the door.

Watson wasn't going to worry about smoothies or peanut-butter-and-jelly sandwiches. He did have three vice captains, but the first two he picked were contemporaries: Floyd, exactly seven years to the day his senior; and two-time U.S. Open champion Andy North (his closest friend), who was six months younger than he was. A few months before the team headed overseas, Watson decided he needed a vice captain closer in age to his players, so he added Steve Stricker, who had played at Medinah at the age of forty-five.

"The fact is if the players had been asked how they felt about Tom being picked as captain, just about all of them would have been against it," Mickelson said. "It wasn't personal. Everyone respected Tom Watson. But none of us really *knew* Tom Watson."

He smiled. "When I was a kid practicing on the putting green behind my house, I always competed with Hogan, Nicklaus, and Watson. My record against them was phenomenal.

"It was more about the thing I'd been talking about for almost twenty years: putting us in a position to succeed or fail. Paul had put us in a position to succeed. Davis certainly tried, but we just couldn't finish the job on Sunday.

"I thought Tom was put in a position to fail when they picked him. Twenty years earlier, absolutely, no-brainer choosing him. I thought I had a chance to make that team [in '93], but he didn't pick me. I won [at the International] the week after the points race was over, and he only had two captain's picks and he went with experience. I got it and, heck, I've been on enough teams, so it's fine.

"This was a different time though. Different players, different mentality."

Mickelson wasn't shy about letting people know he didn't think Watson was the right captain. In July, he played with Ted Bishop in the pro-am at the Scottish Open, and flat out told him that Watson's captaincy was going to be a failure.

"He told me I was wrong, it was going to be great," Mickelson said with a shrug. "I really wish I'd been wrong."

The argument can be made that it didn't help the U.S. team that their leader—"our papa bear," as Zach Johnson calls Mickelson—went to Gleneagles already convinced the week was going to be a disaster. The notion that there was unrest in the American locker room was widespread enough that the Europeans were aware of it—even before the matches started on Friday.

"We heard rumblings," McIlroy said. "And it was pretty apparent just being around them during the week that there were some issues going on in their team room. I guess we didn't really know how serious they were until after it was over."

The simmering Mickelson-Watson rift came to a head on Saturday morning. The U.S. had won the opening session of Friday four-balls 2½–1½. Their most impressive team that morning had been Jordan Spieth and Patrick Reed—both Ryder Cup rookies. The idea for the pairing had come from Spieth.

"I was just looking at some statistics, and I saw that Patrick was the best guy on our team on par-5s, I was the best on par-4s, and we were both pretty good on par-3s," he said. "I thought it made sense for us to go out together. I took the idea to Strick [Stricker], and he took it to Tom."

Given that Mickelson's major criticism of Watson was that the players had "no input," that story is worth noting. Of course, Mickelson was talking more about lack of input *before* the week began more than what happened during the week.

Spieth and Reed went out on Friday morning and blasted Ian Poulter and Stephen Gallacher, 5 and 4. Reed was so tight on the 1st tee that he popped up a three-wood and found himself with a three-iron in his hands for his second shot.

"The rest of them were all hitting wedges," Reed said, laughing at the memory. "It was embarrassing, but I sort of said, 'Okay, watch this.' I got the ball on the green and we all made par. That relaxed me. Walking off the green, I said, 'So, what'd everybody make?' It felt pretty good."

Watson had decided on Thursday night to sit Spieth and Reed out on Friday afternoon. He didn't think they would be as effective in foursomes as in four-ball, and he wanted to get all twelve of his players into the competition on the first day. Jim Furyk, Matt Kuchar, Dustin Johnson, and Hunter Mahan—all Ryder Cup veterans—had sat out the morning. They played in the afternoon, as did Mickelson and Bradley—who had extended their Ryder Cup record as a team to 4-0 in the morning—and Rickie Fowler and Jimmy Walker. Spieth and Reed, along with Bubba Watson and Webb Simpson, who had also won their match 5 and 4, sat out.

Mickelson was upset that Spieth and Reed sat—and told them both so. In fact, the entire team knew that Mickelson wasn't happy with the afternoon pairings. Mickelson and Bradley finally lost a match—to Graeme McDowell and Victor Dubuisson—that afternoon. In fact, the afternoon was a disaster for the Americans. They scored a half point (Walker and Fowler) and trailed at the end of the day, 5–3.

On Saturday morning, Mickelson and Bradley sat out. As with Love at Medinah, Watson didn't want Mickelson playing five matches. He sent Furyk and Mahan out for a second time because they'd played well in losing on Friday, and they won. He paired Kuchar with Bubba Watson and they played very well—seven under par for sixteen holes. The only problem was that Henrik Stenson and Justin Rose were *eleven* under—including nine straight birdies—and won the match.

Still, the U.S. was leading the session 2–1, with the Fowler-Walker/McIlroy-Poulter match still on the golf course, when Watson had to submit his pairings for the afternoon.

Late Saturday morning is probably the most difficult time of any Ryder Cup for a captain. On Friday, most often, he knows who is going out in the afternoon, and he isn't likely to make any radical changes based on the morning play—if any changes at all.

Saturday is different. Almost always, the captain has seen all twelve of his players at least once, probably twice, and sometimes on three occasions. He knows who is hot and who is not, and he has to decide who is tired, who is fresh, and who needs rest. He has his vice captains in his ear telling him what they think.

And he has to submit his pairings before Saturday morning play is over. The Fowler-Walker/McIlroy-Poulter match was on the 15th hole, all square, when Watson was told he had to submit his lineup.

He was torn. Fowler and Walker were playing very well and had played good golf in tight matches for three straight sessions. They had been the only American team that hadn't lost in foursomes the previous day. Mickelson and Bradley were warming up on the range, ready to go, dying to make amends for their Friday afternoon showing.

Watson knew that. He also knew that Fowler and Walker, when on, were his best foursomes team. He decided to play what he thought was the hot hand, scratching Mickelson and Bradley.

Then he had to go give them the news. Mickelson was both disappointed and unhappy. "We're rested and ready to go," he told Watson.

"It's done, Phil," Watson said. Then he added, "You guys just aren't playing well enough for me to put you out there."

If there was any chance at all for the two men to eventually find common ground, it vanished right there. As it turned out, Watson had made a mistake. After playing three straight matches that went to the 18th hole—all halved—Walker and Fowler were gassed, especially Walker.

"I knew I'd gotten it wrong on the 3rd hole," Watson said later. "I could see Jimmy didn't have his legs. If I'd been able to wait until their morning match was over, I might have made a different decision. But I didn't have that luxury. Neither did Paul [McGinley] though. I blew it."

Watson is always blunt—whether criticizing someone else or criticizing himself. That's his style. Some people thrive playing for a leader like that—others don't.

"I *loved* playing for him," Reed said. "I like someone who just puts it out there and tells you what's what. I don't need to be coddled. Hey, if you're good you're good, and if you're not, you're not no matter what the captain does or says. I don't need to be told I'm good when I know I'm not."

Reed was the one player on the American team who kept in touch regularly with Watson after Gleneagles. "I talk or text with Cap all the time," he said a few weeks before the Hazeltine matches. "I learned a lot from him over there. I'm still learning from him. I love the guy."

His teammates were not as enthusiastic. They tended to side with Mickelson—"papa bear."

Saturday afternoon at Gleneagles was just as bad for the Americans as Friday afternoon had been. The score was the same: 3½–½, giving Europe a 10–6 lead going into Sunday. Only Spieth and Reed scored, and Reed was inconsolable after Rose and Martin Kaymer had birdied the 18th hole to steal an extra half point.

"I kept telling him it was okay, that they'd given us everything they had," Watson said. "That's all I could ask. He couldn't stop crying. He was devastated."

Saturday night has now become the traditional night for rah-rah speeches in the team rooms. On the European side, McGinley didn't want to go too far. He had decided before the week began that he didn't want anyone—including the captain—to speak for more than fifteen minutes, and he didn't want the sessions to go on too long.

"You get to a point where the players aren't listening anymore," he said. "Either they've heard it all before or they've just been sitting there too long. I wanted everything quick and hard-hitting."

Poulter, the perennial heart and soul of the team, spoke first. Then came Lee Westwood—which was something of a surprise to the other players. Westwood was Darren Clarke's best friend. He had been the one Cup veteran who had publicly supported Clarke for the captaincy. And yet McGinley had selected Westwood with his last captain's pick over Luke Donald—a good friend, one of his most vocal supporters, and someone with an excellent Ryder Cup record (11-4-1).

"I had to make a cold-blooded decision," McGinley said. "It couldn't be personal or based on Luke having supported me. Lee had played better during the summer, and in fact Luke hadn't played well at all. I had to do what was best for the team."

McGinley asked Westwood to speak because he was the most experienced Ryder Cup player in the room and because he knew he would be succinct and to the point. Then he got up and made his final speech of the week, reminding the players that Europe had been in the exact same position as the Americans (down 10–6 on the road) two years earlier, and they should be prepared for a lot of intensity early from a team that didn't want to go home embarrassed. He also reminded them to stay focused on their own matches.

"I never believed that you can take twelve individuals, put them in a room, and say, 'Presto, you're a team for one week,'" McGinley said. "I focused on trying to get them to play for their individual pride. Martin Kaymer, you're representing the town you grew up in; the people you know back home; your country; and *then* Europe. Play for all the people in the pub in Düsseldorf who want you to make them proud. It was that way with everybody."

In the American team room, the tension was almost palpable. As had become tradition, the players presented a gift to the captain. It was a mock Ryder Cup, signed by all the players and presented by Jim Furyk. Some in the room say that Watson was clearly moved by the gift. Others, not so much. There isn't any dispute though about what Watson said:

"Thank you for this. It's really thoughtful. But it's going to feel a little bit hollow if I can't hold the real thing tomorrow."

To some, Watson was being ungrateful. To others, Watson was making a point: this is really nice, but we've got serious work to do.

Then Watson talked to his team. Again, there is little doubt about what he said. The confusion came in the message his players thought he was sending.

"Look, fellas, you suck at foursomes," Watson said. "But you've been really good playing your own ball [the U.S. had won the four-balls 5–3 and lost the foursomes 7–1]. Tomorrow, you're all playing your own ball. There's no reason why we shouldn't win this thing playing our own golf balls."

Then he began going through the singles matchups. In each case, he talked up the American player and talked down the European.

"Rickie [Fowler], you've played great all week. Are you telling me you can't handle McIlroy? Of course you can."

And: "Phil, you've got Stephen Gallacher. There's absolutely no way you can lose to Stephen Gallacher."

And more along those same lines: Americans good, Europeans not good.

"It was a pep talk, period," Watson said. "I was trying to remind them they were still plenty good enough to win—which I believed they were. I told them we really needed to buckle down on holes 2 through 5 because we'd struggled there. I told them we needed to get a lot of red [U.S.] on the board early because that would make them just a little bit tight. Funny thing is, we did just that."

Some of his players didn't see the talk the way Watson did.

"I think we all knew where he was coming from," Furyk said. "But it didn't come off that way. I think some guys felt like he was talking down to them."

Spieth remembers thinking: "He can't be talking to Patrick and me about foursomes. We only played once and we halved, almost won. So why is he bringing it up?"

The answer, of course, is that he was generalizing about losing the foursomes 7–1 and trying to say, "Hey, the foursomes are behind us."

When Watson finished, Mickelson walked to the front of the room and sat on a chair. He spoke at length, talking emotionally about how much the relationships he'd forged playing in ten Ryder Cups had meant to him. He talked about each of his teammates individually, their strengths, and what he liked about each of them.

As one of the nonplayers in the room put it later: "Tom might not have lost the room that night, but Phil won it."

The sad thing, from the U.S. point of view, was that the room was so polarized. It isn't supposed to be that way on Saturday night at the Ryder Cup.

"If you need a dramatic pep talk on Saturday at the Ryder Cup, that's probably a sign that something's wrong," Spieth said. "Just being at the Ryder Cup should be all the pep talk you need. And yet I felt everyone was searching for something that night."

The U.S. did put red on the board early the next day. Spieth, leading off, was 2 up on McDowell at the turn—but lost 2 and 1.

"I really felt as if I let everyone down by losing that match," he said later. "If I had won, it might have set a different tone for the day."

Reed, following Spieth, *did* win his match—shooting seven under par to beat Henrik Stenson on 18. Reed's legend as a Ryder Cupper began to take clear shape that afternoon when he shushed the European crowd, a finger to his lips after he'd made a birdie putt on the 6th hole. Up ahead, playing the 7th, Spieth and his caddy, Michael Greller, heard all the boos coming from the 6th hole and looked at each other.

"Patrick did something," Greller said.

"No doubt," Spieth said.

The rally fizzled quickly. In the third match, McIlroy played the first six holes in six under par (four birdies and an eagle) and blew Fowler away.

"I played so well it was stupid," McIlroy said. "I really didn't give Rickie a chance—which was what I was hoping to do, knowing how hot he can get."

Mickelson *did* handle Stephen Gallacher, but Sergio García beat Furyk one up (again), and Kaymer handled Bubba Watson. It was left to Jamie Donaldson to score the clinching point with a 5-and-3 win over Bradley.

The next morning, Donaldson was asked by an earnest TV interviewer if it had hit him yet what he had accomplished.

"I don't know," Donaldson memorably answered. "I'm still drunk."

It was the Americans who needed a drink—several—when the matches were over. The final score was 16½–11½, certainly not what Watson, Ted Bishop, or Mickelson had hoped for when the week began.

The Americans had to watch the Europeans celebrate—again—and then had to go through the closing ceremony—again.

"Those are the worst two hours of the whole experience," Matt Kuchar said. "There's no way to get it over with quickly. You have to wait for the ceremony, go through the ceremony, and then go talk to the media. It's fun when you win; torture when you lose."

Just before the Americans walked into the interview room—the Sunday interviews are done en masse—Mickelson gathered a few of the players.

"Let's not give them [the media] anything," he said. "This isn't the time or place. Just say they won fair and square."

Mickelson then made a point of sitting off to the side when the Americans took their places on the podium. He would have been very happy if no one had directed a question at him.

Of course that wasn't going to happen.

After the ritual comments from Watson about how well Europe had played and how proud and honored he was to have captained his team, someone asked the inevitable question about why Europe had now won eight of the last ten matches.

"Well, the obvious answer is that our team has to play better," Watson said. "That's the obvious answer. I think they recognize that fact; that somehow collectively twelve players have to play better."

That answer *was* obvious. Europe had made 135 birdies as a team that weekend. The U.S. had made ninety. There was no doubt the team that had played better golf had won.

But that simple, seemingly harmless answer drove Mickelson over the edge. In his mind, Watson was somehow implying that his players hadn't cared enough, that they hadn't given everything they had to try to win.

Two questions later, Hank Gola, the veteran golf writer for the *New York Daily News,* asked a question that could have been answered by three players—Mickelson, Furyk, and Mahan—or by Steve Stricker, one of Watson's vice captains.

"Anyone who was on the team at Valhalla, can you put your finger on what worked in 2008 and what hasn't worked since?"

Mickelson jumped on the question.

"There were two things I think Paul Azinger did that allowed us to play our best, and one was that he got everybody invested in the process. He got everybody invested in who they were going to play with, who the picks were going to be, who was going to be in their pod, who they would play, and they had a great leader for each pod. In my case we had Ray Floyd and we hung out together and we were all invested in each other's play. We were invested in picking Hunter [Mahan] that week. Anthony Kim and Justin [Leonard] and myself were in a pod that week, and we were involved in having Hunter be our guy to fill our pod. So we were invested in the process.

"And the other thing Paul did really well was he had a great game plan for us, you know, how we were going to go about doing this, how we were going to go about playing together—golf ball, format, what we were going to do if so-and-so is playing well, if so-and-so is not playing well. We had a real game plan. Those two things helped us bring out our best golf. And I think that, you know, we all do the best that we can and we're trying our hardest and I'm just looking back at what gave us the most success. Because we use that same process in the Presidents Cup and we do really well. Unfortunately, we have strayed from a winning formula in 2008 for the last three Ryder Cups and we need to consider maybe getting back to that formula that helped us play our best."

Those 283 words—which came in a torrent—have been analyzed, sliced, diced, and broken down hundreds of times since Mickelson uttered them.

A simple synopsis was this: Azinger listened to me; Watson did not. Watson benched me for an entire day on Saturday. How dare Watson imply that we gave anything but our very best.

Watson stared ahead as Mickelson spoke, his face impassive. Mahan, sitting next to Mickelson, looked as if he was hoping the floor would open up and allow him to disappear.

Later, Watson would admit Mickelson's words stung and surprised him.

"Some of it was just the timing," he said. "I didn't think that was the time or place for comments like that. Later, in private, sure. I would never say that I didn't make mistakes that week, but I was simply doing what I thought at that moment gave our team the best chance of winning.

"You have to be prepared to make changes on the fly as the matches are going on. Did I change some things up from the original plan? Yes. Because I was trying to do everything I could to give us a chance to win."

What shocked Watson the most was the notion that Mickelson thought he had implied that his players didn't care enough. "They tried their guts out—all of them," he said. "I knew that. Nothing different ever occurred to me."

As soon as Mickelson finished his diatribe, a British reporter followed up. "That felt like a pretty brutal destruction of the leadership that's been on this week," he said.

Mickelson backpedaled—briefly.

"Oh, I'm sorry you're taking it that way. I'm just talking about what Paul Azinger did to help us play our best. It's certainly—I don't understand why you would take it that way. You asked me what I thought we should do going forward to bring our best golf out, and I go back to when we played our best golf and try to replicate that formula."

"That didn't happen this week?" came the quick follow-up question.

Mickelson paused for a moment. "Uh . . . no. Nobody here was in any decision. So, no."

Now Mickelson had officially taken down his captain in public. Naturally, Watson was asked for a response.

"I had a different philosophy as far as being captain of this team," he said—not backing down even a little. "It takes twelve players to win. It's not pods. It's twelve players. And I felt—I based my decisions on—yes, I did talk to the players, but my vice captains were very instrumental in making decisions who to pair. I had a different philosophy than Paul. I decided not to go that way. But I did have most of them play practice rounds together who played most of the time in the matches. I think that was the proper thing to do. Yes, I did mix and match a little bit from there, but again you have to go with the evolution of the playing of the match and see who is playing the best with whom, and that's what I did."

Translation: I'm not Paul Azinger. I had my own philosophy, and the reason we lost had nothing to do with pods.

The tension in the room was palpable. When someone asked Jim Furyk how he felt about the back-and-forth between Mickelson and Watson, Furyk shook his head and said, "Oh yeah, thanks for asking me that."

In other words: why are you putting *me* in the middle of this catfight?

The press conference ended a few minutes later after several benign questions about the play of the American rookies. As it turned out, the infighting on the U.S. side was only beginning.

Seven

THE NEXT MORNING, when Tom Watson and his wife Hilary arrived in the lobby of the Gleneagles hotel to check out for the trip home, they found two people waiting for them: Paul and Alison McGinley.

McGinley had planned to see Watson off even before the matches started—regardless of the outcome.

"Hal Sutton was the reason," McGinley said. "When we beat the Americans in Detroit in 2004, we were in the hotel lobby at five o'clock the next morning to fly back home. Most of us hadn't even been to bed. Hal and his wife were there to congratulate us, to tell us they hoped everything had gone well for us off the course during the week and to see us off.

"It was an absolutely classy move—especially given the outcome. I made a note to myself that if I was ever the Ryder Cup captain for matches at home that I would do that—win or lose.

"It became even more important to me to be there after I heard what happened in the American press conference. I felt terrible for Tom. What Phil did was wrong—especially the timing. You don't do that to your captain. You don't do that to a golf legend. And you don't do it right after you've lost. It isn't fair to the winning team either."

Watson greatly appreciated McGinley's gesture. There were a lot of people rallying around Watson that week. There were also a number of people defending Mickelson—saying he was simply sticking up for his teammates by taking on a captain who hadn't treated them with the respect they deserved.

Several Mickelson supporters repeated what had happened in the team room Saturday night, the spin being that Watson had dissed the gift given to him, insulted his team by saying, "You suck at foursomes," and had been disrespectful to the Europeans in his breakdown of the singles matches. None went on the record. All the quotes were anonymous.

Months later, Mickelson admitted to mixed feelings about what he'd said and when he said it.

"My reaction wasn't just directed at Tom," he said, sitting in the champions locker room at the TPC Sawgrass on a quiet Monday afternoon. "It was really twenty years of frustration coming out. It wasn't fair to Tom, really. He just happened to be the captain at that moment.

"I was reacting to my first Ryder Cup [1995] when Lanny Wadkins didn't tell me I'd be sitting out Friday morning and I found out when they announced the pairings during the opening ceremony.

"I was reacting to Hal [Sutton] telling Tiger and me two days before the matches started that we'd be playing together. All of a sudden I had two days to try to figure out how to play with Tiger's ball. I realized it went eight yards shorter with every club, but when the matches started I just didn't trust it.

"I think Tiger and I could have been a good team, I really do, but we weren't given time to prepare to play together.

"I was reacting to no one listening in '08 when I told them Paul [Azinger] should captain again in 2010, and I was reacting to Corey Pavin telling me, 'We have a twelve-man pod' when I suggested to him that he use the pod system that Paul had used.

"If all of that had happened and my record had been 8-2 in Ryder Cups, I probably wouldn't have been so upset. But my record was 2-8. It was embarrassing. When you lose a major, it's sad and it's disappointing. But when you lose a Ryder Cup—playing for your country and for your teammates—it's embarrassing. *They* set us up to lose and *we* got blamed for losing. That's what all that was about."

Some of what Mickelson said made sense. Some of it did not. For example, while having to play with a different brand of golf ball might be difficult in a foursomes match, that doesn't explain why he and Woods also lost in the four-ball match they played that same day in Detroit. It also doesn't explain why they barely spoke to each other for thirty-six holes from early morning to late afternoon.

The bottom line on it all, though, was that Mickelson and many other players felt they deserved—and needed—more input into the process.

Ironically, the man who had started the death march to Gleneagles—in the minds of the players—would be the same man who would come up with the idea that would allow the players more input: Ted Bishop.

Bishop wasn't happy with the outcome at Gleneagles in 2014, or with Mickelson's outburst, but he came to the conclusion that the PGA of America needed to try *something* different. Bishop's Watson experiment had failed: regardless of who was at fault, the final score made it a failure. And so, a little more than a month before he was scheduled to end his two-year term as PGA president, Bishop came up with one final idea: a Ryder Cup task force.

The most important part of the idea was to give Mickelson his wish: player input into everything related to the Ryder Cup. Eleven people were asked to be a part of the task force: Derek Sprague, scheduled to replace Bishop as PGA president in November; Paul Levy, who would be next in line behind Sprague as first vice president; and Pete Bevacqua, the CEO of the PGA. They would represent the PGA, which in the past had been solely in charge of choosing a captain and all the events that led to the matches.

Three past captains were also asked to be part of the task force: Raymond Floyd, the captain in 1989; Tom Lehman, the captain in 2006; and Davis Love, the captain in 2012. The most notable omission in that group was Watson—the most recent captain and, presumably, the person with the most up-to-date knowledge of what had gone wrong and what needed fixing.

Most important was the fact that five current players were asked to take part: Mickelson, Tiger Woods, Jim Furyk, Steve Stricker, and Rickie Fowler. All but Fowler had played at Medinah. Woods was the only one absent at Gleneagles, since Stricker hadn't played but had been a vice captain.

Love was actually a hybrid, since he'd been a captain and a vice captain but was still actively playing the PGA Tour at the age of fifty. Two other notable absentees were Paul Azinger—who had agreed to meet with the PGA officials as a consultant but had asked not to be on the task force—and Fred Couples, who, according to Bishop's book *Unfriended,* published in 2016, had been AWOL on a number of occasions while he was a vice captain at Medinah. Others who were part of that team later confirmed that, and that there had been some friction between Love and Couples over some of Love's decisions. The notion of friction between the two men seemed far-fetched based on their friendship and their personalities, but Couples *was* a noninvitee.

Given that Couples had been an extremely popular three-time Presidents Cup captain, a Ryder Cup vice captain, and a player on five Ryder Cup teams, it would appear to have been logical to ask him to be on the task force. His absence probably had something to do with Medinah and something to do with the simmering rivalry that always exists between the PGA of America—which runs the Ryder Cup—and the PGA Tour—which runs the Presidents Cup.

Bishop had left himself off the task force because he would be out of office by the time the first meeting took place. Of course, he expected to leave amid all the usual fanfare accorded an outgoing president at the annual meeting, scheduled for November 22.

He never made it to those meetings, though, because of one of the most bizarre incidents in golf history.

There is little doubt that one of the things Ted Bishop enjoyed most about being the president of the PGA of America was spending time with some of golf's big names. So it was hardly surprising that he was at the Greenbrier Resort in West Virginia on October 23, 2014, several weeks after the Gleneagles Ryder Cup, taking part in a two-day Nick Faldo clinic for junior golfers.

Faldo was one of a number of name players whom Jim Justice, the Greenbrier's owner, had put on his payroll. Tom Watson had been listed as the "pro emeritus"—even though he'd never set foot on the property before being given that title—and Faldo and Bubba Watson had been given homes at the Greenbrier, among other perks, for spending time there.

A few days prior to the clinic, Ian Poulter's book *No Limits* had been released in Great Britain. In the book, Poulter was mildly critical of both Faldo and Watson as Ryder Cup captains, questioning some of their decisions in much the same way many others had been critical.

In Watson's case, he simply said some of the European players had been surprised by some of his decisions, especially sitting Mickelson and Keegan Bradley on Saturday afternoon. Faldo was different. Poulter didn't actually criticize Faldo's 2008 captaincy—Europe's only loss in the twenty-first century at that point—but the fact that Faldo had said during the Gleneagles matches that Sergio García had been "worthless" that week.

"A lot of us lost a lot of respect for him for saying that," Poulter wrote. "Maybe he should look in the mirror. It sounds like sour grapes."

Bishop took the comments personally. That evening, he tweeted at Poulter: "Faldo's record stands by itself. Six majors and all-time leader in RC points. Yours vs. His? Lil Girl."

The last two words seemed to come out of left field. But if there was any doubt about Bishop's intent, it went away when he took to Facebook.

"Used to be athletes who had lesser records or accomplishments in a sport never criticized the icons," he wrote. "Tom Watson (8 majors and 10-3-1 Ryder Cup record) and Nick Faldo (6 majors and all-time Ryder Cup points leader) got bashed by Ian James Poulter. Really? Sounds like a little school girl squealing during recess. C'MON MAN!"

Even though Bishop deleted both the tweet and the post as soon as he realized there was a problem, it was, of course, too late. There really was no way to walk back the comments, which were sexist, foolish, and stunning.

Bishop's notion that no one was allowed to criticize an iconic player unless his record was equal to or greater than that icon made no sense at all. Poulter was not, in any way, criticizing the playing careers of the two men, but how they had captained Ryder Cup teams. He was certainly not the only one to criticize either in that context.

What's more, within the context of the Ryder Cup—which is what Poulter was writing about—his winning percentage was *better* than Faldo's or Watson's. Watson had gone 10-4-1. Faldo *was* Europe's all-time points leader, but his record was 23-19-4. Poulter's was 13-4-2.

Sure, Faldo and Watson had become Bishop's friends, but Poulter's comments were hardly incendiary. Maybe, as some have speculated, it was an attempt by Bishop to draw some attention to himself by engaging in a cyber-feud with Poulter. There wasn't much doubt that Bishop enjoyed the spotlight given to him as PGA president. He also clearly felt a sense of loyalty to two men who had become his friends.

Reading the tea leaves and the backlash, the PGA reacted quickly.

Bishop was asked to resign the next day but refused, saying he wished to make his case to the PGA board. He was less than a month from the end of his presidency, and—understandably—this wasn't the way he wanted to go out.

According to Bishop's book *Unfriended,* Sprague and Bevacqua agreed to let Bishop speak to the board on a conference call at four o'clock in the afternoon. On that call, Bishop admitted his mistake, pointed out that he had been prevented from walking it back right away because Bevacqua and Julius Mason had told him not to make any comment when the initial furor began, said he would gladly issue another apology, and asked that he be allowed to keep his job.

The board voted to impeach him and take away all the perks that come with being a PGA past president. It was a stunning, dizzyingly fast fall from grace.

In truth, no one came away from the incident looking very good. Even in his book, Bishop fails to explain adequately what in the world he was thinking when he posted the tweet and the Facebook post. He made a case for himself as an advocate of bringing more women into golf—both his daughters are in the golf business—but Bishop still insisted in his book that he was a victim of "political correctness."

Unfortunately, that doesn't explain why he *twice* called Poulter a "girl" in a clearly pejorative way.

In the end, Bishop deserved to be taken down in some form: reprimanded at the very least, perhaps even a second request that he resign after being heard. But the PGA appeared to go out of its way to humiliate him. They took down someone whose leadership for almost two years had been very positive for the organization. And at the same time, ironically, the PGA refused to move the 2017 Senior PGA Championship and the 2022 PGA Championship from golf courses owned by President Donald Trump, who has said and done things about and to women that go way beyond calling someone a "Lil Girl."

Bishop was formally impeached (unanimously, except for one abstention—Dottie Pepper), and Sprague was elected president to fill out the last month of Bishop's term.

It had been twenty-five days since Europe had retained the Ryder Cup and Mickelson and Watson had exchanged barbs during the U.S. press conference. The PGA was officially in shambles. So was American golf.

—

On December 9, 2014—forty-seven days after Bishop's impeachment and seventeen days after Sprague had officially been voted to a two-year term as PGA president, ten men gathered in the second-floor conference room at PGA headquarters in Palm Beach, Florida.

Eight of the ten were members of the newly formed Ryder Cup task force. Three others—Davis Love, Tiger Woods, and Steve Stricker—were on speakerphones placed on the conference table in the middle of the room. There were two non–task force members in the room: Kerry Haigh, the PGA's executive vice president, who had been in charge of every Ryder Cup held in the U.S. since 1989; and Julius Mason, the vice president of communications who had worked for the PGA since 1991.

Mickelson had made the longest trip, flying in from San Diego. Most of the others lived in Florida and had driven to Palm Beach. Woods lived right down the street, but was home sick and, thus, on the phone.

The agenda for the evening was simple: figure out how to put the U.S. in position to play better in the Ryder Cup. What made the meeting unique was it was the first time the leadership of the PGA had said to the players, "Tell us what you need."

Most of what they needed—or wanted—was to copy what Europe had been doing for years.

With Mason transcribing everything that was said on a large easel, the group threw out ideas on subjects ranging from the criteria for vice captains to how many parties the players should be required to attend during the week.

The selection of vice captains was an important issue. For years, Europe's vice captains had always been past captains and players who were considered likely future captains. What's more, Europe had always made a point of inviting past captains to the Ryder Cup even if they weren't officially taking part. Langer's presence in 2012—even though he wasn't a vice captain—had been critical if only because of the pep talk he'd given Martin Kaymer on Friday.

The days when Tom Watson brought Stan Thirsk as his only vice captain or when Tom Kite brought Dennis Satyshur, the pro at Caves Valley in Baltimore, who was a close friend, needed to be put to rest.

The players were insistent they needed more time to themselves during the week. *One* meeting with the media per player; *no* gala banquet less than forty-eight hours before the first tee time on Friday.

There was discussion of the need to try to get potential team members together on more than one occasion during the year leading to the matches. In 2010, Corey Pavin had held a barbeque at the PGA Championship and invited all potential team members. Woods, a likely captain's pick, hadn't bothered to show up. That sort of thing needed to stop: either you were all the way in or you weren't in at all.

As the men in the room and on the phones threw out ideas, Mason kept writing them down. When he finished a page, he took it and taped it to the windows in the room. By the time the meeting was over, all the windows were covered.

Finally, the conversation turned to the most crucial decision of all: who would be the next captain? Rather than discuss specific names, the group started discussing the qualities they wanted in a captain. Among them:

— Someone who could relate to the players who would be on the team. Someone still connected enough to the Tour to actually know the players. (This might have been called "The Watson rule.")
— Someone who was committed to the Ryder Cup, who would be "all in," from day one.
— Preferably someone who had been a vice captain in the past.
— Someone who would be willing to be a vice captain in the future and share his wisdom with the next captain.
— Someone whose selection would be universally supported by the players—not so much in public utterances, but behind closed doors.

Once Mason had written all the various criteria down, specific names were mentioned.

Azinger, the last winning captain. Except he had told the PGA officials in their meetings he didn't want the job. He'd be happy to help out in the background, but didn't want to make another almost two-year commitment.

Couples. He had been wildly successful as Presidents Cup captain on three occasions. The players loved playing for him. "He made everyone feel relaxed," Mickelson said.

"He was always a mess inside, but it never showed," Furyk added. "Freddy was always cool."

In fact, when Love had been asked prior to Medinah what Couples's job was as a vice captain, he'd answered, "To be cool."

Ultimately, though, Couples's cool and his Presidents Cup captaincy probably worked against him. Even though Ted Bishop and Tim Finchem had mended a lot of the broken fences that existed for years between the PGA of America and the PGA Tour, there was always going to be a rivalry—especially when it came to the Ryder Cup and Presidents Cup.

In fact, when Couples had first accepted the job as Presidents Cup captain for 2009, a number of friends—including Love—had warned him that it might cost him a chance to be Ryder Cup captain. Couples knew all that, but accepted anyway.

There was also the very real fact that being a Ryder Cup captain is very different from being a Presidents Cup captain. As hard as the PGA Tour has tried to make people believe the Presidents Cup belongs in the same sentence with the Ryder Cup, it doesn't.

To begin with, it has existed only since 1994, started by the Tour because the Ryder Cup had become so popular and because three of the best players in the world—Greg Norman, Nick Price, and Ernie Els— couldn't play in the Ryder Cup. What's more, if the Tour hadn't gone ahead and launched the Presidents Cup, IMG, the giant management company, was going to start an event of its own.

The U.S. has a 9-1-1 record in the Presidents Cup—the only loss coming in 1998—and most of the matches have been one-sided. What's more, even though all the Europeans don't come from the same country, they come from the same continent and represent the same tour.

The so-called International Team that plays the U.S. in the Presidents Cup is far-flung, players coming from different continents and tours with little in common except perhaps that most play on the same tour as the Americans—the PGA Tour. In fact, the Tour manages *both* teams during the matches, as opposed to the Ryder Cup, where a very real rivalry exists not only between the players but between the staffs of the two tours.

The most enduring description of the Presidents Cup came in 1998 when Lanny Wadkins wondered exactly why the U.S. team was flying to the other side of the world to play the matches.

"Why is everyone going to Australia," he said, "to play against a bunch of guys who live in Orlando?"

Being Ryder Cup captain is almost a full-time job. It involves constant media appearances, sponsor appearances, and made-for-the-public events like the "one-year countdown" celebration that the two captains attend on-site. It requires a great deal of patience and stamina long before you get into the important questions like who will be on your team and who will play with whom.

"That sort of stuff just isn't Freddy," Love said. "The Presidents Cup just isn't like that. In truth, there aren't a lot of guys who would want to do all the stuff I did as captain. Freddy would not have enjoyed a lot of it."

Other names were raised: David Toms, who had been passed over for Watson in 2014. Larry Nelson, also passed over back in the 1990s. The Watson rule eliminated Nelson—he was two years older than Watson.

And then Davis Love's name came up. From 1989 through 2012, the U.S. had not had a repeat Ryder Cup captain. Watson's captaincy had changed that. Love had been captain only two Ryder Cups ago. The consensus, though, was that the loss at Medinah hadn't been his fault and that, in truth, the work he had done in making the Friday-Saturday pairings had staked the U.S. to the 10–6 lead it couldn't hold on Sunday.

Everyone began looking at the criteria on Mason's handwritten pages: *Still relates to the players*—check, Love was still playing the Tour. *Would be supported by the players*—check, few players in golf were better liked or more respected than Love. Furyk, Fowler, Woods, Mickelson, and Stricker all backed that up. *Had previous experience as a vice captain* and *as a captain*. No other candidate had both. *Someone who was "all in" on the Ryder Cup*. Love had been a willing and eager vice captain in 2010 and would have done it again in 2014, if asked.

His father, Davis Love Jr., had been a PGA professional—a renowned teacher—who had taught his son about the Ryder Cup from a very early age. In 1997, after he had won the PGA Championship, Love had climbed onto a plane to fly home with his brother Mark and had said, "Now I can be a Ryder Cup captain."

It was pretty much a given that the PGA wanted captains who had won major championships—especially those who had won the PGA.

As the conversation continued, Love, sitting on the conference call in his office at home in Sea Island, Georgia, began to feel as if all eyes in the room were metaphorically on him. Sprague suggested everyone take a fifteen-minute break. They had been going at it for more than three hours.

Love was on the phone throughout the break.

"By then it was apparent to me that they were probably going to ask me to do it," he said. "I had two concerns. The first was that I might be taking it away from someone who hadn't done it. I'd had my chance already. I wondered if that was fair. But then it occurred to me that the point of all this was to change the culture, to make sure we picked the captain with the best chance of winning, not just someone we thought deserved the honor.

"Second, though, I had to have everyone on board. I called each of the other players and I said, 'If they ask me to do this, I'm not taking it unless I have your absolute assurance that you'll do anything—and I mean *anything*—I ask you to do to help me. I knew that at least one, maybe two of them were going to be vice captains because of the new criteria. But I needed *all* of them to guarantee me they were really on board with all this."

All the players said the exact same thing: anything you need, Davis.

The meeting resumed and went on for another hour. There was no formal vote on the next captain. But when the meeting was over there was little doubt who that captain would be: Davis Love III. There was also little doubt about one other thing: he would be the most scrutinized captain in Ryder Cup history.

The existence of the task force made that a certainty.

Eight

O N FEBRUARY 24, 2015, Davis Love was formally named as the American Ryder Cup captain for the matches at Hazeltine, which were just over nineteen months away.

The task force had met a second time in San Diego on January 26 to firm up everything that had been discussed in Palm Beach and to pick a captain. It was a foregone conclusion by then that Love was going to be the choice.

By the time the PGA held a press conference to announce Love's captaincy—and that Tom Lehman, a Minnesota native and past captain, would be one of his vice captains—word had already leaked that Love was the choice.

That was fine with the PGA, which scheduled the announcement to coincide with the playing of the Honda Classic, just down the street at PGA National Resort and Spa. That meant that much of the golf media—national and international—would be in town, since the tournament traditionally drew a strong field that included a number of international players.

The introduction was more of a pep rally than a press conference. Phil Mickelson, whose outburst at Gleneagles had set the events in motion leading to Love becoming captain, sat almost directly behind Love in a black leather jacket, looking like he had ridden in on a motorcycle.

Derek Sprague and Pete Bevacqua spoke, more or less comparing the task force meetings to the Constitutional Convention in Philadelphia in 1787, and the meetings of the Knights of the Round Table. It was a shame that neither King Arthur nor John Hancock could attend.

When all the dust had cleared and everyone had finished singing Kumbaya, the message that mattered was this: from this day forward, it's all for one and one for all on the U.S. side of the Atlantic.

If that was the goal, then Davis Love was the perfect choice to be captain. There was no one in golf—on either side of the Atlantic or the Pacific—who didn't like Love. Love had already had a hall-of-fame career, winning twenty times on the PGA Tour, including the 1997 PGA. But there were plenty of people who believed he should have won more—a lot more—and the only thing that had prevented him from doing so was that he was just too nice a guy.

Love was competitive and wanted to win every time he teed it up, but he didn't have the mean streak the best of the best always seem to have. If Tiger Woods would step on an opponent's neck in order to win, Love would be the guy calling 911 and tossing aside his clubs to see if he could stop the bleeding.

Golf had been the driving force in his life almost from the day he was born. In fact, on that day—April 13, 1964—his father, Davis Love Jr., had been the first-day leader at the Masters. His dad never played the Tour full-time, but was a very good player and a highly respected teaching pro. He worked often at national teaching clinics with Harvey Penick, who cowrote *The Little Red Book,* which described his teaching philosophy and sold millions of copies.

Davis III—or "Trip," as he was called as a kid—was a phenom at a very young age. He was six feet three with a long, smooth swing as a teenager and, by the time he was in high school, he could hit a golf ball prodigious distances. He opted to go to the University of North Carolina, but wasn't terribly happy there because he never really got along with Devon Brouse, the longtime golf coach.

Love dropped out after his junior year and decided to take a shot at the PGA Tour qualifying school in the fall of 1985. Back then, he hit the ball about as far as anyone had ever seen. He had two problems: he couldn't consistently hit the ball *straight,* and he wasn't a great putter.

But he made it through Q school, rare for a player that young (twenty-one) and even rarer for a player making the attempt for the first time. He played well enough in 1986 to finish seventy-seventh on the money list and easily kept his playing card. Then, in 1987, just after turning twenty-three, he won at Hilton Head, the first of five victories at Harbour Town, arguably famous designer Pete Dye's best golf course.

On November 13, 1988, he and his wife, Robin, flew to Maui for a week's vacation that would include Davis playing in the Maui Invitational, an end-of-the-year exhibition that players lined up to play in because it was, basically, a lucrative vacation. Their six-month-old daughter, Lexie, was home being taken care of by Davis's parents.

When they reached their hotel at about five o'clock Hawaii time, Davis routinely called home to let his mother know they had arrived.

As soon as Davis heard Penta Love's voice, he knew something was horribly wrong. "Your father's plane just dropped off the radar," she said. "They can't find it."

Davis Love Jr. had been en route that day, along with two friends and colleagues, to the annual meeting of the *Golf Digest* instructional staff, scheduled to be held the next day at the Innisbrook Resort, outside Tampa. It was about a five-hour drive from Sea Island, Georgia—where the Loves had moved when Davis was a teenager—to Tampa.

Wanting to spend as much of his Sunday as possible at home, Davis Love Jr. proposed to the two friends he was traveling with, fellow teachers Jimmy Hodges and John Popa, that they fly—first by private plane to Jacksonville—and then on a commercial jet to Tampa. The drive to Jacksonville was only seventy miles and would take only a little more than an hour, but the flight from Sea Island would take about fifteen minutes and wouldn't involve parking at a big airport.

The plane the three men boarded on that Sunday evening was smaller than they had expected. It was a Piper Cherokee Archer, big enough to seat them, but not big enough for them to take their golf clubs along.

The weather in Sea Island was perfect, but by the time the plane reached Jacksonville, a thick fog had enveloped the airport and the pilot, Frank (Chip) Worthington III, was in communication with the tower about the lack of visibility as they approached. According to the audio log recovered from the plane, the controllers in the Jacksonville tower told Worthington that a couple of planes had missed the runway on first approach because of the conditions, but his plane should be clear to land.

That was at 8:52 p.m.—twenty-nine minutes after takeoff. Worthington responded by saying, "Okay, four-two Lima, thank ya."

The last three digits of the plane's tail number were 4-2-L; thus the plane was identified as 4-2-Lima.

That was the last anyone heard from the plane.

As soon as Davis III hung up with his mother, he and Robin went looking for help to get home. A friend whom Davis knew from the PGA Tour policy board had flown to Maui on his private plane. He offered them a ride to San Francisco, where they could change planes to get home.

This was 1988. There was no way of communicating from the airplane. Six terrifying hours later—by then it was early morning on the East Coast—Davis got off the plane, walked to a pay phone, and called home. His younger brother Mark answered the phone. The plane had crashed. All four men on board were dead.

The next two years are a blur in Love's memory. He didn't win again until August 1990, when he won the International, a tournament in thin air in Denver where his drives seemed to carry for miles.

"The hardest part, honestly, was that so many people were crushed by my dad's death," he said. "Every week, when I got to a tournament, I had to steel myself for people coming up to me and telling me how sorry they were and about something my dad had done for them or what a great teacher and person he was. Every single one of them meant well. They were grieving too and wanted to let me know they understood how awful I felt and that they understood the loss I'd suffered.

"But that made it almost impossible for me to move on. Most of the time when a tragedy like that happens, there's a period of mourning you go through and then you have to move on with your life. The person you lost is always there in your heart, but people aren't coming up to you a year later to tell you how sorry they are. I had to go through it all over again week after week.

"My only escape from it was when I got inside the ropes and was able to wrap my mind around trying to play golf. Even when I did that, though, my dad was still there because everything I knew about the game and the golf swing had come from him."

Slowly, with the help of his family, his dad's circle of friends, and the friends he'd made on tour, Love learned to cope with the loss. By 1992, he was a star, winning three times that year.

There were still moments. In 1993, he and Tom Kite got off a plane in San Francisco on their way to play in the Tour Championship, which was held that fall at the Olympic Club. As they walked to baggage claim, he and Kite walked right past the phone that Love had used to call home on that awful morning almost five years earlier. Kite, who had known Davis Love Jr. well, saw the look on his friend's face, understood instantly what had happened, and said quietly, "Just take a few deep breaths."

In 1997, at the age of thirty-three, Love finally won his first, and as it turned out his only, major. It was the PGA Championship, held that year at Winged Foot. After waiting out a rain delay, Love beat his good friend Justin Leonard down the stretch. As he stood over his final putt on 18, a rainbow appeared in the sky. Everyone—including Davis—was convinced his father was looking down and smiling.

It was that night that Davis voiced to younger brother Mark his hope that his win at Winged Foot would pave the way to being Ryder Cup captain someday. That captaincy happened in 2012, only to end in a stunning defeat. Love was surprised to get a second chance in 2016. But he was adamant about making certain the result would be different this time.

When the press conference/pep rally was over, Love posed for photos with almost everyone in the building. The photo sent out that day by the PGA of America showed Love sitting in between Sprague and Bevacqua, with Mickelson, Lehman, and PGA vice president Paul Levy standing behind them.

In front of Love was the Ryder Cup. Of course, *the* Ryder Cup—the one that had been won by Europe five months earlier at Gleneagles— was in Sutton Coldfield, England, the home base of the European Tour.

The photo-op Cup was always on hand in Palm Beach for moments like this one. All six men in the photo knew, just as Watson had known on that Saturday night the previous September, that this was *not* the Ryder Cup they all wanted their photo taken with nineteen months later in Minnesota.

Six days before Love was named the U.S. captain, Darren Clarke was named as Europe's captain. Love had been a surprise to most; Clarke was a surprise to almost no one.

When Paul McGinley had been selected over Clarke in 2013, there had been a general understanding that Clarke was next in line. That understanding was the reason why McGinley had been so surprised when Clarke had thrown his hat into the ring for Gleneagles.

"Everyone knew that Darren was meant to be the captain in America in 2016," he said. "We'd both been vice captains in Wales and at Medinah, but I'd captained the Seve Trophy teams twice. Just about all the players had said publicly that they wanted me to captain at Gleneagles. Darren and I were such good friends that it came as a shock to me when he said at a press conference that he'd like to be considered for '14."

Clarke and McGinley were so close that when Heather Clarke died on the eve of the 2006 PGA Championship, McGinley withdrew and flew home to help Clarke and his family deal with their grief. Alison McGinley and Heather Clarke had been the closest of friends.

Clarke says now that he "made a mistake" by challenging McGinley for the 2014 captaincy. He believed he was ready for the job after having been vice captain twice, and he probably miscalculated the depth of McGinley's support among the players—notably McIlroy, who considered Clarke a hero but had played for McGinley in the Seve Trophy matches and still believes he learned more about team competition from McGinley than from any captain he's played for since then.

"I've played for very good captains along the way," he said. "But Paul was unique. He knew exactly what to say to players as individuals and as a team. I still remember him pulling me aside at that first Seve Trophy I played [2009] and saying, 'I want you to set a quiet goal for yourself. You can't *always* win your team matches because some days your partner might not quite be with it. But you're a good enough player to win all your singles matches. Take some extra pride in trying to do that.' He always found different ways to motivate different guys."

Much like Azinger, although without any mention of "pods," McGinley knew whom he was going to pair with whom well in advance of the matches. When he realized that Victor Dubuisson, a moody but talented young French player, was going to be on the team, he flew to Monte Carlo (Dubuisson's home) to spend several hours explaining what he hoped his role would be with the team.

He also sat down with Graeme McDowell, the hero of the 2010 matches, and told him he was going to play him only once a day on Friday and Saturday and that he needed him to pair with and mentor Dubuisson.

"He told me exactly what his thinking was," McDowell said. "He said there were a several guys he had to have out there pretty much every session—Rory, Sergio, Stenson, Rose—I got that. But he said he needed me with Dubuisson because of my experience, that I had to be the wise old head out there. I liked the idea. I was completely sold on it by the time we got to Gleneagles."

McIlroy and Rose played all five sessions; Stenson and García, four. Dubuisson and McDowell won both their foursomes matches, wrapping up both afternoon sessions with resounding wins.

Europe's system for choosing a captain had always involved players—past and present. In 2016, the five-man committee consisted of the past three captains: Colin Montgomerie, José-María Olazábal, and McGinley, along with George O'Grady, the chief executive of the European Tour, and David Howell, who had played on Ryder Cup teams in the past and was the representative from the European Tour players board.

Clarke was really the only candidate. There might have been some consideration for Thomas Björn, who had been a vice captain in 2012 and come back to make the team in 2014, and there were some who wanted McGinley to captain again. McGinley put a halt to that talk.

"I'm finished with Ryder Cup," he said. "I had an amazing run with it [three wins as a player, two as a vice captain, and one as captain] and loved my involvement. But once we'd won at Gleneagles, that was it for me. I'll turn fifty [at the end of 2016] and go to America and play on the Senior tour there. I'd like to play again."

That left Clarke as the easy and obvious choice.

"It was something I'd dreamed about for a long time," he said. "I knew the day I was selected we were going to have a difficult time at Hazeltine. I knew how desperate the Americans were going to be to win."

He smiled. "And they had a task force."

The task force became the subject of a good deal of joking on the European side. Just the phrase "task force" invited ridicule. In fact, even before the matches began at Hazeltine, the PGA of America had changed the name to "The Ryder Cup Committee."

Clarke wasn't wrong when he said his team would be up against it at Hazeltine. Several players who had played key roles in Europe's past success were struggling or getting older or both. Ian Poulter hadn't been as brilliant in 2014 as in the past. That had gone more or less unnoticed because Europe won so easily. He continued to struggle with his game as 2016 began. Luke Donald, who hadn't made the team in 2014, was still not playing well. Neither was McDowell. Lee Westwood, third on the all-time points list in Ryder Cup history, was forty-three and going through a divorce. Clearly, Clarke's team was going to be much younger and more inexperienced than McGinley's team had been.

Clarke was hardly daunted by the task in front of him. Growing up in Northern Ireland, he'd faced challenges far more difficult than trying to put together a Ryder Cup lineup.

He was born in Dungannon in 1968, a year before "The Troubles" began. He remembers bombings taking place throughout his boyhood and, like almost everyone in the country, lost relatives through the years. Dungannon is about forty miles from Omagh, site of the worst bombing disaster of the Troubles, the August 1998 car bombing that killed twenty-nine people and seriously wounded more than two hundred others.

"The golf club [Dungannon] where I grew up playing was bombed four different times when I was a boy," Clarke said. "We had both Catholic and Protestant members, so I guess we got it from both sides. The schools were segregated—Catholic and Protestant—sport was not."

Clarke was a gifted rugby player as a boy and says to this day it was his first love. "Had I been good enough to play it on the professional level, that's what I would have done," he said. "I loved the physicality of it. I loved the contact. There came a time, though, when I realized I wasn't going to play professionally. That was when I realized I was probably meant for golf."

He had started playing when he was eleven, after caddying for his father when he was younger. Within two years, he was a low-single-digit handicapper and having success in junior tournaments. When he was eighteen, he went to play at Wake Forest, one of *the* college golf powers in the U.S. He didn't stay long.

Jesse Haddock, the coach, was a legend at the school. He'd been there for twenty-six years and had won three national titles, producing stars like Curtis Strange, Lanny Wadkins, Jay Haas, Scott Hoch, and Billy Andrade—among others. Because the Deacons were so deep and just coming off a national championship, Clarke was red-shirted as a freshman.

A year later, he felt he had played his way into the lineup for the fall season, but Haddock didn't play him. The day after the second match in which he hadn't played, Clarke went to see his coach. The conversation was less than cordial. Haddock wasn't used to players questioning him. He suggested to Clarke that if he was unhappy with the way he was being treated, he could leave.

Clarke did. "I packed up and flew home the next day," he said. "Never looked back."

He had to wait until the next summer to turn pro, so he took a job bartending in a local hotel called the Inn in the Park.

One night, Clarke was behind the bar when the phone rang.

"There's a bomb," a voice said. "You better get everybody out. You don't have much time."

In Northern Ireland, bomb threats were always taken seriously. The bar was evacuated. Fifteen minutes later, the bomb went off and the bar was flattened.

"I found out later that the bomb had been behind the bar, about five yards from where I was standing most of the night," Clarke said. "It had apparently been put there by someone at about five o'clock. If it had gone off before it was supposed to, I'd have been dead."

Instead, he played in important amateur tournaments, culminating that summer at the Irish Amateur. The week of the event, a local lawyer who was a friend of Clarke's family called IMG's London office to say that Clarke was planning to turn pro after the Irish Amateur and was interested in talking to IMG about representing him.

The phone call wasn't returned. So the lawyer placed a call to Andrew "Chubby" Chandler, a recently retired player who was in the process of launching his own representation company and looking for players—any players.

Chandler had been a journeyman who realized a couple of years after making his only cut in a major (the 1986 Open Championship) that he probably needed to find a different way to make a living. He was about to turn thirty-six and had young children.

"I wasn't meant to work in a pro shop selling shoes and shirts to people," he said. "Someone suggested I should try PR, and I thought that might be all right until I realized I didn't know what PR stood for. So I decided to have a go at representing players. At the very least, I knew something about *being* a player."

On the morning after Clarke won the Irish Amateur, he met with Chandler and signed a management contract with him. Later that day, his friend finally got a callback from IMG London. Someone there had noticed Clarke's win.

"My friend told them it was too late, I'd already signed with Chubby," Clarke said. "I don't know which agent it was, but he said, 'Your friend just made a very big mistake.'"

Twenty-six years later, Clarke is still represented by Chandler's company, ISM—International Sports Management—and Chandler, who has also represented Ernie Els, Rory McIlroy, Lee Westwood, and Danny Willett, is one of golf's most prominent agents.

Clarke qualified for the European Tour in 1991 and won for the first time in 1993 when he beat Nick Faldo and Vijay Singh down the stretch to win a tournament in Belgium. He finished eighth on the Order of Merit that year and continued to be a consistent money-winner for the next ten years. In 1997 he made his first Ryder Cup team.

"I was thrilled to make the team, but more thrilled to be playing for Seve [Ballesteros]," he said. "I had two heroes in golf as a kid—Seve and Greg Norman. I loved Seve's flair on the golf course, and I loved Greg's flair off the golf course—all the toys: helicopters, Ferraris.

"But then when we got to Valderrama [site of that year's Ryder Cup], I'm not sure Seve spoke five words to me all week. He never even told me I wasn't going to play at all on Friday."

Clarke finally got to play on Saturday morning, pairing with Montgomerie for a 2-and-1 win over Fred Couples and Davis Love—arguably the U.S.'s strongest team. Even so, it was back to the bench in the afternoon. On Sunday, he lost his singles match to Mickelson 2 and 1 as the U.S. almost rallied after trailing 10½–5½ the first two days. Costantino Rocca's stunning 4-and-2 win over Tiger Woods gave Europe just enough cushion to hang on for a 14½–13½ win.

"I was thrilled we won," Clarke said. "But very disappointed to only play twice. I think if I learned one thing that weekend it was how important it is for a captain to communicate with his players. Seve didn't do that. I think he was very lucky we won, because if we hadn't won on his home ground it would have been very embarrassing for him."

Earlier that summer, Clarke had made his first important appearance on the international scene when he led the Open Championship for two rounds at Troon and played with Jesper Parnevik in the final pairing on Sunday. Justin Leonard shot 65 on the last day to beat both Clarke and Parnevik by two shots.

Three years later, Clarke beat *five* major champions en route to winning the World Match Play title. He beat Paul Azinger in the first round, Mark O'Meara in the second, Thomas Björn (the only non–major champion he faced) in the round of sixteen, Hal Sutton in the quarterfinals, and David Duval in the semis.

That put him into the final against Woods. The match was thirty-six holes. Clarke won 4 and 3. Not only was the victory the most important of his career at the time, but the day marked the beginning of a friendship between Clarke and Woods.

"I think he's always enjoyed people who give him a hard time just for the fun of it," Clarke said. "He started calling me an 'f-f' that day, and you can imagine what that means. After I won I found a note in my locker that said, 'Great playing. You're still an f-f. Enjoy the accomplishment.'"

All was well in Clarke's life. He was making a lot of money, was able to afford a lot of the "toys" that Norman had owned when he had idolized him as a boy, and was happily married with two sons, Tyrone and Conor. Then, just before Christmas in 2001, Heather Clarke discovered a lump in her breast. She had cancer. After undergoing treatment for several months, she was pronounced cancer free.

Clarke changed a good deal during that frightening period. He became less temperamental on the golf course, where he was known for occasional volcanic explosions when things went wrong. He had developed a reputation with the British media as being "unplayable" on certain days. He also lost thirty pounds from what had been a six-foot-two-inch, 255-pound frame.

In 2003, with Heather healthy again, he told *Golf Digest*'s John Huggan how the scare he'd gotten, followed by Heather's recovery, had made him understand how lucky he was to be doing what he was doing and making the money he was making—as long as he had a healthy family.

The following year, Heather's cancer returned. She battled it for two years, but this time there was no recovery. Clarke took long breaks from playing to be with her, and when he did play, his mind clearly wasn't all there. On August 13, 2006, Heather Clarke died at the age of thirty-nine.

"By far, the most difficult thing I've ever done in my life was to sit down with my two boys, who were eight and five, and explain to them that their mother was about to pass away," he said, his voice soft but clear almost ten years later. "I mean, it's the sort of thing that you can't possibly imagine."

Because his play had been infrequent and well below his norm, Clarke wasn't close to making that year's Ryder Cup team on points. Ian Woosnam, the captain, had told him, though, that if he felt up to it, he wanted him on the team.

"One of the last things Heather said to me was 'I want you to go and play the Ryder Cup,'" he remembered. "So when Woosy formally asked me to do it, I knew I had to go. I thought it would be good to be around my mates. I had no idea how I'd play. But the support I got—from both teams—was unbelievable."

Clarke dreaded the opening ceremony, knowing he would be the only player walking in alone. That feeling went away when Amy Mickelson stepped between her husband and Clarke and took both their hands.

"Never forget it," Clarke said. "She didn't say a word. There was no need. It's as vivid in my mind right now as if it happened yesterday."

Three years later, when Amy Mickelson was diagnosed with breast cancer, Phil Mickelson remembers the first phone call he got from another player after the news of Amy's illness became public.

It was from Clarke.

"All he said was 'I'm here for you,'" Mickelson said. "And he was."

Nine

I F THERE WAS any doubt about Darren Clarke being a Ryder Cup captain someday, it went away in 2011 when, more or less, he came out of nowhere to win the Open Championship in Kent, England.

He'd been able to keep his emotions together during that weekend in Ireland at the 2006 Ryder Cup, pairing with Lee Westwood to win two matches, halving a third one partnering with Colin Montgomerie, and then winning his dramatic singles match against Zach Johnson.

Not surprisingly, though, he struggled with his game the next few years. In 2007, he dropped to 143rd on the Order of Merit—the European Tour money list—withdrawing from a number of tournaments and not playing well when he did play. A year later his game came back: he won twice and was thirteenth on the Order of Merit. His lost 2007 kept him from making the Ryder Cup team on points, and Nick Faldo didn't pick him, which surprised and disappointed Clarke given that the team had four rookies and he'd played on five teams, four of them winners.

The next two years he had mixed results and no victories. He'd shown a hint of form in the spring of 2011 with his first win in three years, but was an afterthought when the Open was played that year at Royal St. George's. He hadn't had a top ten in a major championship since 2001, and had *played* in only ten of the nineteen majors since Heather's death, making just four cuts and never finishing in the top forty.

But for four windy days in July 2011, at the age of forty-two, the best of Clarke came back. The weather was difficult throughout the week—creating the kind of tough conditions Clarke always preferred. "I never liked playing in good weather very much," he said, half joking.

Ironically, Rory McIlroy, his fellow Northern Irishman, admitted after playing poorly in the third round that he didn't like playing in windy weather, that he preferred warm weather, a golf course where you played the ball in the air (as opposed to relying on getting good bounces and rolls on links courses) and wore short sleeves rather than bundling up against the cold.

McIlroy was pilloried by many in the British media for, in effect, rejecting the style of golf played in his homeland and his weather heritage.

Clarke shot 69 that day to take a one-shot lead over Dustin Johnson going into the final round. McIlroy, who had played solidly the first two rounds, trailing coleaders Clarke and Lucas Glover by four shots after thirty-six holes, skied to a 74 that knocked him out of contention. He shot 73 the final day to finish T-25 amid predictions he would never win his home country's championship. Three years later, he would prove the doomsayers wrong.

At the 2011 Open Championship, Clarke had to hold off charges from Johnson and Phil Mickelson on the final day. Mickelson played the first ten holes in six under par to tie for the lead before losing momentum by missing a short par putt on the next hole. Clarke had eagled the 7th hole to take the lead back, with Johnson two shots back standing on the tee of the par-5 14th.

Johnson decided to go for the green with his second shot but whistled a two-iron out-of-bounds en route to a double-bogey 7. That gave Clarke a four-shot margin with four holes to play, and he cruised home, winning by three over Johnson and Mickelson. He was the only player in the field who shot even par or better in all four rounds, and that consistency on a wet and windy golf course proved to be the difference.

In one of the more emotional post–golf tournament acceptance speeches that anyone could remember, Clarke talked about Heather and his boys.

"In terms of what's going through my heart, there's obviously someone who is watching from up there and I know she would be very proud of me," he said. "But I think she'd be more proud of my two boys and them at home watching more than anything else. It's been a long journey to get here."

That was certainly true. Royal St. George's was Clarke's twentieth Open Championship.

Clarke did quite a bit of celebrating after lifting the Claret Jug and, having achieved the victory he'd spent his life chasing, clearly lost some of his zest for the game. Since that near-perfect weekend on the southwest coast of England, he hasn't won anywhere, and in eighteen major championships, he's made seven cuts—his highest finish being a tie for twenty-first place in the 2013 Open Championship at Muirfield.

"It *is* frustrating," he said, sitting in the clubhouse at Baltusrol on the day he missed the cut at the 2016 PGA. "I still get upset when I play poorly and I still think [two weeks short of forty-eight] that I can play. It took me a while to get motivated again after St. George's, no doubt about that. Now I feel motivated, but there's no question that captaining a Ryder Cup team takes a lot of time and energy away from your golf. There's just so much to do.

"Of course I wouldn't trade it. This is about as high an honor as you can hope to receive, especially since your peers choose you."

Clarke is well known among those peers for being OCD, one of those people who line clothes up in their closet in precise order and choose which shoes they're going to wear a week in advance.

"The one thing that's certain with Darren captaining is that we'll be well dressed," Justin Rose said. "*Very* well dressed."

"Very well dressed and very *expensively* dressed," McIlroy added, laughing. "Our sweaters won't just be cashmere, they will be top-of-the-line cashmere."

Clarke's OCD manifested in many different ways—not just in his almost fanatical studying of the new sabermetric statistics that are the rage in all sports nowadays—but in his planning and attention to every possible detail.

By the time he got to Baltusrol in July 2016 for the PGA Championship, Clarke had already written both speeches he would be expected to give months later at Hazeltine for the Ryder Cup: one for the opening ceremony and one for the trophy presentation ceremony. He had made several trips to the BBC studios in Belfast so that he could practice giving the speeches in front of a teleprompter.

"That's for the opening ceremony speech," Chubby Chandler explained. "That's the most important one. A good opening ceremony speech, especially on the road, can be worth a half point."

Often Clarke would wake up in the middle of the night with an idea or a thought. He would sit up in bed, pick up his phone, and put the thought into it so he wouldn't wake up in the morning and not be able to remember it.

One of those thoughts had come to him at 2:11 a.m. one morning during PGA week.

"I decided I don't want to stand up in front of my team when I speak to them," he said. "I'm going to have all the chairs put in a circle, and we'll sit like that so the message is clear that we're all equal—that no man in the room is more important than any other man—including the captain."

The notion fit with the slogan Clarke had come up with for his team: "Shoulder to shoulder."

"This way, we'll be sitting shoulder to shoulder," he said. "I know that it's going to take a lot more for us to win than any of that. But I don't want to miss any possible detail that might help—even just a little."

He smiled. "After all, we're the first European team that's taking on a country with a task force."

His Irish eyes twinkled. Regardless of the outcome, it was apparent that the Europeans—and their captain—were going to have fun in Minnesota.

"Fun" was not a word in the American lexicon throughout most of 2016.

"We know we're going to get crucified if we don't win," Phil Mickelson said. "No one knows that more than I do. I know—we all know—that the task force wasn't just about *this* Ryder Cup. It's about the next ten. But if we don't win at Hazeltine, very few people on the outside are going to see it that way."

For all the talk about what the task force was created to accomplish, it really came down to one important element: player input.

The players had always had an uncomfortable relationship with the PGA of America—dating to the late 1960s, when a dispute over money (naturally) led to a split.

At the time, the PGA of America was made up of two distinct groups: those who played on the Tour and those who were club pros, men who sold clubs and clothes, gave golf lessons, and booked tee times. The best description of the difference between a tour pro and a club pro is this: a tour pro's entire life is built around making *his* game better; a club pro is paid to make everyone else's game better.

When television money began to make an impact in the 1960s, the PGA's leadership wanted to put the newfound money into its general fund. The Tour players, led by Arnold Palmer and Jack Nicklaus, believed that since TV was paying to watch *them* play, the money should be used to bolster purses.

After Julius Boros won the 1968 PGA at Pecan Valley Golf Club in San Antonio, Texas, the dispute escalated. The players weren't especially happy with the golf courses on which the PGA was choosing to play its annual championship, or that forty slots in the field were taken up by club pros. By then, the days when a club pro like Claude Harmon could win the Masters (1948) were long gone.

At the end of that year, the two groups agreed to split, and a year later Joe Dey was named as the first commissioner of what was then the Tournament Players Association. Six years later, after Deane Beman, a former player, had become commissioner, the name was changed to the PGA Tour. To this day, many golf fans don't understand the difference. They just assume the PGA and the PGA Tour are the same thing.

The split brought about an uneasy peace. The players still weren't happy that forty club pros got spots in the PGA Championship.

"You want to be a major championship, you should have the very best players in the world competing," longtime tour player Peter Jacobsen said in 1993. "Those spots are coveted, and forty of them go to guys who have no chance to win or, most of the time, make the cut."

In 1995, the PGA reluctantly cut the number of club pros in the field to twenty-five and then, eleven years later, down to twenty. No club pro has finished in the top twenty since 1990, and whenever one makes the cut nowadays it becomes a story in itself. From 2011 to 2014 not a single club pro made the cut.

By the 1980s, a number of PGA Tour events were trying to lay claim to being called a major, either as a fifth major or replacing the PGA as the fourth major. The Players Championship—then called the Tournament Players Championship—was launched in 1974 and in 1982 found a permanent home, the golf course that Beman built as a home course for the Tour—TPC Sawgrass—in 1982.

The Tour poured millions of dollars into the golf course and into the purse, and Beman and his minions began whispering in the ears of anyone willing to listen that the Players had a stronger field than the PGA—no club pros—and a huge purse. Nicklaus also quietly campaigned for his Masters-style event, the Memorial, to be considered for major status.

"Tell you what," Jeff Sluman, the 1988 PGA champion, once said. "I'll stop calling mine a major when you tell Nicklaus his *five* don't count."

It never got to that point in large part because Jim Awtrey, who became the PGA's executive director in 1987, aggressively remade the PGA Championship, taking it to high-class golf courses on a consistent basis, upping the prize money, and signing a lucrative TV deal with CBS that happened to coincide with John Daly's stunning victory in 1991.

Before that, Awtrey had to deal with two crises. The first came in 1987 when the PGA Championship was played at PGA National, a wonderful golf course but not the best venue for a tournament in August. The weather was brutally hot and the greens died during the week, leaving the golf course looking ugly both in person and on television. To this day, Awtrey vividly recalls watching a woman in an overcoat being taken out to the scoreboard that floated in the lake to right of the 18th green during the second round. When she arrived, she took off the coat, revealing a tiny bikini, and began putting up scores. Someone had made a deal with one of the PGA's sponsors to send her out to the scoreboard.

"That was when I knew for certain that we had a championship that was in trouble," Awtrey said. "You don't have women in bikinis putting up scores at a major championship."

Three years later, things got worse when Hall Thompson, the founder of Shoal Creek (the host course for that year's PGA), made his infamous comment when asked by a local reporter what would happen if an African American applied for membership at Shoal Creek ("That wouldn't happen in Birmingham, Alabama. We don't discriminate in every other area except blacks.").

Shoal Creek proved to be an historic turning point in golf history. Soon after, the PGA Tour, the PGA of America, and the U.S. Golf Association passed rules saying that no golf club that discriminated on any basis—race, religion, gender—could host one of their events.

The notable exception to this was Augusta National, which did admit its first African American soon after Shoal Creek but didn't admit women until 2012. Not long before the club finally admitted two women, PGA Tour commissioner Tim Finchem basically admitted that the Tour simply couldn't fight Augusta National on the issue because the Masters was too important to risk the club saying, "You can't tell us what to do, we'll just cancel the Masters." Finchem knew the club's leadership was perfectly capable of doing that.

By 1999, the Ryder Cup had become a huge cash cow for the PGA. Beginning with the 1987 matches, the Ryder Cup had become a money-maker, and as the TV rights fees went up, so did the demand for tickets and for corporate tents during a Ryder Cup week.

That led to the next PGA of America–PGA Tour dispute. The players knew the PGA was making big bucks on the Ryder Cup and they were seeing none of it. Not long before the '99 matches at the Country Club, several players—notably Mark O'Meara and David Duval—said they thought it was unfair that the players received no compensation during what had already become the most pressurized week they faced.

The players were heavily criticized for their position. They were representing their country—wasn't that compensation enough? A compromise was reached: the PGA of America would donate $100,000 to a charity of each player's choice. That calmed the waters, but the tension remained.

And then, after the U.S. rally at the Country Club that year, Europe began to completely dominate the matches. Players became sensitive to the criticism they were getting, especially the notion that Europe won because the players *cared* more and because they got along better.

"Simply not true," Davis Love insisted. "I was in those team rooms. We didn't lose because we didn't care and we didn't lose because we didn't get along. We lost because they made more putts than we did."

Which—ironically—was exactly the point Tom Watson made at Gleneagles, the comment that set Phil Mickelson off and led to his mini-tirade.

Love was right—up to a point. The Americans did care—no elite athlete ever wants to lose—but until they started losing regularly, their passion for the Ryder Cup wasn't as great as the Europeans'.

"I think the Americans were about twenty years behind Europe *really,* truly caring about the Ryder Cup to the point where they really *hated* losing," Chubby Chandler said. "The Europeans looked on the Ryder Cup as a chance to prove that their tour was as good as the PGA Tour; that they weren't just the little brothers crying for attention.

"Gradually, that's changed. But I don't think it was until Medinah that the Americans had really had enough with getting beaten every two years."

If you ask almost any American player of the last fifty years what event he was putting to win when he was ten years old and alone on the putting green at dusk, "this putt to win . . . ," the answers will be divided between the Masters and the U.S. Open. Only in recent years has that started to change.

"Masters or the Ryder Cup," Jordan Spieth said. "Those were the two events I most wanted to be part of as a kid."

"Any major or the Ryder Cup," Patrick Reed said. "I played in something in Texas that we called the 'junior Ryder Cup' when I was a kid [there is now an official Junior Ryder Cup played the week of the actual matches], so I was totally into the Ryder Cup from about ten on."

Reed was twenty-six when the 2016 Ryder Cup was played; Spieth twenty-three. The older Americans rarely—if ever—had a putt to win an imaginary Ryder Cup as kids.

For the Europeans, it was different.

"The Ryder Cup has always been massive for all of us, I think," said Danny Willett. "I dreamed about playing in it for about as long as I can remember."

"There was nothing bigger for me than Ryder Cup as a kid," Justin Rose said. "Of course winning a major changes your life, but I *so* wanted to be on a winning Ryder Cup team."

"Just nothing like it," said Ian Poulter. "For me, it's the biggest and best event in golf."

The other issue was the team room. Everyone found a way to get along—even Faldo and Montgomerie—when a Ryder Cup was at stake. The Americans wanted to get along, insisted that they got along, but it wasn't always the case.

A lot of this centered on Woods and Mickelson, who were the two biggest stars in golf and, at least in theory, the team leaders. But in spite of the fact that the two of them get along *now* and insist that was almost always the case, it simply wasn't true. Past players tell stories about Woods sitting on one side of the team room, Mickelson on the other.

They did, as time went by, occasionally play Ping-Pong together. Ping-Pong became the Americans' fallback when questions were raised about team unity. "Well, we really enjoy getting after one another in Ping-

Pong" was the frequently heard response when the question of Euro-unity vs. American-unity was raised. Or "You should see Tiger and Phil teaming up to play Ping-Pong."

Apparently there were no issues over whose Ping-Pong ball to use at those moments.

The desire to win—or, more specifically not to lose—reached new levels after Medinah. Then came the embarrassment and the public tension—to put it mildly—of Gleneagles.

Ted Bishop knew the Watson experiment had failed. It didn't matter how much he admired Watson or how much he believed Mickelson had been unfair to him. The results spoke for themselves.

That was why he came up with the idea to have a "task force" to deal with what in the world was wrong with the U.S. Ryder Cup team year in and year out.

When the task force was announced on October 13, the reaction was mixed. The American players—especially the five who had been appointed to the task force—thought it was an excellent idea.

Jack Nicklaus didn't. "If the task force means we'll make more birdies, then by all means, I'm all for it," he said. "Otherwise, it's ridiculous."

The Europeans were amused. "It's actually quite flattering," Ian Poulter said. "It shows how desperate they are to figure out a way to beat us."

Three of the four major championships in the previous year had been won by Europeans—Justin Rose beating Mickelson at the U.S. Open; McIlroy beating Rickie Fowler at the Open Championship and then beating Fowler and Mickelson at the PGA. The Ryder Cup had been a disaster on and off the golf course.

And the president of the PGA of America, Ted Bishop, had been impeached and publicly humiliated by his colleagues and staff for a senseless tweet and an equally senseless Facebook post.

At the back of his book *Unfriended,* Bishop has a nine-page appendix that lists all the accomplishments of his presidency. There are thirteen categories and a total of 136 achievements he proudly lists—but there is no mention of the Ryder Cup task force. Which, in the end, was both the last and most important thing—social media faux pas aside—that Bishop did as president.

Ten

In the weeks and months leading up to the 2016 Ryder Cup, Davis Love was asked almost daily which four players he was likely to select as his captain's picks if they failed to make the top eight and automatically qualify off the points list.

Love wasn't about to answer the question, so he more or less mentioned anyone who had ever played on the PGA Tour at any time in history. If he could have brought Walter Hagen back, he no doubt would have been an excellent potential choice.

There was only one player Love didn't hedge on in one direction or the other: Jordan Spieth.

"No matter what Jordan does," Love said early in 2016, "he's going to be on the team."

The fact that Spieth was leading the points list at that moment and unlikely to drop out of the top eight made it easy for Love to make the comment. But it went beyond that. At the tender age of twenty-two, Spieth had emerged as the biggest star in golf.

It wasn't as if he had come out of nowhere. He'd been a star junior growing up in Dallas and had first played in a PGA Tour event—the Byron Nelson Classic—at the age of sixteen, finishing in a tie for sixteenth place. In many ways, he was "The Natural"—an apt notion since he had been a talented left-handed pitcher before his gift for golf became so overwhelming that he had to give up baseball.

"I knew it was the right decision," he said. "But I really did love baseball."

He won the U.S. Junior Amateur in 2009 and then again in 2011. (The only person to win the Junior Amateur three times? Tiger Woods.) He also made the cut again at the Byron Nelson in 2011, finishing tied for thirty-second. He was disappointed. He had expected to improve on his performance from a year earlier because he was more experienced.

He stayed near home for college, choosing Texas over the eight million other schools recruiting him. As a freshman, he led the Longhorns to the NCAA championship but that fall had to make a decision.

The PGA Tour had changed the system by which players could gain access to the Tour. The qualifying school, which sent twenty-five players (and ties) directly to the Tour each fall, was being eliminated. Instead, Q school was now going to be a route to the Triple-A Web.com Tour, where a player would have to win enough money during the following year to make it to the big tour.

In the past, top college players would turn pro in the summer and have two ways to reach the Tour: by playing well enough in the seven tournaments they were allowed to play in—if invited by a sponsor—or by going to Q school. Only a small handful of players—Tiger Woods, Phil Mickelson, and Justin Leonard among them—had been able to avoid Q school. Now the more traveled route was being taken away.

Spieth could have stayed at Texas and hoped to play well enough in the summer of 2013 to make it directly to the Tour. Or he could drop out of Texas to play in the final Q school and hope to start his pro career on the big tour in the winter of 2013.

He decided to try Q school. He'd been part of an NCAA championship team and thought he was ready to play with the big boys. Even during his freshman year at Texas, he was mentally preparing to turn pro the next year.

"It was my plan all along, to be honest," he said.

Q school has always been the most tricky and treacherous event in golf. Players often refer to it as "the fifth major" because the pressure can be so excruciating.

Since he was still an amateur with no PGA Tour status at all, Spieth needed to work his way through three stages in order to make the Tour. He made it through the first stage without a problem but stumbled in the second stage, colliding with what players called "the second-stage wall."

Once a player got through the second stage to the final stage, he was guaranteed a place to play golf professionally the next year: the top twenty-five players—and ties—at the finals made it to the PGA Tour. The rest were guaranteed full or partial status on the Web.com Tour.

Spieth shot eight-under-par 280 at a second-stage qualifier held at TPC Craig Ranch, in McKinney, about a thirty-five-mile drive from his home in Dallas. That left him tied for twenty-sixth—three shots above the cut line for the top twenty who advanced to the finals.

"I just didn't make any putts," he said that day, the most familiar golfer's lament. Since he hadn't turned pro to play in the qualifier, Spieth could have returned to Texas. But his mind was already made up to turn pro regardless, so he began 2013 depending on the kindness of others: he needed sponsor exemptions to get into tournaments.

He went to South America to play in the first two Web.com events of the year—he'd been given a sponsor's spot to the season opener in Panama. If he could make the top ten, he would automatically be entered the next week, in Colombia. After that, he'd been offered a sponsor's spot in a PGA Tour event in Puerto Rico—an "opposite" event on the Tour, meaning it was played opposite the big-money limited-field World Golf Championships event at Doral. The field in Puerto Rico wouldn't be as strong as most tour events and the purse was smaller, but there was still serious money to be made if he played well.

Spieth's goal was to gain full status on the Web.com Tour by playing well there so he could use his remaining sponsor's exemptions to play big tour events when he had the chance.

"Basically my plan was to try to play well enough on the Web that I'd make it to the Tour by 2014 in a worst-case scenario," he said. "I never dreamed things would happen as quickly as they did."

Saying that things happened quickly was a vast understatement. He opened by finishing T-4 in Panama. That meant he could play in Colombia without asking for an exemption. There he finished T-7, meaning he'd made about $50,000 in two weeks.

After he finished playing on Sunday in Bogotá, he sat down in the clubhouse with his agent Jay Danzi, his caddie Michael Greller, and Tim West, who has run pro-am events on the PGA Tour for more than twenty-five years and has been an unofficial adviser to young players for almost as long.

The question on the table was simple: should he go to Puerto Rico where he had committed to taking a sponsor's exemption, or should he play in the Web.com event in Chile the next week knowing he needed to make only about $4,000 to qualify for full status on that tour for the rest of the year? A top-twenty-five finish in Chile would have been enough to achieve that.

"I think Jordan was unsure what to do," Greller said. "Part of him wanted to go to Chile and wrap up being able to play Web.com anywhere he wanted the rest of the year. Part of him felt he should keep his commitment in Puerto Rico. Jay and Tim both thought he should go to Chile, because getting the Web.com full status would mean he could jump off to play the big tour pretty much whenever he had a chance to go over there. I thought he should go to Puerto Rico. He was playing well and the field wasn't that strong, so he had a chance to do something there."

They talked for about a half hour. Spieth had to go to the airport and catch a flight—but to where?

"I finally decided on Puerto Rico because I'd made a commitment and because some of my family was planning to come down and see me play," he said. "That decision ended up being a turning point in my career."

He went to Puerto Rico and, after having a chance to win on Sunday, finished tied for second. Finishing in the top ten got him a spot—without needing a sponsor exemption—into the tournament in Tampa the following week. He ended up tied for seventh, meaning he had made $521,000 in two weeks.

The Tour has a rule that if a nonmember earns as much money in his allotted starts as the player who finished 150th on the previous year's money list, he can receive unlimited sponsor exemptions for the rest of the year. The two top tens did that for Spieth.

Suddenly he didn't have to worry about his status on the Web.com Tour. In fact, the Web.com was in his rearview mirror—forever.

In July, two weeks shy of his twentieth birthday, he got into contention again—this time at the John Deere Classic. He came to the 18th hole Sunday needing a birdie to have a chance to get into a playoff. He missed the green, finding the right bunker. That, it seemed, was that. He would have to settle for another high finish and another big check.

Except he holed the bunker shot. Then he won a five-hole playoff, beating local hero Zach Johnson and David Hearn. Even in midsummer, it was almost dark by the time Spieth made the winning putt the third time the three men played the 18th hole.

The victory gave him full status as a PGA Tour member, and all the money he'd made prior to that—added to the $828,000 he made for winning the playoff at the John Deere—became official money, putting him eleventh in the FedExCup standings. He was the first teenager to win on the PGA Tour since Ralph Guldahl had done it—in 1931. The win also qualified him for his second major—the Open Championship at Muirfield the following week. He had finished T-21 at the 2012 U.S. Open while still an amateur. He made the cut at Muirfield and finished T-44, riding on adrenaline and exhaustion all at once.

Spieth had been a prodigy and had been known to those in the golf world as a rising star since the T-16 at the Byron Nelson at age sixteen. But the win at John Deere, his sudden status on tour, and his outgoing, appealing personality quickly made him a star.

He almost won again in August in Greensboro, losing a playoff to Patrick Reed. By then, he'd shown Fred Couples enough that he picked him for the Presidents Cup team. The matches were held in October at Muirfield Village—the same place where the U.S. had lost the Ryder Cup in 1987. This was different; this was the Presidents Cup, an event the U.S. almost always wins. American players always say the Presidents Cup is "more relaxed" than the Ryder Cup. In English that means, "We know we're going to win."

Spieth didn't know that—he'd never played in either. He was scared to death the first day.

"You have to understand the context," he said, laughing at the memory. "In March, I'm sitting in the clubhouse in Bogotá trying to decide if I go to the airport and get on a plane to Chile or Puerto Rico. I have no idea where I'm going to be playing next week, next month, or the rest of the year. I'm just trying to get playing status.

"Fast-forward five months and I walk on the 1st tee and the first two people I see are Jack Nicklaus and George W. Bush. That's a long way from the clubhouse in Bogotá. I'm representing my country—I'm representing Mr. Nicklaus and President Bush! I'm twenty years old. I was shaking."

It took four holes for Spieth to calm down. His partner, Steve Stricker, put an arm around him after he'd come up way short with his tee shot on the par-3 4th hole—"I hit it fat," Spieth said—and Stricker said, "Jordan, you'll be fine. You're a great player. I'll take care of you until you feel better."

"After that, I was okay," Spieth said. "Steve knew just what to say. I'll always be grateful to him for that."

Actually, Stricker wasn't sure what to say. He sent word back to Couples that Spieth was a wreck. Couples sent Davis Love, one of his assistant captains, to try to calm Spieth down.

"By the time I got there," Love said, "he was fine."

Spieth and Stricker ended up winning the match, beating Ernie Els and Brendon de Jonge on the 18th hole. For the week, Spieth was 2-2, although he was disappointed when he lost his singles match, also on the 18th hole, to Canadian Graham DeLaet on Sunday. The U.S.—of course—won.

"Playing in that Presidents Cup helped me the next year at the Ryder Cup," Spieth said. "It's not as if you can match the tension and nerves you feel at the Ryder Cup when you play in the Presidents Cup. You can't. But it does give you a sense of what you're going to feel at the Ryder Cup. It doesn't come as a complete shock to the system."

By the time Spieth played on Tom Watson's team at Gleneagles, he was no longer a rising star, he was a star—period. He had almost won the Masters in his first appearance, leading the tournament until the 8th hole on Sunday before finishing second to Bubba Watson. He'd also had a chance to win the Players Championship. He was in contention so often that the whispers among the golf media were that he was a mega-talent, but could he close?

Given that Spieth had just turned twenty-one and was in his first full season on tour, it was remarkable that the question would come up.

In the 2014 Ryder Cup at Gleneagles, Spieth was paired with Patrick Reed after he suggested to Watson through Stricker that the two of them play together. On the surface, their personalities couldn't have been more different. Although Spieth had a habit of talking to his ball while it was in the air and had occasional bouts of bad body language when he wasn't playing well, he was far more comfortable and smooth with the public and the media than any twenty-one-year-old had a right to be.

Reed, labeled "our new bulldog" by Bubba Watson, wasn't smooth. He could be gruff and, having been through some off-course personal issues that had become public, could be guarded with the media. He could also be charming and funny, but it was a side he didn't show people very often.

"It's true, I tend to get to the golf course, put my headphones in, and go to work," he said. "Every once in a while I'll take one of them out to listen to my coach or Justine [his wife, who was by his side almost all the time], but not very often."

In fact, in his Saturday night assessment of his eleven teammates at Gleneagles, Mickelson had said to Reed, "We need to know you better."

One thing that Spieth and Reed shared was a genuine hatred of losing. Spieth had suggested they play together because of statistics, but truth be told, their personalities meshed too.

"We always play as if we're trying to beat each other, not just the other team," Reed said. "If Jordan birdies a hole, I want to eagle it. If I'm in trouble, he says, 'I got this hole,' but he doesn't say, 'You get the next,' because *he* wants to get the next one too. It keeps us mentally in every hole."

Spieth loves the bluntness of the relationship. "One of us will hit one close in foursomes and the other will say, 'Go make that shit,'" he said, laughing. "It's not like, 'Go get 'em, partner,' it's 'Make this—or else.'"

They played the third match in the morning four-balls on Friday and, after a shaky start, recovered to crush rookie Stephen Gallacher and the iconic Ian Poulter, 5 and 4.

Reed recovered from his popped-up tee shot on 1 to play well, and Spieth, who felt at least as shaky on the 1st tee as he had felt at the Presidents Cup, played equally well.

"Two young guys, first time in the Ryder Cup, they were unbelievable," Poulter said. "I remember thinking, 'If these guys are the future of the Ryder Cup for America, they've got something to build on here.'"

Reed, at twenty-four, and Spieth, at twenty-one, were the two youngest players competing that week for either team. But they played as if they'd been involved in the Ryder Cup forever. In a small way, they had been.

Reed had played in the self-styled "Junior Ryder Cup" since the age of ten, a weekend put together by golf pros and parents from a number of golf clubs in Texas. "If you were from north of San Antonio, you played on the north team," he said. "If you were from south of San Antonio, you played for the south."

Spieth had played in the official "Junior Ryder Cup," which had been launched in 1997. It had been played in a one-day, 12-points format until 2006, when it was expanded to two days. The first day consisted of six foursomes matches—three for boys, three for girls—and six four-ball matches, one boy and one girl on each team. The next day, as with the real Ryder Cup, twelve singles matches were played.

The Junior Cup was always played at a golf course not far from the actual Ryder Cup course early in Ryder Cup week. That meant the junior players had a chance to go to the actual Ryder Cup, walk inside the ropes on practice days, and meet the players.

Spieth had played in the junior cup in both 2008 and 2010.

"It was a lot of fun to play, and then to get to go to the matches was beyond cool," he said. "I was like everyone else, all I could think was 'I want to be part of this someday.'"

The Junior Ryder Cup matches of 2010 had been played at Gleneagles. Four years later, Spieth found himself on the 1st tee at the same golf course but with an entirely different feeling in his stomach.

The European Tour had built a tunnel under the bleachers that the players walked through going from the range or the putting green to the 1st tee. When the players walked out from the tunnel, they found themselves surrounded on three sides by fans—very loud fans—cheering, singing, chanting. It was like nothing else any of them—veterans or rookies—had ever seen in golf.

"It was just an amazing feeling to walk out there into that wall of sound," Spieth said. "Made me feel a little bit like a football player running out of the tunnel onto the field. I loved it. But if I said my legs weren't shaking a little, I'd be lying."

He smiled. "Fortunately, the best shot off that tee was a three-wood. Even if it had been a driver, I might have hit three-wood just to be able to tee the ball a little higher and give myself a little more room for error."

His first tee shot was just fine, his swing as smooth as ever. Knowing how much that moment meant to him, Annie Verrett, his girlfriend since high school, took a picture of it and commissioned a painting based on the picture. The painting hangs in Spieth's living room today.

Spieth and Reed were, by far, the Americans' best team the first two days. They won both their four-ball matches convincingly and were one up in their foursomes match against Justin Rose and Martin Kaymer on Saturday before Rose rolled in a birdie putt on the 18th hole to halve the match.

Reed then played brilliantly to beat Henrik Stenson one up in singles on Sunday, but Spieth, leading off for the Americans, felt he'd let his team down when he lost to Graeme McDowell.

"I just didn't get the job done in the singles," he said. "That's on me, nobody else."

Spieth looked twenty-one but acted thirty-five. Some of this, no doubt, came from the fact that his parents, Shawn and Mary Christine—both athletes in college—treated all three of their children with equal importance. Steven, two years younger than Jordan, was also an athlete. He grew to six-six, which annoyed his six-one older brother no end, and was Brown's leading scorer during the 2016–2017 basketball season. Ellie, the baby, is on the autism spectrum and has severe learning disabilities. Jordan's genuine devotion to her is evident every time he talks about her.

"She's my hero," he said. "Her approach to life is so upbeat. She's the funniest person in our family. I've learned a lot from her about dealing with adversity—real adversity, not golf adversity."

In addition to spending time with his sister, Jordan has worked in the past at her school with classmates who are also disabled. It's given him a view of the world that very few world-class athletes have. He's learned—and is learning—about fame and about being incredibly wealthy at a young age. He occasionally gets annoyed with what people say and write about him when he thinks they're wrong. But he accepts that it's part of the job.

"Look, I understand that until I go back to Augusta and hit that first shot or play the 12th hole again or, more than that, win the Masters again, I'm going to get asked about what happened there," he said in the summer of 2016. "It would be crazy for me to say I'm not going to remember what happened or not going to think about letting that one get away. But I know I've moved on. I get that people are going to have to see it *there* to believe it."

Spieth was talking about what had happened to him at the 2016 Masters, when he had a five-shot lead with nine holes to play and appeared to be on his way to winning the Masters for the second year in a row.

A year earlier, he had led at Augusta from start to finish, opening with a 64 and cruising to a four-shot win, tying Tiger Woods's all-time scoring record with an 18-under-par 270. That win made him a transcendent star, not just a golf star. He'd been on Golf Channel and *SportsCenter* in the past. Now he was on *Letterman* and the *Tonight Show* and *Charlie Rose*.

What he did a week later might have been more impressive. Frequently, when a player wins a major title—especially the Masters because it always involves a victory tour—they will withdraw from the next week's tournament (if they're entered) just because there is almost no chance they're going to be ready to play on Thursday after winning on Sunday and doing nonstop travel and media the next three days.

Spieth had been scheduled to play at Hilton Head. He didn't withdraw. He got to town on Wednesday night and, not surprisingly, shot a three-over-par 74 on Thursday that put him in a tie for 102nd place, well outside the cut line. No one was surprised. At least, most people said, he'd shown up, and once he missed the cut on Friday morning, he could go home and get some rest.

Except he went out on Friday and shot 62, jumping into contention instead of missing the cut.

"I actually thought that I'd play well on Friday," he said, acting as if the 62 wasn't that big a deal. "Thursday I was still tired and it was like my practice round, getting to know the golf course again. Friday, I was rested and made some putts."

He ended up tied for eleventh when all was said and done on Sunday, but his willingness to dig in and grind when no one really expected him to earned him almost as much respect among his peers as winning the Masters.

"Jordan is amazingly mature," Brandt Snedeker said. "He gets it—all of it. He knows playing out here, especially when you're a star, comes with responsibilities. One of them is meeting our commitments. Another is always playing hard because you owe it to the people who came out to watch you play."

Ten weeks after winning the Masters, Spieth won the U.S. Open, putting him halfway to the unthinkable—the calendar Grand Slam. Arnold Palmer had done that in 1960. Jack Nicklaus had done that in 1972. Tiger Woods had done that in 2002. And now Jordan Spieth had also won the Masters and U.S. Open back-to-back.

He was in pretty good company. And he still hadn't turned twenty-two.

Eleven

As it turned out, Jordan Spieth didn't win the British Open, which was played that year at St. Andrews. But he came awfully close. He actually led for part of the final round, which was pushed back to Monday because of a number of rain delays, before finishing one shot out of a three-way playoff between Zach Johnson, Louis Oosthuizen, and Marc Leishman.

His final chip, from the famous "valley of sin" on St. Andrews's 18th hole, swerved just to the left of the hole—leaving him about six inches from making it a four-way playoff.

Spieth signed his scorecard, met with the media hordes—many of whom were far more interested in his losing than in who was going to win the four-hole playoff—and then returned to the back of the 18th green to greet the three playoff contestants and to give Johnson a congratulatory hug after he had won the championship.

The number of players who would have returned to greet the winner under circumstances like that can be counted on one hand. Perhaps one finger of that hand.

That was Spieth.

"You know, when he first came out and I heard about how mature he was and what a great kid he was, I was a little doubtful," Rory McIlroy said. "I mean, he sounded too good to be true. Then I got to know him a little, played with him a few times, spent some time around him, and realized, 'Wow, he really is that person.' He's remarkable."

Three weeks later, at the PGA Championship at Whistling Straits in Wisconsin, Mike Davis, the executive director of the U.S. Golf Association, was standing outside the media tent on Friday afternoon when he saw the U.S. Open champion—Spieth—sprinting in his direction.

Spieth stopped to say hello. "Where are you in such a rush to get to, Jordan?" Davis asked.

"I need to get into the media tent right away," Spieth answered.

"My guess is they'll wait for you," Davis said.

Spieth smiled and shook his head. "It's not that," he said. "I was signing [autographs] for a bunch of kids back there, and they pulled me away and said I needed to get to media. I told the kids I'd get back there to finish signing as soon as possible."

He shook hands again with Davis and said, "Great to see you, Mr. Davis."

He sprinted off to do his media rounds and finish signing all the autographs.

"He's the U.S. Open champion," Davis said, laughing. "I need to get him to start calling me Mike."

As McIlroy said, too good to be true.

Spieth finished second that weekend at Whistling Straits, losing by three shots to a record-setting performance by Jason Day.

He climaxed one of the great years in golf history by winning the Tour Championship in Atlanta, meaning he had won the FedEx Cup. In all, he won five tournaments—two of them majors—and $22 million on the golf course in 2015. In the two majors he didn't win, he finished T-4 and second. No wonder Davis Love was willing to commit a spot on the U.S. team to him before he'd struck a ball in 2016.

There was one other person who was about 99 percent certain to be on Love's team: Phil Mickelson.

Love him or hate him—and there were plenty of people in both camps—Mickelson had been one of golf's most compelling figures for years. He had put himself squarely in the spotlight for Hazeltine with his tirade at Gleneagles and his vocal involvement in the task force. The fact that he had flown in from San Diego to be in the room for the first task force meeting and then had practically sat on Love's lap during the press conference/pep rally introducing the 2016 captain made it apparent how important the 2016 Hazeltine crusade was to him.

Mickelson had played on every American team in the Presidents Cup or the Ryder Cup dating to 1994. That meant Hazeltine would be the twenty-second consecutive U.S. team he'd played on—a record no one else was even close to touching. Jim Furyk had played on fifteen straight teams from 1997 to 2012. Tiger Woods had played on eleven straight teams from 1997 to 2007 before knee surgery prevented him from playing in 2008. Only American players could put together a string like Mickelson's, since the U.S. played in either the Ryder Cup or Presidents Cup every year. The Europeans and Internationals played only every two years.

For a long time, after the Presidents Cup was launched, there were some American players—Mickelson among them—who felt that having to represent their country every year might be hurting the U.S. performance in the Ryder Cup.

"It is something a lot of guys talked about," Love said. "It isn't just that we have to play every year, but we're expected to *win* every year. We never get that much credit for winning the Presidents Cup because everyone says, 'Oh yeah, you're supposed to win that,' but when we lose the Ryder Cup it's 'How can you possibly lose?'"

As the years went by and the Ryder Cup losses continued, the American players objected less to playing the Presidents Cup. Part of it was that younger players had grown up knowing about the Presidents Cup, unlike Love, Mickelson, Furyk, Woods, and others. Making a Presidents Cup team became prestigious—not on the same level as the Ryder Cup, but a notch on the résumé.

Plus, when the Ryder Cup losses came up, there was at least a little bit of fallback from all the Presidents Cup wins. And the Presidents Cup gave players like Spieth the chance—depending on how the calendar fell—to get some experience in a Ryder Cup–light type of atmosphere before dealing with the real thing a year later.

Mickelson had been hurt at various times in his career and had taken time away from the Tour after Amy had been diagnosed with cancer in 2009. He'd dealt with psoriatic arthritis since 2010 but had been able to control it through medication.

One way or the other, though, he had made every American team for over two decades—a truly astounding feat. That record had become a matter of pride, and it was very much on his mind in the summer of 2015.

"I want to make this Presidents Cup team," he said in the locker room at Firestone Country Club in Akron, Ohio, one afternoon. "I want to make it on points. I've never been a captain's pick before, and I don't want to be one now."

Mickelson had not had a good year—for Mickelson. He had finished tied for second at the Masters, four shots behind Spieth's masterpiece. He had also finished in the top five in three other events, but had not played well during the summer.

"I'm going to play four of the next five," he said that day in Akron. "I think I'm ready to start playing some good golf and I don't want Jay [Haas] to have to pick me for the team."

Mickelson knew that Haas *would* pick him, regardless of where he was on the points list. He had earned that, not only because he'd made twenty teams in a row on points but because of his "papa bear" role.

"There's no one on the team who doesn't want Phil there," Zach Johnson said. "It doesn't matter where he finishes on the points list. We want him on the team. We *need* him on the team."

As it turned out, Mickelson wasn't ready to "play some good golf." His best finish in the next four tournaments was a T-18 at the PGA Championship, and he failed to finish in the top forty in the other three. He finished thirtieth on the points list.

And yet when Haas picked him, neither was it surprising nor did anyone question it.

Mickelson ended up playing very well in the Presidents Cup matches in South Korea, going 3-0-1, including a 5-and-4 victory in singles over 2011 Masters champion Charl Schwartzel. The U.S. won—again—although the matches were closer than normal, Bill Haas (Jay's son) having to win the final singles match to secure a 15½–14 ½ U.S. win.

The win was a relief—albeit a small one—for the American players. They were expected to win, and they had won. They had also done it in the middle of the night in the U.S., meaning that even fewer people were watching than normal.

The Ryder Cup remained the holy grail, and no one knew that more than Mickelson.

"I put myself in this position, I understand that," he said in the spring.

"My feeling is if I had to take one for the team to try to help us win Ryder Cups—this year and in the future—it was worth it."

Mickelson is always keenly aware of any media criticism, and he had taken a good deal of it after Gleneagles.

He had been aware of the Ryder Cup as a kid growing up in San Diego. Even though he was right-handed, he learned the golf swing left-handed because he would stand opposite his father and mimic his swing, as if looking in the mirror.

He was a star junior player and first remembers sitting down to watch the Ryder Cup when he was a high school senior.

"It was '87, when Europe won at Muirfield Village. Obviously, I was pulling for the U.S., but I really admired Seve [Ballesteros] and I liked the way he teamed with [José-María] Olazábal. I remember the Americans having a lot of trouble playing the 18th hole on Sunday. I actually kind of enjoyed seeing them dance on the green—not because I liked them winning but because I thought it was a cool thing."

By 1991, when the "War by the Shore" took place, Mickelson was far more than just an interested observer. Earlier that year, Mickelson had won the Northern Telecom (Tucson) Open as an Arizona State junior. He was only the sixth amateur to win a PGA Tour event (no amateur has won once since), and his big smile, dark good looks, and natural charm made him the kind of star sponsors lined up for when he graduated in the spring of 1992.

The win in Tucson meant that Mickelson had full status on tour as soon as he turned pro. He had watched the matches from Kiawah Island thinking he very much wanted to be part of the Ryder Cup in 1993.

"That was the first time I really got caught up in it," he remembered. "I was pretty much glued to the TV that weekend."

Nine months after that Ryder Cup, amid much fanfare, Mickelson turned pro. He had been a four-time all-American at Arizona State and had won three individual NCAA titles. But it was the win in Tucson that made his arrival on tour much anticipated.

This was four years before Tiger Woods showed up to galvanize the game, and golf was looking for a charismatic young star—specifically a charismatic young American star, since the best players in the world at the time were—for the most part—non-Americans: Nick Faldo, Greg Norman, Nick Price.

Fred Couples was briefly at the top of the game after winning the

Masters in 1992, but persistent back problems and inconsistency kept him from being a regular contender in the major championships. He didn't finish in the top five in a major again until the 1998 Masters. During that stretch he had more DNPs (did-not-plays) and cuts missed—six—than top tens—five, the highest being a T-7.

As cool as Couples was, as much as he made female hearts flutter, he was never going to be on Sunday leaderboards week in and week out.

Mickelson didn't win during the second half of 1992, but won early in 1993—in San Diego, by four shots. But he struggled for much of that year before winning again in August at the International. That was one week after Tom Watson had selected Raymond Floyd and Lanny Wadkins as his captain's picks for the 1993 U.S. team.

"I just didn't play well enough to make that team," Mickelson said. "Tom went with experience, plus, I won a week too late, after he'd made his choices. It was disappointing, but I understood. Funny thing is, under today's rules, I probably would have made the team."

Back then, the U.S. had only two captain's picks; now it has four. And the picks were made in mid-August rather than in September.

A year later, in 1994, Mickelson played on the first U.S. Presidents Cup team—one that a lot of American players weren't thrilled about, since they saw it as little more than a PGA Tour money grab.

It was the following year, 1995, when Mickelson finally got his shot at a Ryder Cup—though it didn't quite go according to plan. This was the year when Mickelson was miffed at captain Lanny Wadkins for failing to tell him in advance that he was sitting out the Friday morning match (and he found out only when the pairings were announced at the opening ceremony).

Communication was something that would become vitally important to Mickelson. Wadkins's thinking was actually pretty clear: he believed the boom-or-bust Mickelson would be more effective in four-balls, where making birdies is critical, than in foursomes, where keeping the ball in play is more important. It turned out—at least that year—that he was right: Mickelson sat out both foursomes sessions and was 2-0 playing in afternoon four-balls, first with Corey Pavin on Friday and then with Jay Haas on Saturday. But his logic was overshadowed—in Mickelson's mind—by lack of communication.

"I think I was told at different times I was playing with four different guys on Friday," Mickelson said. "First it was [Jeff] Maggert. Then it was

Jake [Peter Jacobsen]. Then Pavin, then someone else I can't remember, and finally Corey again. You're going into the most pressure-packed situation of your career and you feel like you've got no direction."

The U.S. had taken what appeared to be an insurmountable 9–7 lead on that Saturday after Pavin chipped in on 18 to give him and Loren Roberts a one-up victory over Bernhard Langer and Nick Faldo.

"In a strange way I think Corey's chip-in hurt us," Mickelson said. "We'd never lost a singles session and, with a two-point lead, playing at home our feeling that night was that we had it locked up. I think we let down a little bit emotionally, and it hurt us on Sunday."

Playing Per-Ulrik Johansson the next day in the twelfth match, Mickelson could tell things weren't going well. If he couldn't tell by the lack of cheering, he could tell by looking at the scoreboards.

"Lot of blue," he said. "I knew it wasn't going well. I began thinking my match might decide the whole thing."

After Wadkins had gotten in his face when he was two down at the turn, Mickelson birdied the first three holes on the back nine to take the lead. But the quiet up ahead of him made him nervous. Moments after he'd shaken hands with Johansson on the 17th green, he saw Davis Love standing by the side of the green waiting to tell him that the U.S. had lost.

Mickelson was stunned. The U.S. had been outscored 7½–4½ on the final day, the first time—as Mickelson pointed out—it had ever lost a singles session to Europe.

"I was kind of in shock," he said. "I knew we were struggling all day, that was obvious. But walking off the green feeling so good about winning turned into feeling completely empty because we'd lost."

During the next nineteen years, Mickelson played on two winning teams—Crenshaw's comeback team at Brookline in 1999 and Azinger's "pods" team at Valhalla in 2008. In addition to Oak Hill, there were seven more losses, ranging from routs (2004, 2006, 2014) to close-but-no-cigar (1997, 2002, 2010) to the heartbreak at Medinah (2012). Through it all, Mickelson seethed. His explosion on Sunday night at Gleneagles was the culmination of pent-up frustration that dated to the opening ceremony at Oak Hill.

In effect, Watson took the blows for Wadkins; for Hal Sutton, whom Mickelson blamed for his failed partnership with Tiger Woods in 2004; for the PGA of America for ignoring his pleas to name Azinger captain again in 2010; for Pavin for telling him his team would be a "twelve-man pod."

Right or wrong, Mickelson is very firm in his self-belief. In 2016, Love would joke, "I used to think about half of what Phil said was crazy, now I only think about twenty-five percent of it is."

Mickelson felt like he—even more than Woods because he'd been on ten U.S. teams before Hazeltine and Woods had only been on seven— had become the number-one scapegoat for the U.S. losses.

"They kept putting us in positions to fail ['they' being everyone from PGA presidents to captains], and then we got the blame for losing," he said. "It just wasn't fair."

If there was a moment when the line was drawn in the sand, when Mickelson decided he was going to stop bottling up his anger, it came on that Saturday morning at Gleneagles when Watson delivered the news that Mickelson and Bradley were benched for the day.

"We were pumped, ready to play," Mickelson said. "We were *dying* to get back out there in the afternoon. We'd finally lost a match together on Friday [they'd been 4-0 before that afternoon defeat in foursomes], and we wanted to get back out there and make up for it.

"Then Tom says we're not playing. It wasn't just disappointing, it was deflating."

It was what Watson said next, though, that made it certain Mickelson and Watson weren't going to kiss and make up anytime soon.

Beyond the benching, Mickelson never got over Watson telling him that he and Bradley weren't playing well enough.

" 'Phil, it's done,' " Mickelson said, repeating Watson's words. " 'You guys just aren't playing well enough for me to put you back out there today.' "

That last sentence—those final sixteen words that Mickelson remembered verbatim—sealed the deal. It didn't matter what Watson or Mickelson said when the team met for the Saturday night gathering. If the U.S. had somehow rallied and won, it might have been different.

But that wasn't going to happen. Before walking into the interview room on Sunday, Mickelson told himself—and his teammates—that neither he nor anyone else should say anything about their captain or the weekend.

Four questions in, he began his rant. And Ryder Cup history in the U.S. changed forever.

Twelve

T OM WATSON SAT at the dining room table in the downtown Philadelphia row house owned by his friend Neil Oxman. In real life,
Oxman is a hugely successful political consultant, but he has always had
a passion for three things: caddying, Tom Watson, and Bruce Edwards.

Oxman and Edwards had met in the summer of 1973, when Oxman
was in law school and was caddying on the PGA Tour to make some
extra money. Edwards was just out of high school and also caddying. It
was Oxman who pointed Watson out to Edwards on a hot summer day
in St. Louis and said, "That's Tom Watson, he's going to be a very good
player. Go ask him."

In those days, very few players had full-time caddies. Watson was
twenty-three, a couple of years out of Stanford, and just back from his
honeymoon. He agreed to let Edwards work for him for a week, and they
were together most of the next thirty years.

In 2003, Edwards was diagnosed with ALS. When he became too sick
to work, Oxman—by then the owner of his own political consulting
company—caddied in his place. Edwards died in April 2004, and since
then Oxman has caddied for Watson whenever he's able to take time off
from work.

Watson doesn't pay him, giving money instead to the charity named
for Edwards that has raised close to $8 million for ALS research. For
Oxman, caddying is a true labor of love.

The 2016 Senior Players Championship was being played at the Philadelphia Cricket Club, and Watson and his wife, Hilary, were staying

with Oxman for the week. Watson had shot a solid one-under-par 71 in the opening round that day in blustery conditions, putting him in a tie for fifth place. Even at sixty-six, he was still able to play competitive golf.

"Yeah, but I scored a lot better than I played today," he said with a smile. "If you're driving a car with a five-cylinder engine, the guys with eight cylinders are going to outrun you eventually."

Watson wasn't being modest. He was—as always—being honest. By Sunday, the eight cylinders had gone past him and he finished in a tie for twenty-fifth place.

There are few subjects on which Watson doesn't have firm opinions, and he's never been afraid to voice them. He grew up in a staunchly Republican family in Kansas City, the son of an insurance executive. He learned golf at highbrow Kansas City Country Club and then went to Stanford. There, he went through the kind of transformation many kids go through when they go to college. He grew his hair long, smoked marijuana on occasion, took part in antiwar demonstrations, and graduated in 1971 with a degree in psychology.

A year later, he voted for George McGovern for president. When he told his father that he'd voted for McGovern, Ray Watson looked at him and said, "You're an idiot."

"And he was right," Watson said, years later. Eight years after voting for McGovern, he voted for Ronald Reagan. He hasn't voted for a Democrat for president since McGovern and refers to Oxman—who works exclusively for Democrats—as "my lib friend Neil."

Ninety-nine percent of the time Watson is assertive, almost blustery in any sort of conversation, regardless of setting. On this day, talking about the 2014 Ryder Cup, his voice was soft, regretful.

"What I said about our guys needing to play better was the truth," he said. "They made forty-five more birdies than we did that weekend. That's why we lost. But the notion that anyone might think I didn't believe they were trying their guts out is just flat-out wrong.

"I knew how much they wanted to win. I *never* doubted that."

Watson was thrilled to get a second chance to captain a Ryder Cup team. But, he readily admits, the job in 2014 was very different from the job in 1993.

"There was no one-year-out celebration in 1992," he said. "In 2013, we flew to Scotland for a ceremony that was presided over by the first minister of Scotland. I think we had one trainer with us in 1993. This time we had two PGA Tour trainers, and most of the guys brought their own personal trainers. We had a team doctor—that was my idea—too.

"There were no entourages in '93. Guys brought their caddies and their wives and that was pretty much it. Decorating the team room is a big deal now. The PGA makes all sorts of inspirational videos for the guys to see. Some of it was fantastic—amazing.

"We had, I think, three seamstresses on hand in case the players needed anything done to their clothes during the week. And two tailors.

"When I played on Ryder Cup teams, you basically waited for the captain to tell you who you were playing with and you went out and played. In '93, once I had my twelve guys, I asked each of them if there was anyone they didn't want to play with. I did the same thing this time— and there were a couple who, for different reasons, said they didn't feel comfortable with certain guys. That was good to know and we [Watson and his vice captains] took that into account.

"There's no doubt it was a different job twenty-one years later. But I thought the bottom line stayed the same: you do everything in your power to make sure the players are as comfortable as possible when they go out to play. *They're* the ones in the pressure cooker. Get 'em the food they need. Make sure they have all the towels they need." He smiled. "And the right rain gear."

In fact, remembering the rain gear debacle of Wales, Watson took twelve rain suits, put them on one by one, and stood under a shower to make sure they absorbed water correctly.

"In the end, though, after you've done everything you can, they have to go out and play. I always have said that when a team wins, the captain gets too much credit. And when a team loses, he often gets too much of the blame."

He shrugged. "You know that when you take the job. It's an honor to be chosen. It also makes for two exhausting years—physically and emotionally."

That weekend at Gleneagles hurt Watson. Losing, of course, hurt. But the thought that perhaps Mickelson was speaking for the team hurt more.

"It went downhill after I didn't play Phil on Saturday afternoon," he said. "He's a competitor and he wanted to compete. Until then, I think we'd all gotten along well as a team. But Phil was the leader, he felt he had an ownership in the team, and I get that. He was really upset with me.

"I was doing what I thought was best for the team at that moment. If I had it to do over again, knowing now that Rickie [Fowler] and Jimmy [Walker], especially Jimmy, were worn out physically and emotionally, I'd have played Phil—maybe with Bubba [Watson] as opposed to Keegan, because Keegan was really struggling.

"I should have gotten Bubba out there more than twice the first two days. He was playing well. Again, if I had a do-over, I'd change that too."

He smiled a tight smile. "No do-overs in golf."

Watson believes that some of his players didn't get his message on Saturday night. He wasn't telling them they "sucked at foursomes" to be critical, but to make the point that they had outscored Europe when playing their own golf balls in four-ball play and singles was about playing your own ball. He was stunned when he heard that some players took his comments about the mock Ryder Cup trophy he was presented as dismissive.

"I was very touched by it," he said. "But I did say it would all be a little bit hollow if I didn't get to hold the real one the next day. That was the truth. It didn't mean I wasn't grateful for the gesture they all made. I was very grateful."

Watson paused. "Look, I tend to be very direct in the way I talk—that's just me. I tend to be brutally honest—on all topics. I thought they needed a jolt. I sensed a pall in the room that night, and I knew it came from Phil being angry with me. I wanted to make the point that we were plenty good enough to go out and win the next day."

He shrugged. "And you know what, for a while, early in the day, it looked like we might do it. There was a lot of red on the board."

Of course, it didn't last. What lasted were the hard feelings.

"On the one hand, I understood where Phil was coming from when he said what he said," Watson said. "But dealing with losing is part of competing. Look at how Nicklaus handled defeat. Always gracious, always gave credit to the other guy.

"It wasn't the time or the place. Maybe later, but not then. He took away from the Europeans' win and their great play. That wasn't his intent, but it was the result. The timing was wrong. Just completely wrong."

Watson was deeply touched when he walked into the lobby the next day and found Paul and Alison McGinley waiting.

"He's a class act," Watson said. "He told me how sorry he was when he heard what had happened at the press conference. I told him *I* was sorry that it took attention away from how well his team had played. I won't forget that moment for a long time."

Watson and Mickelson spoke at length on the phone later in the week after the matches. "We talked for a while," Watson said. He smiled briefly. "Phil *will* bend your ear off. He told me what he thought and I told him what I thought."

And the upshot?

This time Watson didn't smile. "Let's say we agreed to disagree and leave it at that."

On November 18, 2015, less than eleven months from the Ryder Cup to be held at Hazeltine, Davis Love named three vice captains for his team to go along with Tom Lehman, who had been named earlier in the year on the same day Love had been introduced as the U.S. captain.

Jim Furyk and Steve Stricker being named surprised no one. Tiger Woods being named surprised a lot of people.

That was because they didn't know the deal Love had struck with the players on the task force on the night of that first meeting when it became apparent to him he was going to be asked to be captain.

"When I called them during that break [Furyk, Stricker, Woods, Rickie Fowler, and Phil Mickelson], they all said the same thing: 'Anything you need,'" Love remembered. "I told them, 'I'm going to hold you to that.'"

Furyk made absolute sense. He had played in nine consecutive Ryder Cups, was one of the most respected players in the locker room, and was a likely future captain—2018 in Paris, as it turned out.

Stricker had been one of Tom Watson's vice captains at Gleneagles. He had played on three Ryder Cup teams—including the last U.S. team that had won—in 2008. He was also a virtual lock future captain. With the 2020 matches set for Whistling Straits in Wisconsin—Stricker's home state—he was already penciled in as the U.S. captain.

Woods was a different story. He had played on seven Ryder Cup teams—winning only in 1999 at Brookline—and his mediocre record (13-17-3) in the team event had been the subject of a good deal of scrutiny and criticism. It was certainly worth noting that Woods was 4-1-2 in singles—the only loss coming to Costantino Rocca in his 1997 debut. There was no doubt failures by his partners at times had affected his record, but there were also those who pointed out that during his dominant period he was probably good enough to win four-ball matches one-on-two if need be.

There was also little doubt that Mickelson was right when he said that the young Woods had difficulty dealing with the idea of being part of a team. Golf is an individual sport 99 percent of the time, and Woods had been raised by his father to believe that anyone with a club in his hand was the enemy—not to be trusted, not to be befriended, but to be beaten. Period.

David Feherty had said it best during one of Woods's early appearances: "On his report card, Tiger's kindergarten teacher wrote, 'Does not play well with others.'"

Feherty said it to be funny, but it had a clear ring of truth.

Woods had softened in that approach as he got older, especially when Tom Lehman and Corey Pavin had finally found him partners whom he felt comfortable with and—just as important—who felt comfortable with him.

"There were guys who didn't want to play with Tiger, not because they didn't like him but because of the pressure," said Butch Harmon, Woods's first teacher on tour. "One of them was Freddy [Couples]. He just felt if he played poorly and they lost because of him, Tiger would unfairly get blamed. When you played with Tiger you were *supposed* to win. That was tough for some guys."

Lehman paired Woods with Furyk in 2006, and Pavin paired him with Stricker in 2010. Both got along well with Woods and weren't freaked out by the notion of playing with him. Woods and Furyk went 2-2 at the K Club and Stricker and Woods went 2-1 in rain-soaked Wales. Love put Stricker and Woods together again at Medinah, and it didn't go nearly as well: the two men were 0-3, at least in part because Stricker was struggling with his game. That's why Love had considered putting Keegan Bradley out with Woods on Saturday afternoon and resting Mickelson and Stricker.

Now all three would be working together as Love's vice captains. Lehman had been named in the past captain's role that the task force had mandated. Furyk, Stricker, and Woods were all potential future captains.

For Woods, this was something brand-new: being in a supportive role, where, as much as was possible for him, he would be in the background. That part of the job probably appealed to him.

"I had no idea what I was going to get from him," Love said. "He hadn't hesitated at all when I told him I needed him to do whatever I asked. Right from the beginning, though, he was all in."

Love smiled. "I did wonder—we all wondered—what would happen the first time someone asked Tiger to run and get him a towel or a sandwich."

That question was answered quickly the week of the matches. Woods brought his pal Notah Begay with him to be his cart driver and unofficial assistant. Begay, a friend since junior golf, gave up working that week for Golf Channel and NBC in order to help Woods out. When players needed something and Woods was the nearest vice captain, they usually bypassed Woods and went straight to Begay.

At the very least, it saved some time.

In making the formal announcement of the three new vice captains, Love left open the possibility that he would name one more before the matches began. Europe had been using five vice captains, and the captain's agreement for 2016 had formalized the fact that each team could have up to five vice captains.

The official PGA of America release noted that if Furyk, Stricker, or Woods made the team as a player, Love would probably name someone to take their place on his staff.

At the time, Woods was still recovering from back surgery and a long way—another thirteen months, as it turned out—from even thinking about playing competitively again. Furyk was also on the shelf, having had wrist surgery just prior to the Presidents Cup. He had gone to South Korea as one of Jay Haas's assistant captains and had actually been asked to mentor J. B. Holmes, who had taken his spot on the team. Furyk wasn't likely to play before the spring, limiting his chances to be on the team.

Stricker was forty-eight and had cut his schedule back several years earlier to have more time at home with his wife, Nicki (who had caddied for him early in his career), and their two daughters. He had played only nine times in 2015 and planned to play—if healthy—a little more than that in 2016.

As a result, all three were likely to be available to assist Love at Hazeltine.

Love, though, thought Furyk might play his way onto the team. He had played well prior to his injury in 2015, ending a four-and-a-half-year winless drought with a victory at Hilton Head in April, and had finished fifth on the Presidents Cup points list.

"Knowing Jim and how consistent he is, he almost certainly would have made the team on points for Hazeltine," Love said. "I really wanted to see how he would play when he came back from the injury. If he played like Jim Furyk, I was pretty sure I wanted him on the team."

Furyk's first tournament back turned out to be the Wells Fargo Championship in Charlotte in early May. On Tuesday of that week, he and Love played a practice round together.

Not surprisingly, they spent the first few holes discussing plans for the Ryder Cup—logistics, possible captain's picks, potential pairings.

Standing on the 4th tee, Love turned to Furyk and said, "You know, I don't want you to just think about what you're going to be doing as a vice captain. I want you to think about yourself as potentially a member of the team."

Furyk was actually surprised by the comment. "After my surgery, I hadn't seriously thought about it," he said. "Davis caught me off guard there. My mind-set at that point was on how I could help him as an assistant."

As it turned out, Love's belief that Furyk could contend for a spot on the team proved to be accurate. It took him a while to find his post-injury groove—he missed two cuts and finished T-35 and T-52 in his first four tournaments back—but, playing the U.S. Open at Oakmont, where he had finished tied for second in 2007, he again tied for second. That gave him a huge boost in the FedEx points list and the Ryder Cup points list.

He then finished tied for thirteenth in Canada and tied for fifth in Hartford. There, he shot 58 on Sunday, becoming the first player in the history of the PGA Tour to shoot that score in tournament play. At that point, even though he wasn't going to finish in the top eight on the points list because of the time he'd missed, he was very much in play as a possible captain's pick.

"Let's be honest," Love said. "If Jim's not hurt and he plays the way he played in the summer, he probably finishes fourth or fifth on the points list. I had to take that into consideration."

There were a number of people who disagreed with Love's thinking. Stricker had also played well during the summer, notably in Memphis, where he had finished T-2, and at the Open Championship, where he'd finished solo fourth.

Fairly or unfairly, though, Furyk and Stricker—along with Woods and Phil Mickelson—were closely tied to the American failures in the twenty-first century. All four had losing Ryder Cup records as individuals. The teams Woods had played on had gone 1-6; Mickelson's were 2-8; Furyk's were 2-7; and Stricker's were 1-2.

The thinking went that it was time for new blood—players who didn't have the scar tissue from all the U.S. losses of the past twenty years. What's more, the team that was shaping up did have experience. Among the top ten on the points list as the weeks dwindled, only one player—Brooks Koepka—would be a rookie. There were younger players like Rickie Fowler, Jordan Spieth, and Patrick Reed who had experience, but not so much that losing was in their Ryder Cup DNA. Brandt Snedeker and Jimmy Walker were older but had been part of only one losing team—Snedeker at Medinah and Walker at Gleneagles.

Dustin Johnson had played only in Wales and at Medinah. He'd gone 1-3 in Wales but had bounced back to go 3-0 at Medinah. He had not played at Gleneagles because he had decided in August to take a "leave of absence" from golf. There were all sorts of rumors attached to Johnson's decision—including a *Golf Magazine* report that he had been suspended by the PGA Tour after testing positive for cocaine in a drug test—the third failed test of his career.

Johnson and the Tour denied the report, but rumors persisted that Johnson had made a deal with the Tour allowing him to take a "voluntary" leave so both he and the Tour could honestly say he hadn't been suspended. This was all part of the Tour's never-ending campaign to be about as transparent as a concrete wall.

"I just needed to do it," Johnson said in June 2016, having returned to the Tour in February. "I had issues I was dealing with [he had admitted to having a drinking problem], and we all agreed I had to do it. The only thing I regretted about it was missing the Ryder Cup. That killed me. But it was the right thing to do."

Looking back on the matches at Gleneagles, Tom Watson had lamented Johnson's absence. "We were missing some key guys," he said. "Tiger was out, Jason Dufner, who'd played well at Medinah, didn't make the team, and we didn't have D.J., who was playing well. I'm not saying we win if we have those three at their best, but I'd have liked our chances a lot more."

Johnson's talent was such that he was often looked on with awe by his fellow pros. He'd grown up in South Carolina and made the varsity golf team at his high school in the seventh grade. He was six foot one by then and could dunk a basketball.

"You could play noncontact high school sports before ninth grade in South Carolina," he said. "I had played basketball until then, but when I made the varsity in golf, I focused on golf. I was good enough to play number three that year, and we finished second in the state."

He smiled. "The older guys didn't like having a cocky seventh-grader on the team at first," he said. "I got a lot of wedgies on the early road trips. Then, when I started beating them, they stopped."

Nowadays Johnson plays with a quiet confidence that comes with the ability to hit the ball into space and to play, at times, at a level rarely seen.

"Back then I *was* cocky," he said. "I was kind of a little shit. I remember telling people when I was fifteen that I was going to play on the Tour someday. I knew I wanted to be in golf in some way, shape, or form. My dad was a club pro, and I grew up working all the jobs you could at the golf course: pro shop, cart boy, ground crew. I wanted to be around golf, and the best way to do it was to play."

By the time Johnson graduated from high school, he was six-four and a celebrated junior golfer. He chose to stay close to home, going to Coastal Carolina, not exactly a golf power. It was during his sophomore year that he first *really* believed he was good enough to take a shot at the Tour.

"We were playing in the East Regional of the NCAAs at the Golf Club of Tennessee," he said, his memory very clear, especially for someone who often says, "My memory sucks."

"First day, first hole. It's a 155-yard par-3. I chunked a cut nine-iron right into the water. Might have been the worst shot in the history of golf. I made double [bogey]. All day, I'm grinding, and I get to 17 and I'm still two over par. It's a par-5 and I hit driver, seven-iron to 15 feet. As I'm walking onto the green, they blow the horn for a delay.

"After we came back, I made the putt. Then I birdied 18 and birdied 1, 2, 3, and 4 to start the second round. I shot seven under that day and won the tournament. Plus, we made the NCAA nationals for the first time in school history—knocked Clemson out. We ended up tenth at nationals. That was when it occurred to me that I had the potential to be really good."

Johnson led the Chanticleers back to the NCAAs the next two years (the school hasn't returned since) and turned pro at the end of 2007, making the Tour right away by finishing fourteenth at Q school. Less than a year later, he won the Turning Stone Classic. He won at Pebble Beach in 2009 and again to start 2010. He was twenty-five and well on his way to stardom.

Then the roadblocks began to crop up. After three rounds of the 2010 U.S. Open—played at Pebble Beach—Johnson led by three shots. Given his clear affinity for the golf course, his first major win was not only very much in sight, but seemed likely.

That changed quickly on Sunday. An awkward lie on the second hole forced Johnson to play a shot left-handed. He moved the ball four feet. Two more chunks and a short missed putt later, he had a triple-bogey 7. Unnerved, he pulled his driver on the 3rd tee, hit the ball way left, and never found it. That led to a double-bogey 6. By the time he bogeyed the 5th hole he was six over par for the day and his lead was long gone. He ended up shooting 82 and finished tied for eighth.

Johnson didn't talk to the media that day, but when he did talk a few weeks later, he insisted that putting the brutal final round at Pebble Beach behind him wouldn't be a problem. Most golfers would need months, maybe years, to recover from a meltdown like that.

Not Johnson. He really is as laid-back as he appears, the ultimate "whatever, dude" sort of guy. Less than two months after Pebble Beach, he found himself leading the PGA Championship coming to the final hole at Whistling Straits on Sunday.

This time he was done in by nerves, by his own lack of attention to detail, by a goofy golf course setup, and by an official who failed to do his job.

The nerves came into play on his drive, which flared way right—so far right that Johnson was outside the ropes. Whistling Straits is a faux links course, and it has hundreds of sandy areas outside the ropes that are never raked, which spectators walk through all week during a tournament. In spite of this, the PGA of America has always designated them as bunkers. That means the rules of a hazard apply.

There were signs all over the locker room that week reminding players that any sandy area, regardless of what it looked like, was considered a bunker. If you sat down on a stall in the bathroom, you would be staring at a sign reminding you of that fact.

Johnson's ball came to rest in one of those sandy areas. In the heat of trying to win his first major championship, his mind wasn't on signs in the locker room. It was on trying to figure out a shot.

"People had been walking there all day," he said almost six years later. "You could see the footprints. There was garbage in there. I know I should have known the rule, but that wasn't what I was thinking about. It didn't *look* anything like a bunker. Never once did it cross my mind that I was in a bunker."

When Johnson reached his ball, he waved rules official David Price over. Price, a club pro from Austin, Texas, was one of the most experienced and respected PGA of America officials—which is why he was walking with the last group.

"What do you need?" Price asked.

"I need you to move all these people back so I can have a clear shot to try to get to the green," Johnson answered.

"You got it," Price answered.

Off he went to clear the crowd. Which was his mistake.

A full-time rules official—like the ones who work on the PGA Tour—would have said to Johnson, "You got it. Just remember you're in a bunker under the local rule."

It's called preventive officiating. In all sports, the best officials will try to keep a player from committing a penalty if they can. In basketball, when teams come out of a time-out, an official handing the ball to an in-bounder will always point at the floor and say, "Spot," to indicate to a player he can't move while in-bounding—which is allowable only after a made basket. Officials in football and basketball can often be heard yelling, "Watch your hands," to let a player know if he doesn't stop holding (in football) or hand-checking (in basketball), he's going to be penalized. If the player persists, *then* the whistle blows.

In golf, given the chance, rules officials will often remind players when they are in a place where they can commit a violation.

"You'll say something like 'You know that's a red stake there,'" said David B. Fay, the former executive director of the U.S. Golf Association and current rules expert for Fox Sports. "You can be in a water hazard without being in the water—so you remind the player that if he's inside that stake, even if his ball is dry, he's in a hazard. In a case like that one, the first responsibility to know the rule lies with the player. The second lies with the caddie. But a rules official isn't under the kind of pressure they're under. That's why he should be—if possible—the last line of defense."

Price failed to be that last line of defense. Later, he defended his actions by saying, "All he had to do was ask me."

Actually, he shouldn't have had to ask.

Once Price had cleared an alley, Johnson stepped into the bunker, grounded his club behind the ball, and swung. The ball flew into a bunker right of the green, giving him a reasonable chance to get up and down to win the championship.

Except it didn't. As soon as he grounded his club, Johnson was finished. Because he was in a bunker, he had to be assessed a two-stroke penalty. Fortunately for the PGA, Johnson missed the eight-foot putt he thought was for par and the win. If he had made that putt, he would have been celebrating what he believed to be the biggest win of his life when Price walked up to him.

As it was, Johnson thought the missed putt had put him into a three-way playoff with Martin Kaymer and Bubba Watson. Instead, Price, a hand on his shoulder, explained that he had ground his club in the "bunker" and needed to sign for a triple-bogey 7 on the last hole—leaving him two shots outside the playoff—which was won by Kaymer.

Johnson had another chance to win a major—this time at the British Open in 2011, but the two-iron that flew out-of-bounds on the 14th hole on Sunday finished him.

He had come back to play well after his six months away from the Tour, winning a World Golf Championships event at Doral a month after his return. He had two goals beginning 2016: finally win a major and play on a winning Ryder Cup team.

The U.S. Open victory at Oakmont checked off the first of those goals. He took a two-week break, returned to play at the WGC event in Akron, and won again. His talent continued to leave people who understood the game breathless.

The week before the Open, Phil Mickelson and Justin Rose had gone to play Oakmont. On a windy Monday, they played in an outing with some members.

"I can't remember playing a tougher golf course," said Jim Mackay, who had been Mickelson's caddie since the day he turned pro. "Literally, between the two of them, Phil and Justin didn't make a single birdie that day. Next day, they went out to play again—just the two of them. It wasn't quite as windy. On the 13th tee, we ran into Dustin and A.J. [Johnson's brother Austin, who caddies for him]. By then I think they'd each made a birdie—maybe two. I went over to say hello to Dustin and A.J. and I said, 'Have you ever seen a harder golf course?'

"They both kind of shrugged, didn't really say anything. So, I said it again: 'Boy, this place is brutal, isn't it?'

"Dustin kind of smiled sheepishly and said, 'Well, maybe, but I'm six under so far.' That's when I thought, 'This guy is going to win the Open.'"

Which he did. Then he won Akron. Love's team was very much starting to take shape.

Thirteen

D ARREN CLARKE'S TEAM was starting to take shape too—but not necessarily in the way he had hoped.

He had a cadre of veterans who not only had Ryder Cup experience, but knew what it felt like to win. Rory McIlroy had now played in three of them and had gone from not understanding why the event was so meaningful to knowing the time had come for him to take the role of leader in the team room. Henrik Stenson and Justin Rose would be playing in their fourth Ryder Cup and, like McIlroy, had won major championships.

Lee Westwood's place on the team had been in doubt until April. At forty-three, he was going through a difficult and—as is always the case with star athletes, especially in Great Britain—very public divorce. His play had suffered. Then, at Augusta, he found his missing game and finished tied for second with Jordan Spieth, three shots behind Danny Willett. Clarke had breathed a sigh of relief. He knew he needed Westwood's calming—and often funny—voice in the team room and his Ryder Cup experience on the golf course.

But there were clearly problems, especially for a captain who knew he would be facing a desperate American team and a desperate American fan base.

Graeme McDowell, who had played an important role in the last three victories, had rebounded from an extended slump briefly, winning a PGA Tour event in Mexico in the fall, but was struggling again. He was nowhere near making the team on either points list—Europe uses a worldwide points list and a European Tour points list to pick its nine players—and Clarke didn't think he could pick him if he didn't show *some* form during the summer.

Victor Dubuisson, the taciturn Frenchman who had played so well at Gleneagles, was also nowhere to be found on either points list. The same was true of Jamie Donaldson, who had scored the clinching point at Gleneagles.

Worst of all, Clarke knew that Ian Poulter wasn't going to be on the team. Poulter had just started to show some life in his game in the spring when the pain he had been feeling in his right foot for almost two years began to worsen. Poulter had an arthritic joint in the foot and had taken cortisone shots, which had helped lessen the pain.

But after finishing tied for third in Puerto Rico in March and steadily making cuts for most of the year—without contending anywhere else—he began to have trouble walking when the Tour got to Texas. He missed two cuts there and went back to see his doctor, who told him the only way he was ever going to get better was to shut down completely for at least four months.

This was the last week in May. If he shut down, Poulter couldn't possibly play on the Ryder Cup team, because the earliest he'd play again would be right around the time of the matches and Clarke certainly couldn't pick someone for the team who hadn't picked up a club in four months.

"It really wasn't a choice at all," Poulter said. "At that point I couldn't walk, much less play. The doctor told me it was only going to get worse, not better, without complete rest. I honestly believed earlier in the year that I was going to find a way back into the team. I knew if I showed any form at all, Clarkie would pick me, regardless of where I was on the points list."

Clarke certainly would have done that. It wasn't just that Poulter was 12-4-2 in five Ryder Cups; it was the fire he brought to the team room. So he did the next-best thing: he added Poulter to his list of vice captains. He'd already named Padraig Harrington, Paul Lawrie, and Thomas Björn. None was especially fiery. Poulter would fill that role.

"Not the same though, is it?" Poulter said. "Can't be. It's a helpless feeling knowing all you can do is try to support the guys who are actually playing."

Westwood had been half kidding at Medinah when he had announced that the new European selection system would be "eight guys on points, three captain's picks, and Poults." But there was a ring of truth to it. Just as Mickelson was a lock to be on the U.S. team regardless of where he stood on the points list, Poulter almost certainly would have been on the European team as long as he could walk.

The problem was, he couldn't walk. And so, Europe was likely to be down several key players, much the way the U.S. had been down several important men at Gleneagles.

As the summer began, Clarke was looking at a points list that made it almost certain he'd be taking five rookies to Hazeltine: Danny Willett—granted, the Masters champion, but nonetheless a Ryder Cup rookie; twenty-nine-year-old Andrew Sullivan; Matthew Fitzpatrick—who was twenty-one but looked fourteen; Rafael Cabrera-Bello, a solid Euro Tour player at thirty-two, but still a first-time Ryder Cupper; and twenty-eight-year-old Chris Wood.

All—except Fitzpatrick—were experienced players. But none had played in a Ryder Cup, and only Willett had experienced the heat late on Sunday at a major.

"They'll have to grow up quickly," Clarke said. "The good news is, I've got some veteran guys I can pair them with. Keep them calm, as calm as possible—I hope."

The most experienced of those veterans, outside Westwood, was Sergio García. Once, he had been "El Niño"—the boy—who charmed the world at the age of nineteen and seemed destined to become Tiger Woods's great rival.

At the 1999 PGA, played at Medinah only a few months after he had been low amateur at the Masters and then turned pro, he chased Woods to the finish, literally and figuratively. García came to the 453-yard 16th hole on Sunday trailing Woods by one. His chances of catching him seemed to go a-glimmering when his pushed tee shot came to rest on a root under a giant oak tree to the right of the fairway. The lie was impossible—and dangerous. Trying to take a full swing off the root could lead to a serious wrist injury.

Plus, even if he could get the ball moving, steering it 189 yards down the fairway in the direction of the green would hardly be easy. But García was nineteen and fearless. He took a six-iron, swung as hard as he could, his left foot coming off the ground, and watched the ball start in the direction of the green.

Unable to see the green from where he was standing, he ran down the fairway and jumped in the air, performing a graceful scissors kick, to see where the ball had ended up. Miraculously, it was on the green. He made par, but Woods hung on to win by one.

Even so, no one ever forgot that moment. The boldness, the swing, the run, the leap, and the result. The tree became known as the "Sergio Tree," and thousands of hackers—much like with Tom Watson's chip-in from left of the 17th green at Pebble Beach—would drop a ball as close to the spot as possible and take a swing. Most could barely move the ball. Some hurt their wrists. Eventually, Medinah removed the tree for reasons of age and pace of play. According to club management, pace of play improved by about fifteen minutes a round after the Sergio Tree was removed.

Six weeks after the PGA, García played for Europe in the Ryder Cup matches at the Country Club. He was the first teenager (nineteen years, eight months) to ever tee it up in a Ryder Cup. To this day, he is still the *only* teenager to play in a Ryder Cup.

The first two days, paired with Jesper Parnevik, he won three matches and halved the fourth one. On Sunday, as part of Europe's collapse, he lost his singles match to Jim Furyk.

"Losing the singles was disappointing . . . that whole day was disappointing," García said, years later. "But I *loved* the Ryder Cup from the very beginning. I never enjoyed a week more in my life than that one. There's no pressure like the Ryder Cup, and there's nothing more fun than the Ryder Cup. I felt both right from the beginning."

His 3-1-1 record was the start of a superb Ryder Cup career. He played all five sessions in Europe's victories in 2002, 2004, and 2006, compiling an 11-3-1 record in those matches. He stumbled in 2008 under Nick Faldo's captaincy at Valhalla, going 0-2-2. He was sick that week and emotionally drained, having just broken up with his girlfriend, Morgan Leigh Norman—Greg Norman's daughter. On Saturday afternoon, he sat out a session for the first time ever.

Six years later, Faldo took a shot at García for his poor play that weekend. On the opening morning of the Gleneagles matches, he was working on Golf Channel with Terry Gannon.

Gannon made the comment that, even though García had never won a major championship, he had been a spectacular Ryder Cup player.

"Apart from the one," Faldo said—referring, obviously, to Valhalla.

When Gannon asked Faldo if he was still brooding about 2008, Faldo answered, "He was useless. A half a point and a bad attitude. It's six years later and we move on."

Well, not exactly. To begin with, García had scored one point, not a half point. More important, Faldo had made the comment *during* a Ryder Cup, making it news.

"He sat out one of the best Ryder Cup teams ever Saturday afternoon [García and Westwood]," Graeme McDowell said that night. "He's right, he was useless—because he wasn't playing."

García and Morgan Leigh Norman had been dating seriously, and no one disagreed with the notion that García had taken the breakup hard. Plus, he was sick, taking antibiotics.

Later, Faldo agreed that the "useless" comment was harsh.

Two years later, García had put it behind him—but hadn't forgotten it either.

"When he said it in '14, it didn't really affect me," he said. "Why? Because it was Faldo. If it was someone else, a friend, a member of my family, it might have bothered me. But it was Faldo."

García's record that weekend at Gleneagles backed up the notion that he wasn't bothered. He sat out the Saturday morning four-balls—as planned—then he and McIlroy won their foursomes match in the afternoon. On Sunday, he beat Jim Furyk in the singles—again winning on 18, just as he had done at Medinah.

As Gannon noted, prior to the 2017 Masters, García had never won a major. He had come achingly close on a number of occasions, most notably at the Open Championship in 2007, when he had an eight-foot par putt on the 18th hole at Carnoustie that would have given him the title. The putt slid a couple of inches right of the hole, and he lost a playoff to Padraig Harrington.

There were other chances—though none *that* close. García has finished in the top four at least once in all four majors and has finished in the top five eleven times, including another second at the PGA (behind Harrington again) in 2008 and a tie for second (with Rickie Fowler) at the Open Championship in 2014, when Rory McIlroy took a big lead into Sunday and García and Fowler almost tracked him down.

McIlroy played superbly down the stretch to beat both García and Fowler—each seeking his first major title—by two shots. García shot 66 on that final day. "I gave it everything I had," he said. "Rory was just a little too good."

It had taken García a long time to get to a point where he was comfortable with himself and with his place in the game. His expectations were as high as anyone's after he became a star at such a young age. The near misses in majors clearly frustrated him.

In 2002, playing the U.S. Open at Bethpage, he was tormented by the New York crowd because he had developed a habit of gripping and regripping over the ball before finally swinging the club. The crowd took to counting his regrips and García snapped. He made a profane gesture to the crowd at one point during the second round, and when it was over—having played all afternoon in a downpour—he claimed that the USGA would have delayed play if the conditions had been identical and Tiger Woods had been playing in the afternoon. Woods had played in the morning and was warm and dry and leading the golf tournament while García struggled.

Deep down, García knew that the lack of a delay was because there was no lightning in the area and, the next day, put a note apologizing to Woods in his locker. Woods is not the most forgiving person in the world, and he and García had certainly never been friends, dating to the '99 PGA, when Woods won the championship but García charmed the crowd.

They ended up paired together in the final group on Sunday. García, thinking peace had been made, walked onto the 1st tee with a smile on his face and shook hands with Woods. Then he walked over to the table stocked with things the players might need—tees, snacks, candy, water—on it, picked up some tees, and turned to Woods.

"Need some?" he asked cheerfully.

The photographers who had rushed to take a picture of their handshake had turned away at that moment.

Woods glared balefully at García, said no, and turned away. The next time the two men spoke was when they shook hands on the 18th green—Woods the U.S. Open champion; García having finished fourth after a final round of 74.

By 2010, García's lack of a major title was bothering him. After losing the PGA to Harrington at Oakland Hills two years earlier, his play began to slide. By the time he got to the PGA that summer at Whistling

Straits, he was clearly burned out and not happy to be playing golf. He had dropped out of the top fifty in the Official World Golf Rankings for the first time since 1999 and badly needed a break.

He shot an opening-round 78 and then came back to shoot 69 the next day. He still missed the cut by two shots, but the 69 was proof that the real García was still somewhere inside—if he could just find his motivation and something resembling a reasonable putting stroke.

The turning point, though, came at that year's Ryder Cup. Colin Montgomerie asked him to be a vice captain and García decided to accept—even though he knew it would be painful not to play after having been part of the previous five Cups.

"It did hurt," he said. "It made me realize how much I loved to play and how much I loved golf. I had been going through the motions, just playing because I was supposed to play. I wasn't enjoying myself. I'd forgotten how much I loved it."

He changed his putting stroke and his attitude and his game started to rebound. He actually had to qualify to get into the U.S. Open the next June, but he made it and finished tied for seventh. A month later, he finished tied for ninth at the Open Championship. That fall he won twice in Europe, and the next summer he won in Greensboro—breaking a four-year PGA Tour drought.

Nine months later, he was in contention at the Players Championship—an event he had won in 2008. The Players is generally considered the fifth most important annual tournament in the world, a step below the four majors, a step up from the week-to-week events on tour.

He and Woods were paired together in the final group on Saturday, García leading by one at the start of the round. On the 2nd hole, García was getting ready to hit his second shot from the fairway. Just as he started his swing, Woods—who was left of the fairway—pulled a club that indicated he was going for the green from a tough lie. The crowd reacted during García's backswing.

García was convinced Woods had timed the pulling of his club to interfere with his swing. Woods hotly denied it, saying he'd been told that García had already hit.

Marshals came forward—two saying Woods was lying; two more saying Woods was telling the truth. In the end—as was almost always the case on the golf course—Woods had the last laugh. Tied for the lead on Sunday after birdieing the 16th hole, García pumped two balls into the water at the island green 17th hole, then drowned a third ball on the 18th. He ended up tied for eighth; Woods walked off with his seventy-eighth PGA Tour victory.

Several days later, García made things much worse for himself at a European Tour awards dinner. The night was, for all intents and purposes, a celebration of Europe's win at Medinah, and each team member was called up to applause and to answer a few softball questions from the emcee, Golf Channel's Steve Sands.

Half jokingly, Sands asked García if he would try to get together to talk to Woods during the U.S. Open—the next time they'd be playing in the same event.

"Oh, sure," García said. "We'll have him round to dinner every night. We'll serve fried chicken."

García later said that he knew almost as soon as the words were out of his mouth that his attempt at humor was way out of line. In fact, he apologized publicly before the night was over and again the next morning.

After first issuing a statement through the European Tour saying he had made a "silly" attempt at humor in response to what he thought was a humorous question, García was much more honest when he met with reporters. "My answer was totally stupid and out of place," he said. "I feel sick about it."

Neither Woods nor most of the public was going to let him out of the hole he had dug for himself.

In response to García's apologies, Woods tweeted, "The comment that was made wasn't silly. It was wrong, hurtful and clearly inappropriate."

As with Fuzzy Zoeller in 1997—Zoeller had made an even worse comment while Woods was winning the Masters about Woods serving fried chicken, "or whatever the hell they serve" at the champions dinner the next year—Woods had no interest in saving a drowning man.

Had it been a friend, Woods would have been more sympathetic. In 2008, when Golf Channel's Kelly Tilghman jokingly said on-air that the best way to keep Woods from dominating golf might be to "lynch him in a back alley," Woods and agent Mark Steinberg helped quell the outrage by issuing a statement that Woods knew there was no ill intent in the comment and considered the matter closed. Tilghman and Woods were friends; in fact, Tilghman had worked with Woods at a Nike demonstration and was also involved in some of his video games.

Tilghman was suspended by Golf Channel for two weeks for the comment, but her career continued to flourish—in large part because she's very good at what she does—but also because Woods came to her defense.

García, as a longtime Woods antagonist, wasn't going to get off the hook that easily.

"Tiger and I have never been friends, we just never connected," García said. "I put myself in a bad spot with that comment—it was my fault."

García won again on the European Tour early in 2014 and had another chance to finally win a major at the Open Championship—before falling to McIlroy. He then played well in the Ryder Cup at Gleneagles.

In May 2016, he won the Byron Nelson Classic for his twenty-fourth worldwide win. The victory was a relief for both García and Darren Clarke because it boosted García high enough in the point standings that Clarke wouldn't have to use a captain's pick on him.

"Unless he was playing really horrible, I couldn't see leaving Sergio off the team," Clarke said. "He, Poulter, and Westwood have been rocks for us for a long time."

Poulter wasn't going to play. Westwood probably wasn't going to make the team off the points list but, after Augusta, was a lock captain's pick. García would be on the team. Along with McIlroy, Stenson, Rose, and Westwood, they would form the veteran corps that Clarke would build his team around.

And finally, there was one other veteran Clarke wanted on the team: the hero of 2012.

There's an old saying about athletes: sometimes you can be too smart. The greatest athletes in any sport have tunnel vision. They see nothing, hear nothing, and often know nothing if it isn't related to their sport.

When quarterback Jared Goff, the number-one pick in the 2016 NFL draft, was asked if he knew where the sun rose each morning, he was stumped. The moment was captured by a film crew from HBO's *Hard Knocks* series.

In a later show, Goff was shown taking a blimp ride with fellow rookie Pharoh Cooper. When Goff asked Cooper if he knew where the sun rose, Cooper said, "In the air?"

"No," Goff said. "In the east. Apparently it's well known."

Cooper went to the University of South Carolina for three years. Goff went to California-Berkeley for three years. Apparently sunrise was not part of the curriculum at either school.

Golfers were perhaps best summed up as a group by David Duval, who graduated from Georgia Tech, making him a minority on the PGA Tour; most players don't have college degrees.

Duval had been described in a magazine piece as one of the Tour's "intellectuals." As proof, the writer cited the fact that he read Ayn Rand. Duval was amused and bemused.

"Hang on, reading Ayn Rand makes me an intellectual?" Duval said. Then he paused and added, "I guess everything's relative. In a locker room where most guys think of *USA Today* as heavy reading, I guess reading Ayn Rand would make me an intellectual."

Martin Kaymer hadn't gone to college. He had pursued his dream of playing professional golf as soon as he graduated from high school in Dusseldorf. He'd spent winters in Florida, grinding on his game, spending hours on the range and the golf course.

"I lived in a small apartment and had to manage my money very carefully," he said. "I made myself pasta six nights a week because it was all I could afford." He smiled. "One night a week I'd treat myself and get sausages.

"It was actually a great time in my life. I matured, learned to appreciate how lucky I was to have that opportunity. But there were times when it was quite difficult. I look back on it now, though, and realize how happy I was because I had a clear goal and everything I did was about reaching that goal."

Kaymer was the classic driven young golfer. He had the tunnel vision needed to clear a path to stardom. He was twenty-five when he won his first major championship in August 2010 and barely twenty-six when he became the number-one player in the world six months later. At that point, only Tiger Woods had been younger than Kaymer when he first ascended to the number-one ranking.

The achievement left Kaymer feeling . . . empty.

"I remember going to dinner with my father, who flew in from Germany to be there, and my friends and they were all so excited," he said. "I sat there thinking, 'So what now?' I'd worked so hard to achieve an end—to become the number-one player—and I was thinking, 'So what now?'

"I never dealt with it well. It felt like almost everyone I knew treated me differently, looked at me differently. I had close friends, even some [extended] family members who wanted to take pictures with me or even get my autograph. I think there were three people in my life who looked at me the same way—my father, my brother, and my girlfriend.

"I look now at Rory and Jordan and how they handled being number one [both were younger than Kaymer when they reached that ranking], and there's no doubt they've been able to handle everything that comes with it better than I did.

"I've wondered why that's true. Maybe it has something to do with the fact that they were stars very young, they got used to all the attention. Maybe for Rory being an only child helped because being the center of everything was a comfortable place for him. I can't be certain. All I know is, I *didn't* handle it well."

Kaymer's theory on McIlroy and Spieth rings true. McIlroy talks often about being an only child and a prodigy and how he needs to push back from that every once in a while.

"I realized at a certain point that I'm not a great judge of character," he said one night. "If you live in a world where everyone treats you well because they think you're a star or important, it's tough to judge who is really a good guy and who is not. At least I've figured out that the real test is how you treat people who you don't think are important or can't help you make money."

When Danny Willett won the Masters, he talked about the changes in his life. "One thing that's been hard is getting to the range at tournaments and feeling surrounded," he said. "Used to be just my caddie and me, maybe my coach and that was it. Now there's cameras all over, people wanting to talk to me, equipment people—everyone. I miss the quiet."

When Spieth heard what Willett had said, he shook his head and said that hadn't been a problem for him after his Masters win or even after his extraordinary 2015 season. "Honestly, not to sound arrogant, but I always had people watching me on the range when I was a junior," he said. "Once I started to win a fair bit, I was never alone on the range."

Kaymer was more in the Willett category. He hadn't been a prodigy; in fact, his first love was soccer. One of the things he loved about that game was that you were a part of a team.

"Golf is such an individual sport," he said. "I liked having the friends you have on a football [soccer] team. If I hadn't gotten decent at golf and realized it was my true calling, I would have never stopped playing soccer.

"Even now when I go to a Bundesliga [German's soccer major league] game, I find myself wondering, 'Could I have . . . ?' The guys who are stars are about my age. But it got to a point where I knew golf was the sport where I had a chance—a reasonable chance—to become quite good."

Kaymer became very good, very quickly. And then he crashed. A lot of people attributed his dive to a swing change. Wanting to play well at the Masters, which he considers to be *the* major, Kaymer worked on hitting a draw more often off the tee, because Augusta National is built for a right-to-left player or, in the case of successful lefties there—Phil Mickelson, Bubba Watson, Mike Weir—a right-to-left fade. Kaymer had always been a left-to-right player, much like Lee Trevino, who won every major except the Masters.

"People forget I won a tournament at the end of 2011 after I'd changed my swing," Kaymer said. "It was more about not being able to handle the spotlight than anything else."

The two years after that—with the exception of Medinah—were difficult. His world ranking dropped steadily, reaching a nadir at number sixty-three early in 2014. He went back to grinding on his swing and his game—able to do so because he'd dropped out of the spotlight he'd had so much trouble dealing with.

Almost unnoticed, he slipped into the lead early at the Players Championship and hung on after a rain delay on Sunday to win on the PGA Tour for the first time since his win at the PGA in 2010. What had once been a four-shot lead was down to one by the time he got to the infamous island green 17th hole. His tee shot found the bunker—fortunately—in front of the green, the only place to miss the green without getting wet.

His bunker shot came up 28 feet short. Facing the specter of a bogey that would drop him into a tie with Jim Furyk, who was already in the clubhouse, he rolled the putt in for par, then got up and down at 18 for a par and the win.

"Honestly, making that putt on 17 was just about as emotional as the putt at Medinah," he said. "Not because it meant more but because it was *hard*. I knew I was going to make the putt at Medinah. I didn't feel that way at Sawgrass."

The win at the Players led to an even more impressive win six weeks later at the U.S. Open. Kaymer shot 65-65 the first two days at Pinehurst and cruised to a remarkable eight-shot win for his second major title.

"I think I appreciated that one more," he said. "When I won the PGA, honestly, I had started that week trying to finish high enough to make the Ryder Cup team. When I won [the Open] at Pinehurst, I think I appreciated it more."

Suddenly, Kaymer was again one of the best players in the world. His world ranking skyrocketed—again. He was ranked number twelve when the Ryder Cup was played that year and went 1-1-2, including an impressive singles win over Bubba Watson.

Once again, though, he couldn't stand prosperity. He struggled so badly in 2015 that he didn't even make the PGA Tour playoffs— finishing 139th on the points list.

It wasn't as if he wasn't trying. In fact, needing a top-ten finish to make the top 125 and qualify for the playoffs, he went to Greensboro, the last tour stop of the so-called regular season. Every year a number of top names end up in Greensboro, trying to get into the playoffs. Ernie Els once called it "the last chance saloon."

Kaymer finished tied for fourteenth—not good enough. What's more, because he had counted on making the playoffs when he put his schedule together, Kaymer had played in only thirteen tour events—two short of the fifteen required in order to qualify to play a full schedule the following year. It was a minor headache, but one Kaymer had to deal with nonetheless.

"I miscalculated," he said with a smile at the Players Championship—a PGA Tour event he could play because he was a past champion. "I'll try to play well enough so that it doesn't happen again."

He did play better in 2016, but focused his attention on the European Tour, playing in twenty-four events there. His game began to come around in the spring—not anywhere near what it had been at its peak, but solid: five top tens in Europe going into the PGA Championship.

"I need Kaymer and Graeme [McDowell] to play well the next couple of weeks, especially here," Darren Clarke said on the eve of the PGA. "Martin is very close, G-Mac, honestly, right now, is not. Same with Luke [Donald]. The two of them will have to show some real form the next couple of weeks. Martin has been a lot more solid."

Kaymer gave Clarke what he needed at Baltustrol, finishing T-7. A T-6 a couple of weeks later in Denmark, the last event before Clarke made his three captain's picks, ensured that he and Westwood would be two of Clarke's picks.

The third pick was up in the air going into Denmark. Clarke would have loved to be able to pick another veteran—Donald or McDowell, specifically. Donald did pick up his game as the deadline neared.

But not enough. In the end, Clarke had to go with another rookie. Russell Knox had played well, winning at Hartford, and most people believed he'd get the last spot. But Clarke was intrigued by Thomas Pieters, a twenty-four-year-old from Belgium who had won the NCAA championship three years earlier while playing at the University of Illinois.

Clarke asked to be paired with Pieters for the first two rounds of the "Made in Denmark" tournament. He wanted to see Pieters up close to see how he handled the pressure of playing alongside Clarke, knowing that he was essentially auditioning for the Ryder Cup captain. Pieters knew exactly why Clarke was paired with him and that a spot on the Ryder Cup team was at stake.

"I think it's fair to say he handled it pretty well," Clarke said with a laugh.

Pieters shot 62 on Thursday and went on to win the tournament. He'd been put into a crucible that wasn't the Ryder Cup, but was still pretty intense.

On Monday, August 29, Clarke announced his picks: Westwood, Kaymer, and Pieters. Russell Knox was disappointed, but no one was that surprised.

The European team was set: six veterans, six rookies. No Poulter. No McDowell. No Donald. No Dubuisson. No Donaldson.

Now it was Davis Love's turn.

Fourteen

Davis love was in a very different position from Darren Clarke when it came to his captain's picks. To begin with, Love had four, not three.

For years, the U.S. had two captain's picks and Europe had three. That had changed when Paul Azinger asked the PGA for four in 2008. Each side had the right to choose how many captain's picks it would have, so the PGA granted Azinger's wish. In 2014, the U.S. had gone down to three captain's picks because Tom Watson believed the playing field should be level.

Which made absolute sense. Why the U.S. and Europe had never agreed to have the same number of captain's picks, no one seemed to know. When he was named captain, Love had decided to go back to four picks. He was far more interested in winning than a level playing field. Which was understandable.

Love also benefited from the way the points list was shaping up as the summer wore on. The only potential rookie consistently inside the top eight was Brooks Koepka, who had missed the Presidents Cup a year earlier only because he had spent most of 2014 playing the European Tour and had accumulated points on a regular basis only in 2015.

Koepka was twenty-six, hit the ball into outer space, and had the kind of "bring it on" attitude that would make him an ideal Ryder Cup player. Love was hoping he would make the team.

There were other potential first-timers lurking in the top twenty-five, including Bill Haas, who had scored the winning point at the

2015 Presidents Cup; Scott Piercy, a thirty-seven-year-old late bloomer playing the best golf of his career; Charley Hoffman, another veteran (thirty-nine) who had been in contention to make teams in the past; and—most intriguing to Love—two youngsters: Justin Thomas and Daniel Berger.

Both were twenty-three—born twenty-two days apart in April 1993; both had won on the PGA Tour; both were pals with Jordan Spieth (another 1993 baby) and Rickie Fowler. And both were dying to play Ryder Cup.

Thomas's father was a club pro, who had taken his son to the Ryder Cup on three different occasions when he was a boy. Thomas had been awed by the event; the crowds; the atmosphere; the intensity. When he became a star as a junior golfer and then at the University of Alabama, the Ryder Cup became one of *the* goals for him.

"I had the sense, even just watching, that it was an amazing thing to be part of as a player," he said. "I could see the pressure written on the faces of the players and I remember thinking, 'I want to feel that pressure.'"

In fact, when Thomas sat down for an interview with Mark Rolfing on Golf Channel in Hawaii in January, he told Rolfing that his number-one goal for 2016 wasn't necessarily to win a major—though he wouldn't mind—but to "play on a winning Ryder Cup team."

Rolfing, who loves the Ryder Cup as much as anyone, was so surprised by the answer that he asked the question again, just to be sure he'd heard right. He had. The Ryder Cup was Thomas's number-one priority for 2016, even though winning a major is worth millions of dollars. Remarkably, Thomas heard blowback for that comment. People were stunned: The Ryder Cup first, a major second? How could that be?

"I didn't think it was that big a deal," Thomas said later in the year. "I wasn't putting the majors down at all. I was just saying that having grown up as the son of a PGA professional, having seen the Ryder Cup up close, I wanted to be part of it *and* I wanted to *win.*"

Berger's father, Jay, had been a top-ten tennis player who had represented the U.S. in the Davis Cup. He worked for the U.S. Tennis Association and was Davis Cup captain Jim Courier's right-hand man during Davis Cup matches. The U.S. had won the Davis Cup more times than any other country (thirty-two), but had won it only once since 1995 (2007). As a result, Daniel had a sense of how important the one team event in men's tennis was to his father and how frustrating it was to not have won it very often during a twenty-one-year period—which was most of his life.

All of that made him someone who would fit perfectly on the 2016 U.S. Ryder Cup team. When he won for the first time on the PGA Tour at Memphis in June, Berger jumped into contention, not only on the points list, but also as a potential captain's pick.

Love had all but decided on four players he would take as captain's picks if they didn't make the team on points: Zach Johnson, Patrick Reed, Rickie Fowler, and Matt Kuchar. He was fairly certain that all four wouldn't miss the top eight but was prepared to pick any of them who did.

At forty, Johnson wasn't just a veteran of four Ryder Cups, he was one of those guys everyone in the locker room respected and looked up to—not to mention, he had won the Open Championship in 2015. Johnson had a choirboy face, was deeply religious, and almost never said anything even a little bit controversial in public. But beneath the dimpled smile was an absolutely manic competitor who could putt the eyes out when he was on. Love knew all that.

Reed was far more likely to say something that would land him in trouble than Johnson. He wouldn't turn twenty-six until August but had already won four times on tour. More importantly—at least to Love—he had played superbly at Gleneagles, going 2-0-1 in his partnership with Spieth and then beating Henrik Stenson in what might have been the best-played singles match of Sunday.

"He's our new bulldog," said Bubba Watson—like Reed, an ex-Georgia golfer. Watson and Reed had become friends after Gleneagles. "We need someone like him on the team," Watson added.

Most players didn't know Reed very well. He'd started his college career at Georgia before transferring to Augusta State, where he'd played a key role in winning two national championships.

Because he'd been thrown off the team at Georgia, there were numerous stories about *why* he'd been tossed. In a book called *Slaying the Tiger,* author Shane Ryan reported that Reed had been accused of cheating during a team qualifier for a match and for stealing from his teammates. Reed vehemently denied those charges and got Georgia coach Chris Haack to sign a document saying those had *not* been the reasons for his dismissal.

By then, Reed was one of the Tour's young stars. He had won three times in an eight-month period from August 2013 to March 2014, including a win at the WGC event at Doral. After that victory he had said he believed he was one of the top-five players in the world, even though the Official World Golf Rankings had him at number twenty-one.

That comment produced a lot of clucking and tutting in both the locker room and the media room. Golf is a very insular world, and anyone who goes outside the box is automatically viewed with suspicion by many players and most in the golf media.

What you're supposed to do when you win on tour is thank the sponsors (first, last, and always), the volunteers, and your family, and then talk about how amazing it is to win against such great players. If you'd like to give glory to God while you're at it, that's fine too.

Reed had said—in essence—"Hey, I'm twenty-four years old, and I think I'm just about as good (or better) than any of these guys."

During that eight-month period, he *had* been one of the five best players in the world—regardless of what the rankings said. The Official World Golf Ranking is a flawed system anyway. Instead of starting at zero each year, it rolls over for two years, meaning a player who won a couple of tournaments twenty months ago (but hasn't been able to—as the players say—"play dead" since) might be ranked ahead of someone who has played steadily with one win in the past year.

There are plenty of other things wrong with the system beyond that, but that wasn't the point. Reed had gone outside the norm, and that's frowned on in golf world. When he didn't play as well in the next few months, voices in both the media room and the locker room could be heard saying very clearly, "Top-five player in the world, huh?"

They were much quieter after Gleneagles, where he was one of the few bright spots for the U.S. Still, he remained something of a mystery, even to his Ryder Cup teammates. This led to Phil Mickelson—while talking about each player on the team on Saturday night at Gleneagles—saying Reed needed to let the players in the room "get to know you better."

"He was right," Reed said with a smile. "I have a tendency when I get to the golf course to go into my own little world. I go out on the range or to the putting green, put my headphones on, and focus on my golf and the music." Remarkably, during 2016, Reed had exactly one song playing repeatedly as he practiced: "Radioactive," by Imagine Dragons.

"I think it's fair to say I know it backwards and forwards," he said.

On occasion, Reed will take one earbud out so he can talk to his wife,

Justine, who is a constant presence when he's practicing most weeks; his coach; or his caddie . . .

"Sometimes when I have an earbud out, guys will come over and talk," he said. "If I've played well, they might congratulate me or they might talk about the golf course—whatever. I'm fine with that. If I don't want to talk to people, I just put the other earbud in and go back to work."

Gleneagles was something of a turning point in Reed's relationships with other players. Because of the rumors about his college career and his ever-present headphones, he was viewed with some suspicion by other players. Just the *thought* that someone might have cheated can make someone persona non grata in the locker room. Vijay Singh is in the Hall of Fame, but there are still players—some of whom weren't born yet—who bring up the incident on the Asian Tour in 1985 in which he was accused of intentionally signing for a wrong score.

Asked about Singh's induction into the Hall of Fame in 2006, one top player shrugged and said, "Once a cheat, always a cheat."

Singh was suspended for the scorecard incident. Reed was never sanctioned for anything; he was just the subject of rumors.

During that 2014 Ryder Cup, many players got to know him for the first time. Spieth, whose reputation was as pristine as Reed's was clouded, found common ground with him on the golf course because each was so competitive and they'd both grown up in Texas.

Bubba Watson, himself shy by nature and often a polarizing figure in both the locker room and the media room, went out of his way to take Reed under his wing, becoming an unofficial mentor after that weekend.

"It was an amazing experience," Reed said. "I loved being a part of it and the competition, but I also really enjoyed getting to know the guys on the team. I remember Phil making the point that one of the best things about being on a Ryder Cup team was that you developed relationships during that week that would go on for years afterwards. He's right about that."

Reed is refreshingly blunt and self-deprecating.

Always a little overweight, Reed liked to tell people he was on a "seefood diet: I see food, I eat it . . . especially a big steak."

Tip your waiters and try the . . . steak.

Reed started 2015 with a win—at the Tournament of Champions on Maui, coming from behind to catch Ryder Cup teammate Jimmy Walker and then beat him in a playoff. Two months later, he almost won again, losing in a three-man playoff to his pal Jordan Spieth at the Valspar Championship in Tampa.

That victory turned out to be the springboard for Spieth's amazing 2015, during which he won two majors and almost won two more. Reed didn't win again but had another solid year. He continued to play well in 2016 but didn't have a win during the so-called regular season that wound up in Greensboro—the site of his first tour win in 2013.

"It's frustrating," he said. "I understand that golf is a sport where you lose a lot more than you win, but when I tee it up on a Thursday, my only real goal is to win. When I get in contention and don't win, it bothers me. I'm not knocking top tens, but that's not what I'm out here for, I'm out here to win."

Reed may love to play more than any other top player in the game. In his first four years on tour, he played in 111 tournaments—averaging just a tad under twenty-eight events per year—not counting the Ryder Cup or Presidents Cup or exhibitions or overseas events. Most top players will play about twenty times a year. Jordan Spieth, who has also been on tour since 2013, played ninety-six times during that period—including twenty-one tournaments in 2016, the year after his two major victories.

"I love to play, I love to compete," Reed said. "Realistically, I know I need to play less. I need to be better rested for the major championships [where he has yet to record a top-ten finish]. I get that. The problem is when I'm home, I'm just dying to be out there playing. The fact that I can still have my family [he and Justine have a three-year-old daughter] out there with me makes it easier. When she's in school, that will make it different, I know that.

"In 2015, I skipped Greensboro. I wanted to be rested for the next week when the playoffs started. It almost killed me. I'm sitting at home watching them play a golf course I really like, a golf course where I've *won* and I'm saying to myself, 'What am I doing here?' "

In 2016, Reed *did* play Greensboro. That was part of a stretch in which he played thirteen weeks out of fifteen, beginning in June at the U.S. Open and stretching through the Ryder Cup, which ended on October 2. In early August, he played Hartford, flew to Rio to play in the Olympics, and then flew back to play in Greensboro.

Part of the reason for the frenetic schedule was the Olympics—he was one of a handful of top players who were going to play in Rio regardless of schedule, the Zika virus, or security concerns. "I've always loved the

Olympics," he said. "I love the idea of playing for my country in anything. And you never know if you'll get another chance."

The third reason he played so much was that he wanted to guarantee his spot on the Ryder Cup team. He knew there was an excellent chance that if he finished outside the top eight, Love would make him a captain's pick. But he didn't want to leave it to chance.

"If you need to be a pick, you never know what can happen," he said. "We've seen guys who finished ninth get left off the team. [Anthony Kim in 2010 and Hunter Mahan in 2012 were two examples.] I want to know I'm playing—period."

He went into the Barclays, the first playoff event but the last tournament before the standings were finalized, in eighth place. Knowing he needed to play well to cement his spot, he won—his first victory since Hawaii twenty months earlier.

"Winning is always great," he said a week later. "Knowing that I had pretty much clinched my spot on the team even if I didn't actually win but finished in the top three or four made playing that back nine on Sunday a lot easier."

Reed was paired that day with Rickie Fowler. Like Reed, Fowler was almost a lock to be a captain's pick if he didn't make the top eight. Like Reed, he didn't want to leave it to chance, especially since he'd had a difficult summer.

Fowler was a star on the PGA Tour—had been almost since his rookie year. Kids loved him because he wore his dark hair long and wore an orange flat-brimmed cap that set him apart from everyone on tour. Often, he wore it with the brim turned around backward. He defined cool. Girls loved him because of his boyish good looks, he'd been a dirt biker as a kid, and had an easy smile that made their hearts melt. He defined hot.

Perhaps most surprisingly, players loved him too. In many ways, Fowler should have been the guy they resented. He was making big money in endorsements—see above—almost from the minute he left Oklahoma State (thus the orange cap) to turn pro in 2009. There was no doubt he could play—he had lost a playoff at the Frys.com event in October of that year that would have given him a two-year exemption and allowed him to skip Q school. Instead, he went to Q school, finished fifteenth, and earned his card that way.

He finished second twice in his first full season, 2010—at Phoenix and at the Memorial—and was thirty-second on the FedEx Cup points list. He was also twentieth on the Ryder Cup points list, a pretty good start for a twenty-one-year-old who no doubt would be on the team in the near future.

The near future turned out to be that year. Corey Pavin asked Davis Love, one of his vice captains, to talk to some people about the possibility of picking Fowler, even though it would mean skipping over a number of people on the points list—including, as it turned out, Anthony Kim, who finished ninth, and J. B. Holmes, who finished nineteenth. Both had been a part of the winning U.S. team at Valhalla. Also skipped over was Lucas Glover, who had won the U.S. Open in June and was tenth on the list.

"Everyone I asked about Rickie as a possible captain's pick said the same thing," Love said: "'Take him. He'll do well under pressure and he'll be not good, but great in the team room.' I remember [past PGA champion] Bob Tway [whose son Kevin had played with Fowler at Oklahoma State] looking me in the eye and saying, 'He shouldn't be your last captain's pick, he should be your *first* captain's pick.'"

Pavin went with Tiger Woods, Zach Johnson, Stewart Cink, and Fowler for the 2010 captain's picks. The first three were major champions. Fowler was a little more than a year removed from being a sophomore at Oklahoma State.

Fowler's personality is the opposite of Patrick Reed's. He's very comfortable around his peers, the guy who is always looking to play a joke to loosen things up. He also has an endearing, self-deprecating sense of humor.

Sitting at lunch with Dustin Johnson one day, he heard Johnson mention to someone that he'd been six-one as a seventh-grader.

"What's it feel like to be six-one?" he asked Johnson.

"Don't remember," Johnson answered. "I wasn't six-one for that long. I've been six-four for a long time now."

"I'd have loved to have spent one day being six-one," Fowler said, laughing. "Come to think of it, I'd have loved to have spent one day being five-nine."

The PGA Tour media guide lists Fowler as being five-nine. "Someone was being nice to me," he said. "I'm five-eight standing up straight."

Being small had never deterred Fowler as an athlete. He'd started riding dirt bikes as a kid and was a good baseball player. But golf had always been the sport he aspired to from a very young age.

"I can remember telling people when I was seven that I wanted to play on the PGA Tour," he said. "I always followed golf as a kid. I remember the comeback at Brookline [he was ten] very well, and I knew what the Tour was about—as much as you can as a kid."

Fowler's father owned a sand and gravel company and would often trade sand with the owner of a nearby driving range in return for unlimited free range balls for Rickie. His father never played—it was his grandfather who introduced Fowler to the game—but he supported his son's aspirations.

Fowler loved team sports. Motocross is a team sport, and he might have stuck with baseball if he'd had a little more size and power. While in college, he played on a Walker Cup team and remembers the experience fondly.

"I always enjoyed being part of a team—in any sport," he said. "The Walker Cup was a lot of fun . . ." He paused. "Maybe because we won." A smile. "Actually, I think I'd have enjoyed it even if we lost. I've played on two Ryder Cup teams and we lost both times, and I can still honestly say they were my best experiences in golf. You develop relationships during those weeks that just don't happen the rest of the time on tour.

"I hardly knew Jim Furyk when we played together in Wales; now we're good friends. Jimmy Walker and I hang out all the time. Phil [Mickelson] is my big brother figure out here. It's hard to explain why it happens given that we're all *so* individual the rest of the time, but it does."

In spite of his lack of size—he may weigh 150 pounds dripping wet—Fowler can hit a golf ball plenty far. And just as Love had predicted, he proved to be a perfect guy in Pavin's 2010 team room—right from the start.

When the players arrive at a Ryder Cup, the first thing they see waiting for them is a huge box filled with their clothing for the week. The PGA of America (and the European Tour) hire tailors to measure the players for all their clothes, give them each a chance to pick the dress clothes—including shoes—they want, and then ship them to the site of the matches.

Every American player who is given any chance to make the team is asked to spend an hour or so selecting clothes and being measured during Jack Nicklaus's Memorial Tournament. That's considered a perfect site because almost all the top American players show up and it's a more relaxed atmosphere than a major.

"The clothes we get are unreal," Jordan Spieth said. "I haven't had to buy a suit or any dress clothes the last three years because of it."

When Fowler unloaded his box of clothing after arriving in Wales, he had an idea. The next morning, as players and wives came down the hall, still a little groggy as they headed for breakfast, they saw a box sitting there. Zach Johnson had helped Fowler climb in. As soon as anyone got close to it, Fowler, hiding in the box, popped out of it, sort of like a jack-in-the-box yelling, "Wake up!" or "Welcome to Wales!" or something along those lines.

"A lot of guys jumped out of their skin," Fowler said, grinning. "I got some of the wives too." He smiled. "Tabitha Furyk and Robin Love really freaked out. Phil [Mickelson] was eating chips. He just looked up, shrugged, and kept going."

Fowler was exactly the kind of relaxing presence the normally uptight Americans needed. The leaders of the team—Mickelson, Woods, Furyk—weren't exactly laugh-a-minute guys, even though Mickelson was a nonstop needler. The only other American on that team who had a knack for making people laugh was Matt Kuchar. Fowler provided some backup.

"He was perfect," said Paul Goydos, like Love, a vice captain. "A twenty-one-year-old playing his first Ryder Cup, you might have thought he'd be intimidated or overwhelmed by it all. He wasn't. *He* helped the veterans relax."

Fowler played reasonably well in Wales in his two team matches, although he was guilty of an embarrassing rules gaffe in his first match. Because of the rain delay Friday, the second session was backed up into Saturday. Playing with Jim Furyk in a foursomes match against Martin Kaymer and Lee Westwood, Fowler found Furyk's tee shot on the 4th hole in mud. He was allowed a free drop. Unfortunately, he dropped his *own* ball instead of the ball Furyk had hit off the tee. Even though both balls were Titleists, foursomes rules require a team to finish a hole with the same ball used off the tee.

Fowler and Furyk were penalized the hole and were 2 down at that point. They recovered to halve the match. The next day Fowler lost a four-ball match with Mickelson to Kaymer and Ian Poulter.

On Monday, he was 3 down in his singles match against Edoardo Molinari with four holes to play. He had to birdie 15 just to halve the hole and keep the match alive. Then he birdied 16, 17, and 18—rolling in a curling 18-footer at the last—to win all three holes and steal a half point for the U.S.

His comeback gave the Americans life, and they almost rallied for a 14–14 tie that would have allowed them to retain the Cup. Only Graeme McDowell's victory over Hunter Mahan in the last singles match allowed Europe to hang on and get to the magic number: 14½ points.

"When I made the last putt, it was as cool a feeling as I'd ever had in golf," Fowler said. "Edoardo had played so well. I had to get up and down for birdie just to halve the 15th and stay alive, so getting that half point meant a lot. It was just a shame we couldn't quite finish."

Two years later, Fowler was a spectator, watching his friends fail to finish at Medinah. He had won for the first time on tour in May, beating Rory McIlroy in a playoff in Charlotte with a birdie on the first playoff hole. But he started to experience back and shoulder pain soon after that.

"I tried to play through the pain," he said. "I took a couple shots, but they didn't help much. I knew it was going to be a close call when I didn't make it off the points list because I hadn't been playing well. It wasn't like Davis could say, 'Hey, it's okay, Rickie, I know you're playing hurt.'

"I wasn't shocked when he called to tell me I hadn't made it, but it was pretty brutal anyway. It's a terrible call for both sides, kind of like when you break up with a girlfriend."

Fowler watched on and off throughout the Medinah weekend but found himself averting his eyes as things went south for the U.S. on Sunday. "I thought they were going to do it," he said. "Then it turned around. I'd been there, I knew what losing felt like, except we hadn't had the lead in Wales. It was hard to watch as an American; harder to watch because those were my buddies; hardest to watch as someone who thought he should be playing."

Fowler eventually learned that he had stress fractures in the L-4 and L-5 joints of his back. Trying to get healthy, trying to get his swing back to where it was, he struggled in 2013. That was when he made the decision to go see Butch Harmon. Fowler was a self-taught player. He'd never really needed a swing instructor. Now, though, he was frustrated. He didn't want to spend his life being the pretty boy who made millions in endorsements but never won anything that mattered. That's why he went to Harmon.

Fowler was a different player in 2014. His hair was shorter and his game under pressure much better. He contended in all four majors, finishing T-5 at the Masters; T-2 at the U.S. Open; T-2 at the British Open; and third at the PGA. At the British Open, both he and Sergio García made moves on Rory McIlroy on Sunday before McIlroy found an extra gear late. At the PGA, it was more of the same, he and Mickelson chasing McIlroy down the stretch. At one point, Fowler had the lead on the back nine, but again McIlroy found the extra gear, aided—at least to some degree—by seeing Fowler and Mickelson exchange a fist-bump after Fowler had made a birdie on the 10th hole.

"I'm not sure why but it bothered me seeing that," McIlroy said later. "This wasn't the Ryder Cup. They were supposed to be playing *against* one another. They weren't teammates. For some reason, seeing that got me going."

Fowler laughs at the notion that McIlroy was upset. "Phil and I are close friends," he said. "We're both trying to win, but when one of us pulls off a shot, we're happy for the other guy."

His play in the majors made Fowler a lock to be on the U.S. team that went to Gleneagles—he finished second on the points list, behind only Bubba Watson. He and Walker formed one of the best U.S. teams during the first three sessions, halving all three of their matches against top European teams. It was only in the Saturday afternoon foursomes that they sputtered—losing 5 and 4 to Graeme McDowell and Victor Dubuisson.

"We were on the 14th hole in the morning match when Tom came out and said, 'You guys ready to go after it again this afternoon?' Of course we said yes, absolutely. We both wanted to play. I didn't know at the time it was Phil and Keegan he was going to sit out. All I knew was I wanted to play. But I know Phil and Keegan were dying to get out there again."

Fowler had played superbly in 2015, winning the Players Championship, the Scottish Open the week before the British Open, and the second playoff event in Boston. But he hadn't been able to maintain his remarkable play in the majors—a T-12 at the Masters was by far his best finish. He missed the cut by a wide margin at the U.S. Open, although his horrific opening-round 81 did lead to one of the funnier lines in Tiger Woods's career.

Woods shot 80 that same day, playing in the same threesome with McIlroy. "Well, I said my goal was to kick Rickie's butt," Woods said at the end of the day. "And I did it."

Fowler's win at the Players was especially gratifying because it came the same week that an anonymous poll of players on tour came out naming Fowler and Ian Poulter as the two most overrated players in golf. As soon as he saw the poll, Butch Harmon made sure to get it in Fowler's hands. On Sunday, he rallied on the back nine to catch Sergio García and Kevin Kisner before beating them in a playoff.

By midsummer 2016, Fowler was fighting his swing and his putter. He had started the year well, finishing in the top ten in four of his first five events, including a playoff loss to Hideki Matsuyama in Phoenix. He finished T-4 at Charlotte in early May and then went into a complete funk. He missed three cuts in a row, including his title defense at the Players and again at the U.S. Open, and had one top ten—a T-10 in Akron—in nine tournaments. Suddenly, he went from a lock for the top eight on the Ryder Cup points list to needing a top-three finish at the Barclays.

For three rounds, he played superbly and had the lead going to the back nine on Sunday. But a disastrous back nine dropped him from first place to a tie for seventh and all the way down to eleventh in the final points standings.

"Now I have to try to make sure I play well enough the next two weeks to be a captain's pick," he said. "I'm still planning on being in Minnesota."

He had good reason to feel that way. Just as in 2010, Davis Love knew he wanted Fowler on his team. He hoped that the first sixty-four holes on Long Island at the Barclays had been a harbinger. He knew what he'd get from Fowler in the team room. He had to hope he'd get the "good Rickie" on the golf course.

Fifteen

RICKIE FOWLER DIDN'T play especially well the next two weeks, but it really didn't matter. His play at Bethpage Black in the Barclays—the last nine holes notwithstanding—was more than enough for Davis Love to justify his selection.

The same was true of Matt Kuchar. If Fowler was everyone's little brother figure—even though he was no longer the youngest player on the team—then Kuchar was the court jester. Most golf fans would never have known that.

"His image with the public is a hundred percent different than who he really is," said Zach Johnson, a close friend and a neighbor on Sea Island, the Georgia enclave where a number of tour players live. "He smiles and says all the right things, and then you get behind closed doors and he's the devil."

Johnson meant that—of course—in an endearing way. He was a frequent victim of Kuchar's, often opening his locker to find some kind of poster—sometimes of a man, sometimes of a woman, usually without any clothes on—hanging prominently from the door. Kuchar's hope was that Johnson might open his locker in the presence of a media member or perhaps a pro-am partner and be forced to explain himself.

His explanation was always quite simple: Kuchar.

Kuchar has a wide, ever-present smile, one that earned him the nickname "Smilin' Matt," and has long been a fan favorite because of that smile and his easygoing manner. Beneath it, though, Kuchar's not only a nonstop prankster, he's one of the brighter, more thoughtful people in the game.

He's a college graduate in an era when most golfers leave college without a degree. "What was my major in college?" Patrick Reed often says with a smile. "Golf."

Kuchar could have made a large chunk of money had he chosen to leave Georgia Tech after his sophomore year. He had won the U.S. Amateur in 1997, meaning he was invited to play in the Masters, U.S. Open, and British Open the following year. He became something of a sensation at the Masters, playing alongside defending champion Tiger Woods the first two days. In the summer of 1996, Woods had beaten Kuchar in a close U.S. Amateur semifinal, denying Kuchar a Masters spot since both U.S. Amateur finalists qualify for the Masters.

The following April, Woods had won the Masters by twelve shots in his first major as a pro. In 1998, as the Amateur champion, Kuchar was paired with the defending Masters champion—Woods. He made the cut, then shot 68 on Saturday and finished tied for twenty-first—giving him a place in the next year's Masters, since the top twenty-four finishers were given automatic invites.

Then, at the U.S. Open at Olympic Club in June, Kuchar finished T-14—meaning he got to play in the Open the following year since the top fifteen Open finishers qualified.

By then, sponsors were coming out of the woodwork wanting to throw money at Kuchar. He turned them all down and went back to Georgia Tech. Two years later, he graduated with a degree in business management and stunned the golf world by not turning pro.

"I just wasn't sure it was the lifestyle I wanted to lead," he said. "Even in my limited experience, I could see that traveling that much wasn't easy and that it could be pretty lonely spending that much time on the road. I thought maybe going into the business world and continuing to play well as an amateur might be the route I wanted to go."

He smiled. "I went to college in Atlanta. Bobby Jones was from Atlanta. I thought maybe I could model myself at least a little bit on what he had done."

Jones won fourteen major championships, including what was then the Grand Slam in 1930: the U.S. and British Opens, and the U.S. and British Amateurs. Soon after that, he retired from competitive golf at the age of twenty-eight and went to work as a lawyer. It was then that he and his friend Clifford Roberts purchased the Fruitlands Nursery, a tract of land in Augusta, Georgia, and Jones and Alister MacKenzie designed a new golf course called Augusta National Golf Club. In 1934, they began a golf tournament there called the Augusta National Invitational. Five years later, the tournament became known as the Masters.

Jones is as revered a figure as there is in golf, especially in Georgia. Kuchar thought he might be a good role model.

Except that working in an office proved to be even less enjoyable than the notion of sleeping in hotel rooms. After six months, he decided to give the PGA Tour a shot.

Playing on sponsor exemptions in 2001—he was still the kind of young "name" player sponsors wanted in their event—he earned enough money to become a full-fledged tour member in 2002, and early in that year he won the Honda Classic. Little did he—or anyone else—know that it would be seven years before he would win again.

By the end of 2005, he had lost all his status on tour and had to go all the way back to the second stage of Q school, where he failed to advance. At that point, it looked as if Kuchar would be one of those players who had a brief moment in the sun and then faded quickly. Ty Tryon, who played in that same second-stage qualifier as Kuchar in 2005, had made it all the way through Q school in 2001 at the age of seventeen and never won on tour. Years earlier, Marty Fleckman had led the U.S. Open for three rounds in 1967 as an amateur—leading Arnold Palmer and Jack Nicklaus by a shot—before fading to a tie for eighteenth place on Sunday.

Fleckman turned pro that fall and won in his first tournament, one of four players in history to accomplish that feat. He never won again and was off the Tour several years later. There were plenty of other flash-in-the-pan stories. Two of the other players who had won their first time out were Robert Gamez and Garrett Willis. Gamez had reasonable success on tour, winning five times. Willis never won again.

The fourth player who won his first time out was Ben Crenshaw. He's in the World Golf Hall of Fame.

Kuchar had to play the Triple-A Nationwide Tour in 2006. He managed to finish tenth on the money list, regaining his status on the PGA Tour for 2007. He also began working with a new swing coach, Chris

O'Connell, who changed his swing radically, flattening it considerably. Kuchar became a new—and improved—player.

He won again late in 2009 and became one of the game's most consistent players. He had played on three consecutive Ryder Cup teams and Love very much wanted him to be on a fourth, if only to keep Zach Johnson on his toes.

Love was scheduled to name the first three of his four captain's picks at a press conference at Hazeltine on the Monday after the conclusion of the BMW Championships, the third of the four PGA Tour playoff events. That was September 12—eighteen days before the matches were to begin. His fourth pick wouldn't be made until the night of September 25, the day before most players would be traveling to Hazeltine to begin preparations for the matches.

This was known as the "Billy Horschel Rule."

In 2014, Horschel had won the last two playoff events and, by winning the Tour Championship, the FedEx Cup. But Tom Watson had made all three of his captain's picks by then.

The day after Horschel had won the $10 million bonus in addition to a second straight first prize of $1.44 million, Watson called him.

"Billy," he said, "unfortunately you're a day late. But you certainly aren't a dollar short."

Horschel would have been a lock to make the team had there been a captain's pick spot available after the Tour Championship. And so one of the decisions made by the task force was to hold back the final captain's pick until the night of the Tour Championship.

"It's not as much of a no-brainer as people might think," Love said. "The reason you do it is because of Billy Horschel. You don't want to have someone who might be the hottest player in the world sitting on the sideline. But when you pick a guy that late, he's got almost zero time to get logistically squared away. He's playing in Atlanta, presumably late on Sunday, and then he's got to get to Hazeltine and dive right into all the pre–Ryder Cup events. It's definitely risky."

Love smiled. "Less risky, though, than if we were playing in Europe."

Not surprisingly, the PGA saw the announcement of Love's first three picks as a public relations opportunity. That's why Love flew to Minneapolis to make the announcement. That's why, once Love had let the PGA know on Sunday night who the picks were going to be, arrangements were made so that all three could speak via Skype to the media assembled at Hazeltine and to the audience watching live on Golf Channel.

Love was scheduled to make the final pick on the night of the twenty-fifth during halftime of an *NBC Sunday Night Football* game. NBC was the PGA's longtime television partner—it had been televising the Ryder Cup since 1991. What better way to promote the upcoming matches than for Love to dramatically announce his final pick on one of television's highest-rated programs?

One person who didn't like the idea was Paul Azinger.

"What you're doing is giving the most attention to the twelfth pick, the guy who just squeezed onto the team after the first eleven," he said. "If anything, that kind of attention should go to the guy who finished first on the points list, not the guy picked last."

That made sense, but it wasn't going to happen. There was no suspense in announcing that Dustin Johnson—number one on the points list—was on the team. The final pick meant that someone was elated, and one or two or perhaps three others were disappointed.

No one was surprised on a bright, beautiful September morning at Hazeltine when Love announced that he had picked Fowler and Kuchar. The third pick was a little bit of a surprise: J. B. Holmes.

Holmes had played on the last winning U.S. team, one of the three so-called rednecks on the team at Valhalla—along with Kenny Perry and Boo Weekley.

He had been the medalist at Q school in 2005 and had started using "J.B." instead of John at the suggestion of CBS announcer Gary McCord. John Holmes had been a porn star in the 1980s. He had gone by the screen name of "Johnny Wadd Holmes." Given that John Holmes was known for hitting the golf ball long distances, the nickname "Long John Holmes" was almost inevitable. Since few people had heard of the young golfer, McCord suggested to Holmes he go by "J.B." before he was tagged with a more crude nickname.

Holmes was a remarkable comeback story. In the summer of 2011 he had experienced symptoms of what doctors thought was vertigo. After he'd been forced to withdraw from the PGA Championship in August after shooting a first-round 80, further testing had revealed that he had something called "Chiari malformation," a defect in the brain's cerebellum. He had surgery in September, then needed to be airlifted to Johns

Hopkins Medical Center after it was found that he was allergic to the adhesive used on the titanium base during the surgery. There, he had surgery again. Remarkably, four months later he was back on tour, and in April 2015 he beat Johnson Wagner and Jordan Spieth in a playoff to win the Shell Houston Open.

Holmes was a feast-or-famine player. When his massive drives found fairways, he could compete with just about anyone. When they went awry, not so much. His spring and summer had been proof of that. He'd tied for fourth at the Masters, his first top-ten finish in twenty-two starts in major championships. Then he'd missed the cut at the U.S. Open, only to turn around and finish third—behind the Henrik Stenson–Phil Mickelson shootout—at the British Open. After that, he'd missed three straight cuts. But he finished T-4 at the BMW, the last event before Love made his first three picks.

Holmes had one other thing going for him: two of Love's vice captains, Steve Stricker and Jim Furyk, were very much in his corner. Stricker believed that Holmes's style was perfect for better-ball play: he'd make a lot of birdies, and his bad holes wouldn't matter so much. Furyk had spent a lot of time with Holmes at the Presidents Cup the previous year. Holmes had taken Furyk's place on the team after Furyk's wrist injury, and Jay Haas had informally assigned Furyk, who went to the matches as a vice captain, to work closely with Holmes.

"I really got to know him well for the first time in Korea," Furyk said. "I was impressed, not just with his play but with the way he approached being part of a team."

Plus, both Stricker and Furyk believed he was the perfect partner for Bubba Watson. For most of the year, the assumption had been that Watson was a lock for the team and Holmes—who finished tenth on the points list largely on the strength of the Masters and the British Open— was a possibility.

Which is why it was somewhat shocking when Love made Holmes the third pick along with Fowler and Kuchar on the morning of September 12. All of a sudden there was only one spot left, and it appeared that Watson—ranked seventh in the world and, more important, ninth on the Ryder Cup points list—might have to play his way onto the team at the Tour Championship.

The press conference and the Skype interviews were exactly what you might expect: Love was thrilled to add these three to the team; it had been a really tough choice because there were so many guys who deserved to be picked. The three players were honored, happy, and relieved to be on the team.

Yada yada yada. Except for Matt Kuchar.

"I've been hearing some rumors," Kuchar said with his wide, choirboy smile during his Skype interview, "that the fourth pick might be Tiger Woods. That would be legen . . . dary."

To his everlasting credit, Julius Mason, moderating the show, thanked Kuchar for making "legendary" into two words.

Woods was not going to be the fourth pick. Kuchar had totally made up the "rumors." He knew that some in the media would somehow take him seriously or even semiseriously, and sure enough, stories began popping up that maybe Love was going to do something legen . . . dary and pick someone who hadn't played a competitive round of golf in more than a year to play in the sport's most pressure-packed event.

An email to Kuchar accusing him of having made the whole thing up got this response: "No, I did hear rumors . . . inside my head."

Of course he did.

There was now one pick left for Love to make. At that moment, he had no idea who it was going to be. Watson was the leading candidate. Furyk was still under consideration. And there were three rookie possibilities: the youngsters, Justin Thomas and Daniel Berger; and Ryan Moore, an eleven-year tour veteran who had played well through most of the summer.

Tiger Woods would not be the pick—legen . . . dary or not. But he would have some say in whom Love would choose.

It had not been an easy year for Woods. He had actually hoped early in the year that he might be able to make it to the Masters, even after being forced to have back surgery twice in the fall.

His last tournament had been the Wyndham Championship in August—Ernie Els's "last chance saloon"—where he had entered for the first time in his career, in the hope that he could play himself into the FedEx Cup playoffs. He had missed the cut at the U.S. Open, British Open, and PGA Championship—all comfortably—and his only hope to keep playing when the top 125 players on the points list went to the Barclays was to win in Greensboro.

He was fading on Sunday, but still on the fringes of contention, when a triple bogey at the 11th hole ended his chances. He finished T-10. That was easily his best finish of what had been an embarrassing year. He'd shot 73-82 in Phoenix and then withdrawn the next week during the first round in San Diego, famously claiming, "My glutes didn't fire."

He managed to overcome the chipping yips that had befallen him early in the year to finish T-17 at the Masters, but then shot a third-round 85 at the Memorial on a golf course where he had won five times in the past. Then came the opening-round 80 at the U.S. Open—the day he "kicked Rickie's butt"—and the missed cuts at St. Andrews in the British Open and at Whistling Straits in the PGA.

His play in Greensboro had sent the Tigeristas—those who still believed golf existed only when Woods was playing—into paroxysms of joy, since clearly Woods was "back" again. Except he wasn't, because he needed the two back surgeries in the fall.

The Masters came and went without Woods—only the second time he had failed to play there since 1995—and so did the rest of the summer. For a long time, Woods couldn't even practice. That left him with a lot of time on his hands. Some of it was spent playing video games. Much of the rest of it was spent obsessing about the Ryder Cup.

"You don't understand," Davis Love said on a spring morning. "When I asked Tiger to commit to giving me a hundred percent, I never dreamed he would dive in the way he has."

According to Love, Woods was constantly texting him and calling him to talk about who should be on the team. Four months before the matches, he was putting together hypothetical teams for Friday and Saturday based on who would be on the team; who might be on the team; and who might not be on the team. He had even put together singles lineups for Sunday, each dependent on what the score was after the first sixteen matches.

He had also gone back to his notes on Hazeltine from the two PGAs he'd played there—finishing second both times—to make suggestions to Love on how he and Kerry Haigh might make changes that would benefit the Americans. Clearly, they didn't want as much rough as there had been at the previous PGAs. The Americans liked wider fairways and faster greens. The Euros preferred more penal rough and slower greens. Love and Darren Clarke both had plenty of statistics that backed up those notions.

Woods called Love so often and kept him on the phone for so long that Love began passing on picking up Woods's calls when he was doing something.

"I would look at the phone, see it was Tiger, and I knew I didn't have an hour to talk to him right then," he said. "So I'd let it go to voice mail, and then I'd call back when I had more time to talk."

Love wanted the world to know how involved Woods was because he thought it was important for his players to know that Woods wasn't just along for the ride, that he had come to genuinely care about the Ryder Cup and about helping this U.S. team win.

"I think Tiger's just like me on this," Phil Mickelson said. "He doesn't like to lose. He's not the same guy he was all those years ago when everything he'd been taught by his dad said, 'Don't give any of your secrets away.' Now he's willing to share pretty much anything he thinks will help us win."

Once the first eight players had made the team on points, they too started to hear from Woods on a regular basis. There was talk about who would make the best teams, who wouldn't, and whom they'd all like to play against in singles. Early on, Love assigned Woods to work with Spieth, Reed, and Snedeker as their "pod captain," even though the title was never formalized at least in part because the pods weren't locked in the way Azinger's had been. Woods began calling the first three guys—and, when Kuchar was added to the pod, Kuchar too—on a regular basis.

At one point, as Woods rattled on to Snedeker about when he might play and whom he might play with and why this was the best way to line the team up, Snedeker said to him, "You know something, Tiger, you need a hobby."

He was probably right. The Ryder Cup was clearly *not* his hobby. It had become his passion.

Woods's teammates of old would have been stunned by this development. Love, who had played with Woods on three teams, was surprised by it. But unlike much of what Woods says and does in public, this was genuine. Maybe the most genuine thing he'd done in golf that didn't involve winning tournaments.

Much to his surprise, his involvement as a supporting player—nonplayer, actually—would turn out to be one of the most gratifying experiences of his career.

Sixteen

WHILE DAVIS LOVE was announcing his first three picks on the morning of September 12, three men stood near the back of the room in the Hazeltine clubhouse virtually unnoticed, even though all would play important roles in the Ryder Cup.

One was Chandler Withington, Hazeltine's head golf pro. The second was Chris Tritabaugh, the club's superintendent. The third was Jeff Hintz, who had been working on-site for the PGA for two years.

All were young—not yet forty. Withington and Tritabaugh had both come to the club four years earlier to replace men who had almost iconic status at Hazeltine.

Mike Schultz had been Hazeltine's pro for thirty-seven years, having been hired in 1975 to replace Don Waryan, who had been the pro during the first thirteen years of the club's existence. When Schultz decided to retire, Withington, only thirty-four at the time, had been hired to take his place.

Withington was tall and soft-spoken. Tritabaugh was not as tall but just as soft-spoken. Hintz was tall and outgoing. He and Tritabaugh were Midwesterners—Tritabaugh born and raised in Minnesota; Hintz born in Iowa, raised in Indiana.

When the jobs had opened up in 2012, Tritabaugh had been working at a club called Northland, which was in Duluth, about four hours north and east of Hazeltine. Withington had been an assistant pro at Merion and was as East Coast as Tritabaugh and Hintz were Midwest. He had a sneaky sense of humor, the kind where the joke might be missed if you weren't paying close attention. His first passion in life had been hockey, and he was still a devoted fan of the New York Rangers.

"I still get the skates on during the winter," he said with a smile. "One of the appealing things about this job was the notion of being in a place where hockey was a big deal."

Hockey wasn't a big deal in Minnesota—it was a huge deal. It wasn't just that the Minnesota Wild consistently sold out, even though they'd never reached the Stanley Cup finals in sixteen years of existence; it was high school hockey and college hockey. The high school tournament was one of *the* events of Minnesota winters, and the University of Minnesota (better known locally as the "U") hockey team consistently contended nationally. It had also produced Herb Brooks, the legendary coach who had led the U.S. hockey team to the Miracle on Ice at Lake Placid in 1980.

Withington had been introduced to golf by Mike Grubbs, the pastor at his local church in Bernardsville, New Jersey, at the age of thirteen. He'd been a hockey player and a baseball player but fell in love with golf when his family took a vacation to Hilton Head in April 1992 and rented a house near the second hole of Harbour Town Golf Club during the annual Heritage Classic. Given the chance to walk the golf course, Withington wandered out to the par-5 5th hole and watched a young pro put his tee shot into orbit.

"I couldn't believe how easy he made it look," Withington said. "I followed him around the rest of the week, and he won. After that he was my golf guy."

The guy was Davis Love.

"I liked the way he played, the way he carried himself, the way he handled himself win or lose," Withington said. "And I wanted to have his golf swing."

After Grubbs, who liked to build golf clubs as a hobby, built him his first clubs, Withington frequently stood in front of the TV set, watching Love swing the club—first in slow motion and then in stop action. He would go outside and try to mimic what he'd seen. He was a late starter and a late bloomer as a golfer, but by the time he graduated from high school, he knew he wanted to make a living in golf—somewhere, somehow.

"I had thought architect or engineer as a kid," he said. "But I didn't have the grades. When I heard about the PGA training program at

Campbell [North Carolina] I knew that was what I wanted to do. Problem was, when I got to college I couldn't break 90, and I knew to become a PGA pro, I'd have to pass the PAT."

That would be the PGA's Playing Ability Test, which every pro has to pass in order to be certified. On October 26, 1999, a day Withington remembers vividly because it was the day after Payne Stewart was killed, he shot even par for the first time in his life and passed the test. The scorecard hangs on a wall in his office.

From there he embarked on a fairly typical club pro odyssey, landing, after several years, at Merion, outside Philadelphia. He had promised Scott Nye, the pro at Merion, he would stay at least three years when he first got there. He stayed six—but not for lack of trying.

"Scott had wanted me to stay at least through the [2009] Walker Cup, which we were hosting," Withington said. "That year, a head [pro] job opened up right down the road at a place called Llanerch. Scott said to me, 'It's time.' Honestly, I was pretty sure I'd get it. I didn't. I finished second."

That began a series of frustrating second places for jobs around the country. In 2011, Withington thought he was finally going to break through. He interviewed for the job at Charlotte Country Club and—when the search committee asked if he could come back for another interview and bring his wife—figured it was a slam dunk.

"I told them that we were about to have our first child, but if there was any way she could make it down, I knew she'd love to come," he said. "A week after our daughter was born, we got in the car—all three of us—and drove [nine hours] to Charlotte. We thought everything went really well, and on the drive back we were talking about places to live and how Charlotte was going to be a great place to raise a family.

"About halfway back we got a call. They'd picked the other finalist. The rest of the trip was very quiet."

The Charlotte loss caused Withington to reexamine his approach to being interviewed. He decided that instead of telling the search committees why he'd be a great hire, he'd turn the tables and ask what *they* were looking for in a pro, what was important to *them*.

The next summer he got a call from Nathan Ollhoff, the pro at the historic Interlachen Country Club. Interlachen had been founded in 1909 and had been redesigned twice: once by Donald Ross and once by Robert Trent Jones. It had hosted the 1930 U.S. Open, won by Bobby Jones on his way to the Grand Slam. Ollhoff and Withington had worked together once upon a time at Seminole Golf Club in Florida. Ollhoff wanted Withington to know the job at Hazeltine, seventeen miles to the west of Interlachen, was about to open.

Hazeltine is probably one of the best-known "young" golf clubs in the country. It was founded in 1962 by a man named Totton P. Heffelfinger, a former USGA president. One of Heffelfinger's main goals from day one was to attract major championships to Hazeltine—which was named after the lake it is built around. In fact, part of Hazeltine's mission statement reflects that. Inside the front door of the clubhouse (renovated in 2010 with the Ryder Cup in mind) is a plaque that contains the club's mission statement. It begins this way: "The mission of the founders of Hazeltine is to build and maintain a golf course suitable for the conduct of national championships. An important part of the mission was to develop a membership that supports this concept."

The club has about 300 members, and anyone who applies for membership is shown the mission statement so they understand that there may be times when sacrifices have to be made to allow the club to host major events like the U.S. Open, the PGA, the Ryder Cup, or—in 2019—the women's PGA Championship.

Heffelfinger was able to use his USGA contacts to quickly carry out that part of the club's mission. In 1966, the club hosted the U.S. Women's Open. Four years later, the men's U.S. Open was staged there. For an eight-year-old club, this was almost unheard of, although the USGA had broken with its tradition of going to older clubs like Oak Hill, Baltustrol, Olympic, Bellerive, Congressional, the Country Club, and Oakmont— the hosts, in reverse order between 1962 and 1968—to go to Champions, in Houston, in 1969. But even Champions was twelve years old.

That year's Open was a huge success—for Tony Jacklin, who followed up his British Open championship in 1969 by winning at Hazeltine. It wasn't quite so sweet for the club. Dave Hill, who finished second, commented that the only thing the course was missing was "eighty acres of corn and a few cows."

Many other players were critical of the course, although it was Hill's comment that stuck. There were, in fact, cows on the property. In 2016 the cows' former home was used as a parking lot during the Ryder Cup.

Robert Trent Jones had originally designed the course, and the feeling was that there were too many doglegs—seven—and that the doglegs were too severe. When the USGA awarded the 1991 Open to Hazeltine in 1986, many people in the golf community were shocked. But Rees Jones—Robert Trent Jones's son—was hired to renovate the course. Jones did such a good job that the USGA began hiring him so regularly to renovate future Open venues that he became known as "the Open doctor."

The '91 Open got off to a less than auspicious start (to put it mildly) when lightning moved in late in the first round. Six spectators seeking shelter under a tree on the 16th hole were struck by lightning—one fatally. The championship continued the next day, and Payne Stewart ended up beating Scott Simpson in an eighteen-hole playoff on Monday when Simpson bogeyed the last three holes after leading by two shots through 15.

The reviews for the renovated course were very good, and in 1996 Hazeltine "invited" the USGA to stage the championship there in 2001. Technically, the USGA asks clubs to "invite" them to stage championships.

"At that point, I think our hope was to be like Winged Foot and be able to host both the Open and, at some point, the PGA," said Reed Mackenzie, a longtime Hazeltine member and former club president who was on the USGA's executive committee at the time. "I honestly thought we'd get the '01 Open. But, at the last minute, Southern Hills came in with an invitation, and there were a number of executive board members [notably incoming president Judy Bell] who thought it was time to go back there."

Southern Hills got the '01 Open, and Mackenzie and his fellow club members decided it was time to take their case to the PGA.

Often, when the USGA abandons a course, the PGA will come racing in to fill the void. Very quickly, the club and the PGA agreed to hold PGAs there in 2002 and 2009. In 2002, the PGA added the 2016 Ryder Cup to the menu, breaking with precedent by naming a Ryder Cup venue fourteen years in advance.

Rich Beem won the PGA in 2002 and Y. E. Yang won in 2009. Both championships had one important thing in common: Tiger Woods finished second. In 2002, Beem denied him a third major title in the same year—he'd won the Masters and U.S. Open. In 2009, Yang made history when he became the first player to catch Woods from behind in the final round of a major. Until then, Woods had gone 14-for-14 when leading or sharing the lead in a major going into Sunday. Little did anyone know that Woods's life and career would change radically a little more than three months later with his postmidnight "accident" outside his house on Thanksgiving night.

In the clubhouse basement at Hazeltine, there's a museum filled with memorabilia from the club's history. One of the photos is of Yang chipping in for birdie at the 14th hole on Sunday to take the lead for good. As 2017 dawned, that was the last moment that Woods led a major on Sunday.

In 2012, when word reached Withington that Hazeltine was looking for a new pro, he utilized his new interview approach—and it worked. The search committee had one major concern: We've had two pros here in fifty years. We're a little concerned about hiring someone who may jump at the chance to go back to the East Coast to a more traditional club in five, six, seven years. Withington was ready for the question.

"I told them then, I tell them now when the subject comes up, that I've got very young kids who, by the time something comes up like that—if it does—will have known only this place. Their friends will be here, and so will my wife's friends. If I were to go in and say, 'We're uprooting to go to a club that, basically, has the same things Hazeltine has,' that would be selfish."

He smiled. "The only way I'd leave is if my family didn't like it here. They love it here. So do I."

Withington was thrilled when Love, his boyhood hero, was named Ryder Cup captain again. He had never expected that.

"I got the job a week after Medinah," Withington said. "Of course, knowing we were going to host the Ryder Cup was a big thrill, but I was kind of sad that Davis had just been captain because I assumed that meant there was no chance he'd be captain here. It was great when they named him. Working with him has been everything I could have expected—and more."

Love had included Withington in his circle almost from the beginning. He had asked him to work with Scouts Inc., the analytics firm he had hired. Paul McGinley had used statistics more than any other Ryder Cup captain in history, both before and during the matches, charting every shot his players hit in practice rounds and every shot both teams hit during the matches.

Both Love and Clarke had followed McGinley's example and were working with analytics people throughout the year. Clarke's most difficult captain's pick had come down to Thomas Pieters or Russell Knox. Pieters had undoubtedly wrapped up his spot by playing so well when paired with Clarke in Denmark, but analytics had played a role too. Pieters made a lot of birdies, which is critical in four-ball play. Knox's greatest strength was bogey-avoidance—which is almost irrelevant in four-ball play since at least one of the four players will birdie most holes.

This was going to be especially true at Hazeltine. In spite of its length—it would play at about 7,600 yards most days—it was not going to be set up to play that hard, since Love wanted wide fairways, little rough, and relatively easy pin positions. Birdies would be at a premium all week.

Clarke knew this, which is why the stats told him Pieters was a better pick than Knox. In the end, so did his gut.

Since Withington knew the golf course better than anyone, Love wanted his input. As detailed as they are, after all, statistics can be misleading. For example: Even with the redesign, there were still five doglegs on the golf course. Because players could cut corners on those holes off the tee, their length was deceiving.

Love's faith in Withington—and the fact that his circle of advisers was wider than just his vice captains—was evident on the morning of September 7 when Withington was sitting in his office awaiting the arrival of Kerry Haigh, the PGA's czar of golf course setup. He was a little worried that Haigh was going to be concerned because the course had been inundated with rain the previous two weeks: "Ten inches in fourteen days," Withington said.

Even though the golf course drained extremely well, it was still muddy and soft after all the rain. Haigh wouldn't be thrilled.

Just before Haigh arrived, a text popped up in Withington's phone. It was from Love: "So," it read, "who should I pick?"

Withington laughed. He knew Love was going to pick Fowler and Kuchar the following Monday and wasn't quite certain about his third pick.

"I think he wants to pick Bubba," he said. "He's the seventh-ranked player in the world, and he's got experience. But he might want to go with Holmes, because he hits it a mile, or one of the young guys—Thomas or Berger."

When he texted back, Withington told Love what Love wanted to

The two captains—Darren Clarke and Davis Love: good friends, but only one could go home with the "real" Cup. (PA Images / Alamy Stock Photo)

Jordan Spieth and Tiger Woods. Yup, Woods is laughing on a golf course. Sight rarely seen. (PA Images / Alamy Stock Photo)

No one was under more pressure at Hazeltine than Phil Mickelson. (PA Images / Alamy Stock Photo)

Jordan Spieth, J. B. Holmes, and Ryan Moore: The champagne flowed . . . and flowed . . . and flowed. (ZUMA Press Inc. / Alamy Stock Photo)

In the midst of the most electrifying stretch of golf in Ryder Cup history, Rory McIlroy and Patrick Reed walk to—as it turned out—the climactic 8th tee. (ZUMA Press Inc. / Alamy Stock Photo)

McIlroy held nothing back from start to finish all weekend.

(Tribune Content Agency LLC / Alamy Stock Photo)

Darren Clarke (center) with vice captains Padraig Harrington (left) and Ian Poulter. The Euros sorely missed Poulter's presence between the ropes. (PA Images/Alamy Stock Photo)

Sergio García laughed off the barbs of the "one percenters" to again play superbly in the Ryder Cup. (PA Images/Alamy Stock Photo)

Argument can be made that Brandt Snedeker was the unsung hero—on and off the course—of the American team. (ZUMA Press Inc. / Alamy Stock Photo)

Matt Kuchar and Mickelson celebrate their Saturday afternoon victory (Martin Kaymer is walking over to congratulate them). At least they didn't do another shimmy. (Tribune Content Agency LLC / Alamy Stock Photo)

No one had a more difficult week in Minnesota than Danny Willett—even though he did nothing wrong. (PA Images / Alamy Stock Photo)

McIlroy, Henrik Stenson, and Justin Rose tee off during a practice round. Note the massive crowd for a practice day. (PA Images / Alamy Stock Photo)

McIlroy and Reed after Reed's victory. The two men were almost too drained and exhausted to shake hands—but they did. (PA Images / Alamy Stock Photo)

In his third Ryder Cup, Rickie Fowler starred—carrying Phil Mickelson on day one and winning his singles match on Sunday. (ZUMA Press Inc. / Alamy Stock Photo)

Captain America. (Tribune Content Agency LLC / Alamy Stock Photo)

Four years later, Captain Love finally gets to hold the most cherished seventeen-inch trophy in sports—for real. (PA Images / Alamy Stock Photo)

hear: "Go with what you think the eight guys already on the team want. That's the most important thing."

Love went with Fowler, Kuchar, and Holmes. It was the fourth and last pick that would be his most difficult.

On the same day that Withington was texting with Love, Tiger Woods was announcing that he would return to golf (again) in October—two weeks after the Ryder Cup—in Napa, California.

While Golf Channel was breaking into programming to analyze Woods's latest comeback, Jeff Hintz was standing on Hazeltine's 1st tee. Hintz had been working at Hazeltine for two years as the PGA's on-site representative. Kerry Haigh was in charge of everything that happened inside the ropes, and Hintz was in charge of everything outside the ropes.

That included training the four thousand volunteers who would be working on-site during the week; planning bus routes to get people who would be parking off-site—which would be most people—to the golf course; working with the sales and corporate staffs on ticket sales and corporate chalet sales; and working on the logistics of where to put concession tents, the massive (forty-eight-thousand-square-foot) merchandise tent, the media tent, and, perhaps most important, the portajohns that would have to accommodate almost all of the nearly sixty thousand people who might be on-site over the weekend.

Hintz had played golf and basketball in high school, but knew he wasn't good enough to play either on the Division I level, so he went to Indiana—which was his dream school anyway. He was a senior when Bob Knight had the infamous run-in with a student inside Assembly Hall in the fall of 2000 that led to his firing. "I realized later I was in the building when that happened," Hintz said. "I wasn't right *there,* but I wasn't far away either."

He got an internship that summer working at a Senior tour event in Minnesota and was hooked. "I knew I wanted to manage golf tournaments someday," he said. "I loved the sport, and I loved the challenge of trying to put everything together."

He hooked on at the PGA of America a year later, first working as a "swamper"—meaning he worked *on* the golf course—and then moved inside. He ran the Senior Players Championship in Michigan for three years before the Ryder Cup opportunity popped up as a surprise in 2014.

"We had just bought a house in Michigan three months earlier [Hintz is married with three children], but when Brett Sterba, who was supposed to run the Ryder Cup at Hazeltine, got a chance to go to Augusta National, he took it. I was offered his spot. No way I could turn it down."

And so, he was as familiar to everyone at Hazeltine as any member or full-time employee. With three weeks left before the crowds—at least fifty thousand people a day—began arriving, Hintz felt as if almost everything was in place, but there was still much to do.

Which is where the 1st tee came in. There is no 1st tee in golf like a Ryder Cup 1st tee. With each passing Ryder Cup, the atmosphere each morning on the 1st tee every morning had grown more intense as more grandstands were built and the players' entrances became more dramatic—almost, as Jordan Spieth had noted, like football players running from the tunnel before kickoff.

At Gleneagles there *had* been a tunnel that the players walked through to reach the 1st tee. "You walked out there and it felt as if all the oxygen had been sucked right out of the place," Patrick Reed said.

Hazeltine did not set up logistically for a tunnel or a bridge—like the one at Medinah—to be used. Instead, the players would walk along a path that led to the right of the tee, which would have grandstands that could seat about 1,500 people behind and to the players' left. There were no grandstands right of the tee because they would have blocked the view of the members' tent that was about a hundred yards down the fairway to the right. Once they got to the tee, the players would walk up fifteen steps—each marked with the new slogan, "Where Legends Are Made"—onto the tee.

On Friday and Saturday, the gates would be open at six thirty—about forty minutes before sunrise, and sixty-five minutes before the first tee time. On Sunday they would open at seven thirty—a little more than three and a half hours prior to the first singles match. Since people would scramble to get to the 1,500 seats in the 1st tee grandstand, that would leave a lot of dead time—especially on Sunday—before the players showed up.

Hintz had an idea: music. Not a live band or anything like that, but a DJ playing different songs throughout the morning. "Singing and chanting has become such a big part of the Ryder Cup experience, we decided to take it up a notch," Hintz said. "We're going to put microphones there so people coming in the gates and around the grounds can hear it too. Kind of liven things up early in the morning."

Hintz had talked with Kerry Haigh about keeping the music going after the first group teed off, maybe turning the microphones down and being careful not to interfere with anyone getting ready to play a shot out on the golf course. That idea had been nixed. First ball in the air meant the last note of music.

Hintz also had to be certain that the PGA's corporate customers would be well taken care of when they arrived. There were, in all, seventy-nine chalets/tents on the grounds. Eight of them could accommodate up to 150 people. They had been sold for $600,000 or $650,000 apiece, depending on location—as in view of the golf course. There were forty-two more for up to a hundred people that cost $425,000 each, and the rest, for up to fifty people, cost between $200,000 and $250,000, again depending on location. There were also two "captain's clubs"— one behind the 1st green, the other next to the 1st fairway.

The one behind the 1st green was considered a prime location because it opened up to the golf course. As a result, a table of ten for the week cost $69,000. If you chose the second location, the cost was only $59,000.

How many "captain's clubs" tables were available? "As many as we can get in there," Hintz said, smiling.

For the rest of the forty-five to fifty-five thousand people who would come through the gates each day, a grounds pass for the week cost $560. If you wanted access to the massive International Pavilion, the cost for the week—three practice days, plus three competition days—was $750.

At those prices—from the 150-person chalets to the grounds passes— what were the odds that the PGA and Hazeltine would sell out?

"We're completely sold out," Hintz said. "Have been for months."

The third person in the room when Love announced his first three picks probably wouldn't come anywhere close to a corporate chalet during the week unless he walked past one.

And, in all likelihood, Chris Tritabaugh would be walking. "Too tough to get around with a cart," he said, smiling. "So much traffic outside the ropes. I figure if I walk inside the ropes, I get where I'm going a lot faster."

Tritabaugh always feels more comfortable inside the ropes on a golf course. He had gone to high school in the tiny town of Albany, Minnesota (population two thousand), and found a home at the local golf course—Albany Golf Club—as a teenager.

"We moved there when I was in ninth grade, and all of a sudden there was this cool place to hang out. We hadn't had a golf course in my old hometown. My brother and I began riding our bikes down there and hanging out. I was always fascinated with the guys who worked *on* the golf course. Sometimes I'd just stand and watch them mowing greens or setting pins, getting the course ready.

"When I was a junior, I got a call one day from the pro, Paul Wellenstein, saying that Tom Kasner, the superintendent, had an opening on his crew and did I want to work for them part-time? They had me fill in some potholes on a cart path as a tryout. I must have passed, because they hired me and I was hooked right away. I liked sitting on a mower, things like that, but I wanted to know how you made different kinds of turf do different things on a golf course."

He went to the University of Minnesota, his goal to be a golf course superintendent someday. He had been at Northland Country Club for six years when he heard the Hazeltine job was about to open.

"At first I wasn't even going to apply," he said. "I liked Northland. It's a beautiful club and I was very comfortable there. Plus, I knew the Ryder Cup was coming to Hazeltine. I figured they'd have experienced guys from big-time clubs lining up for the job."

He changed his mind after a conversation with Bill Larson, whom he had worked for early in his career at Town and Country Club outside Minneapolis.

"We had bentgrass at Northland, and Hazeltine was converting to bent," Tritabaugh said. "They'd tried all sorts of different grasses on their greens but never seemed to get it where they wanted it. We had a hard, fast golf course with bent at Northland. Bill was convinced the search committee would like that."

Tritabaugh didn't know anyone at Hazeltine, but he did know *of* one important member: Reed Mackenzie, who had been president of the USGA and was a semilegendary figure in Minnesota golf circles.

"I didn't even know if he'd be on the search committee," he said. "But I just felt as if he was on it, he would understand that I was the right guy for the job. Don't ask me why. But when I walked into the boardroom to meet with the committee, Reed was sitting at the far end of the table. As soon as I saw him, I had this feeling in my gut that I'd get the job."

His gut was right. He was hired in January 2013 and spent most of the next two years working on the conversion to bentgrass. Midway through 2015, it began to hit him that the Ryder Cup wasn't that far away. That became his focus.

All went well until early August 2016. Kerry Haigh visited several times and declared himself happy with the golf course.

Then, on August 10, it rained. And for the next six weeks, it rained and rained . . . and rained. Hazeltine is located in the town of Chaska (population 23,770), which is thirty-five miles south and east of downtown Minneapolis. The town has a rain gauge that dates to 1925. Never in ninety-one years had the town experienced more than fifteen inches of rain in August and September. From August 10 until September 25, seventeen inches of rain fell.

"For the most part, I was okay with it," Tritabaugh said. "It was frustrating because there were days we couldn't get any work done at all. But the course drains quickly and I wasn't all that worried. Neither was Kerry.

"Then he came up here on September seventh and eighth, and the course was just soaked. Still, plenty of time. We had a good weather report for the ninth, and I had a big day planned to make up for lost time.

"I woke up in the morning and it was raining—still. It looked like (and was) an all-day rain. I walked in to meet with all my guys and I just lost it. I'm usually very low-key, but that day I just lost it. I wasn't mad at *anyone,* I just couldn't take the rain anymore. I ranted for about two minutes, then pushed over a whiteboard where I'd written down what everyone was supposed to be working on. I felt terrible, embarrassed, upset—you name it."

Tritabaugh retreated to his office to try to calm down. Finally, he called his wife, Leah, who suggested he call Mackenzie. Tritabaugh and Mackenzie had become very close since Tritabaugh's hiring. Mackenzie suggested they meet for coffee the next morning at the Caribou coffee shop just down the road from the club entrance.

Mackenzie reminded Tritabaugh of a story he had once told him about how Bruce Edwards, the legendary caddie who had worked for

Tom Watson for twenty-seven years and Greg Norman for three, had described the difference between working for Watson and working for Norman.

"Bruce said that if Greg hit a shot that rolled into a divot he'd look at it and say, 'Woe is me, I'm so unlucky,'" Tritabaugh said. "Tom would look at a ball in a divot, pull a club, and say, 'Watch this.'

"My birthday is September fourth, same as Watson's. I've always been a Watson guy. From that day forward, my approach when something went wrong was 'Watch this.'"

On September 25, the day before the teams were due at Hazeltine, it rained all day. The weather was cold and miserable. There was mud all over the golf course; standing water in many places.

"It's supposed to be windy the next couple days," Tritabaugh said. "That'll dry the course by Wednesday, Thursday latest. We'll be fine when it matters on Friday."

Watch this.

Seventeen

O<small>N SEPTEMBER</small> 18—<small>EIGHT</small> days before the teams were to arrive at Hazeltine and twelve days before the start of the forty-first Ryder Cup—the U.S. team got together for the first time since the eleven players who had made the team or been selected for the team had been named.

Davis Love had invited fifteen players to Hazeltine for a couple days of practice and team bonding. He wanted them to get to know the golf course and, to a lesser extent, one another, in a team setting.

In addition to the eleven players who were already on the team (Dustin Johnson, Jordan Spieth, Phil Mickelson, Patrick Reed, Jimmy Walker, Brooks Koepka, Zach Johnson, Brandt Snedeker, Matt Kuchar, Rickie Fowler, and J. B. Holmes), Love had invited the four finalists for the last spot: Bubba Watson, Justin Thomas, Daniel Berger, and Ryan Moore. Only Moore had declined the invitation. He wanted to rest for a couple of days before the Tour Championship began in Atlanta, since he had qualified to play for only the third time in his eleven-year career. Moore asked Love if not going to Hazeltine would affect his chances to be selected for the team. Love told him it wouldn't.

The golf course the Americans played was wet because of all the rain that had engulfed Minnesota for most of two months. It was soft and muddy in some spots and was playing very long. Even though Chandler Withington and Chris Tritabaugh told Love the chances were good that the course would be dry and play much faster by the time the matches started, Love wanted to see it from the back tees, to get a feel for the options he and Kerry Haigh would have when it came time to set up the course.

The captain's agreement had been amended after Medinah to remove the home captain from input into course setup beginning on the Sunday before the matches started. In reality, this was a minor change. Love had been working with Haigh almost since the day he'd been named captain, and Haigh knew exactly what Love wanted. But the Europeans had requested the change after the golf course at Medinah had changed markedly from the one they had scouted a few weeks before the matches to the one they played during Ryder Cup week.

"We arrived at Medinah, and the rough was completely gone," said Richard Hills, the longtime managing director of the Ryder Cup for the European Tour. "It had completely disappeared."

There wasn't going to be a lot of rough when the Europeans arrived at Hazeltine. The greens were going to be fast—probably running between 13 and 14 on the Stimpmeter—because the Americans putted better on fast greens (according to the statistics) than the Europeans. What's more, the hole locations weren't going to be too difficult either. Love had spent four years beating himself up for tucking too many pins on Sunday at Medinah—most notably at 17 and 18—and wasn't going to make that mistake again.

"The setup is an important part of home course advantage," said Phil Mickelson. "We're better putters than they are, so why wouldn't we put the pins in places where we're going to get a crack at making a lot of birdies? It would be insane not to do that. If we're better at getting close to the hole with our wedges, we want the par-5s to play as three-shot holes, not holes where a lot of people can get home in two. It's just common sense.

"When we get to Paris [in 2018] there'll be lots of rough, the greens will be slower, and the pins will be tucked. We know that. We expect that. But this year is our turn."

In Love's mind, there were actually five candidates for the final spot. He was still considering Jim Furyk, even though Furyk hadn't qualified for the last two playoff events—hurt, again, by not playing at all the first four months of the season because of his wrist surgery.

In the end, it was Furyk who took himself out of the mix. He and Love played together on Monday. When they got to the par-4 12th, which played 518 yards from the back tee, both he and Love had to pull three-woods for their second shots.

"Actually, neither one of us got to the green," said Love, once one of the longest hitters on tour but not nearly as long now, at fifty-two, as he'd been at twenty-two when he first reached the Tour. "Walking off the green Jim said to me, 'If it's wet at all, I won't be able to handle the longer holes. You can't pick me.' I knew he was probably right."

Six of the eleven players already on the team had played in the 2009 PGA—additionally, Mickelson had played in 2002—so they had some familiarity with the golf course. The bunkers had all been redone since then—one of Kerry Haigh's "suggestions" when he'd first arrived to look the course over—and there had been other nips and tucks to all eighteen holes.

But the major change was the routing. Instead of walking from the 4th green to the 5th tee, players in the Ryder Cup would walk behind the 5th tee to the 13th tee, which was now officially known as "Ryder Cup number 5." They would then play what had been 14, 15, 16, 17, and 18 as 5, 6, 7, 8, and 9. Then they would play 10, 11, 12, and 13 before finishing on what had been 5 through 9 as 14 through 18.

It was a bit confusing and would have been impossible in a full-field event because of the need to cross over holes that would be in play at the time. But with only twenty-four players, that wasn't a problem.

There were two major reasons for the change in the routing: money and darkness—or, more specifically, money and darkness/alcohol.

Hazeltine's "real" back nine was about as far away from the entrance/exit to the course for spectators as one could get on the six-hundred-acre property. Most of the buses that would shuttle spectators from remote lots to the course would park at Chaska High School—which would be closed during Ryder Cup week. (The students weren't getting extra days off; they were being made up later in the year.) Chanhassen High School, which was on the other side of the golf course, was also closed for the week.

From the parking lot at Chaska High, it was a short walk to where most people would be entering the property in the morning and—more important—exiting in the evening. With daylight savings time winding down—it had five weeks left in its annual thirty-four-week run—the days were getting shorter. That would mean the matches would end on

Friday and Saturday not that long before dark—*if* there were no weather delays. If there were any delays at all, the matches would end at nightfall, meaning close to forty-five thousand people would be trying to get to the exits in the dark.

More than a few would have had more than a few beers. The PGA was planning to sell six hundred thousand beers during the week.

"Probably not the best idea to have all those people, a lot of them having consumed a fair amount of alcohol, trying to find their way all the way across the property in the dark," Jeff Hintz said. "That was definitely one reason we did it. But of course, it wasn't the only reason we did it."

The other reason was corporate tents. Hazeltine's signature hole was 16, a breathtaking par-4 that had Lake Hazeltine running down the right-hand side. It had originally been a par-3 but had been converted to a par-4 when Robert Trent Jones realized there was room behind and to the right of the 15th green to put in a back tee. It had been there that Scott Simpson's bogey-bogey-bogey meltdown had started in the 1991 U.S. Open playoff against Payne Stewart. Trailing by two, Stewart had birdied the hole to pull even and ended up winning by two.

But there was very little room on the 16th for corporate tents or chalets. The 7th hole had lots of room for tents and chalets and, with the hole playing as the 16th, would afford the corporate types a spectacular view of what could be a critical hole in many matches. Since it was a risk/reward par-5, it was entirely possible that many matches would turn one way or the other at that hole.

"There's one other thing," Chandler Withington pointed out. "Some matches may not get to 16. This way, the prettiest hole on the course is guaranteed to be part of every match."

It had been the club's idea to reroute, but the PGA had liked the idea from the beginning. The members had played the "Ryder Cup" course all summer to get accustomed to the new routing so they would be familiar with it in their roles as volunteers once the matches began.

The Hazeltine members were making, arguably, more sacrifices than any club was ever asked to make before hosting a major golf event. Beginning in August, everyone had to carry mats around with them on the golf course to play off, not just on tees, but on fairways. And at the request of the PGA, the course was shut down for the year on August 29—four weeks before the practice rounds for the Ryder Cup would begin.

Complaints? "Very few, I mean *very* few," said Patrick Hunt, who was the club's Ryder Cup chairman. "When people sign up to become members here, they know about the club's mission statement. They're told about it very specifically, so they aren't taken by surprise. Plus, we tend to embrace these events in Minnesota. We don't get them here all that often."

Minneapolis had hosted one Super Bowl (1991) and two Final Fours (1992, 2001), with another Super Bowl scheduled for 2018. The Stanley Cup finals had come to town twice—in 1981, when the North Stars lost to the New York Islanders, and ten years later, when they lost to the Penguins—and the NBA Finals had never been played there. The Twins had won the World Series in 1987 and 1991 but hadn't been back to the Series since.

"If we're lucky, we may get an event like this every eight to ten years," said Irv Fish, who had been a longtime Hazeltine member and had also served for many years on the USGA's executive board. "Minnesotans tend to be very gung ho when something like this comes to town because they know it will probably be a while before it happens again."

The rerouting of the golf course wasn't a big deal for the players. If it had been attempted for a PGA or U.S. Open, it would have been—at the very least—extremely difficult logistically. But on an empty course that Monday in mid-September, the change in the order of the holes was almost irrelevant.

On that Monday afternoon, Phil Mickelson stood in the middle of the 2nd fairway and made an announcement: "I would like it noted by everyone here that I have now hit two fairways—*two* in a row—with my driver," he said.

He was smiling and, to those around him, clearly having fun. Mickelson had always struggled to find fairways with his driver, so his self-deprecating "boast" was something everyone understood. Mickelson was obviously comfortable—very much in his element—as this team's "papa bear."

If Kuchar was the team's number-one prankster, Mickelson was—without a doubt—the team's number-one shit-giver. He took pride in it, although he admitted there were two people he more or less stayed away from: Kuchar and Tiger Woods.

For a long time the notion of Woods and Mickelson exchanging friendly barbs was laughable. Mickelson, though, had seen a gradual change in Woods's demeanor around him and the other players.

"I honestly think it has something to do, a lot to do, with his father's death [2006]," Mickelson said. "When his father was alive, I think he was being told to keep his distance, to never lose that intimidation factor that he had for all those years. Some of that changed with age and injuries, but I think dating as far back as 2008 or 2009, you could see him starting to change. He went from being apart from the guys to being one of the guys. It didn't happen right away; it was gradual."

There were times when Mickelson did engage Woods, but he knew he couldn't win the battle. "He has the ultimate trump card," Mickelson said, laughing. "Fourteen and seventy-nine. Whenever things get going, he pulls that out and I'm done."

Fourteen was the number of times Woods had won major championships; seventy-nine was the number of tournaments he had won in all. Mickelson's numbers were extremely impressive for a mere mortal: five and forty-two. He wasn't afraid to roll them out—especially the five—when he engaged with other players.

"You have to know where to pick your battles," he said.

On that Monday at Hazeltine, he pulled a hybrid on the tee at the short par-4 (352 yards) 5th hole. Brandt Snedeker, a pretty good needler himself, couldn't resist.

"Hybrid, Phil?" he asked.

"Just trying to make sure I find the fairway," Mickelson answered.

Except he didn't. The ball found the rough. Snedeker couldn't resist. "How'd that hybrid work out for you?" he said.

Mickelson responded by holding up five fingers. "You know what this is, Brandt?" he said. Snedeker knew, but Mickelson wasn't going to be stopped. "It's, one, two, three, four, *five* more majors than you've won, isn't it?"

Game, set, match, Mickelson. Fortunately for him, Mr. Fourteen-and-Seventy-Nine wasn't around.

Mickelson tried to avoid shit-giving combat with Kuchar for a different reason. "He's too quick," Mickelson said. "I'm good. I'm *very* good. But I *never* beat him."

Example. Several years earlier, Mickelson had showed up at a tournament wearing custom-made alligator (or Augusta) green shoes. He walked onto the range and began loosening up. Kuchar was right next to him.

"What are *those*?" Kuchar asked, pointing at the shoes.

"These?" Mickelson answered. "These are shoes you can only get after you've won three Masters."

Mickelson grinned. He had him. He'd played *his* trump card. Only not so much.

"Well, if that's the case," Kuchar said, starting to turn away to resume his warm-up, "I hope I only win *two*."

Game, set, match to the man married to the former Georgia Tech tennis player.

Mickelson was about as relaxed as he had ever been pre–Ryder Cup. The task force—which was now being called the "Ryder Cup committee" by the PGA because so many people had made fun of the term "task force"—had done just about everything he had wanted.

He wasn't listed as a vice captain, but he had as much of a voice with Love as any of the four vice captains. He and Love had started talking early in the summer about whom Mickelson wanted to play with in the four-ball and foursomes matches. It was unlikely that Keegan Bradley was going to make the team. Mickelson liked the idea of playing with either Snedeker or Kuchar. But he loved the idea of playing with Rickie Fowler. He liked playing with one of the young guys; someone he had played a lot of Tuesday matches with; someone he had mentored.

He wouldn't have minded playing with Jordan Spieth (who wouldn't?), but Spieth was locked in with Patrick Reed. So he and Love had pretty much agreed that he would play with Fowler—at least on Friday. They had also agreed he would sit out one session, most likely Saturday morning in foursomes play. What was most important to Mickelson—as he'd said repeatedly—was that he knew whom he was playing with and when he was playing.

"There were no ifs or buts involved," he said. "The goal of the task force was to give us the best chance possible to play well. Davis did that.

"When we left Hazeltine that day, we all felt good about the way the golf course was going to be set up, about the team, about what was going to happen.

"We knew we were going to win. In my mind, there just wasn't any doubt about it."

—

The Europeans had decided to pass on a preview look at Hazeltine. It wasn't that they were cocky, but that they simply believed three full days—even four for some of them—would be plenty to know and understand the golf course.

"It isn't rocket science, is it?" Danny Willett asked. "You go to a major, you might play thirty-six holes to get ready and that's usually enough. If we don't win, it won't be because we didn't see the golf course soon enough."

Willett was living proof that you didn't necessarily need a lot of prep before an important event to succeed. He had been the last player to arrive at Augusta in April, flying in Tuesday night because he'd been uncertain whether he was coming. His first child—a son—had been born ten days earlier in England.

Then he won the Masters.

Stardom was new to Willett, but he appeared to be well equipped to handle it. He was the third of four brothers. His mother, Elisabet, was a math teacher; his dad, Steve, was a vicar in the Church of England. Danny's language can turn salty at times—not what you might expect from a vicar's son.

"My dad uses more profanity than I do," he said, laughing. "He kind of figures there are worse things people do."

Willett is very quick and funny, and is one of those athletes who takes his job seriously but doesn't take himself too seriously. On the first practice day of the U.S. Open, he walked across the street from the house where he was staying to the front gate of Oakmont Country Club. He had walked so that his wife, Nicole, could have the car for the day to get around with their three-and-a-half-month-old son.

When he reached the gate, he was stopped by a security guard.

"Can't walk in here," the guard said.

Willett was baffled. On the other side of the gate was the players parking lot and, a few steps beyond that, the locker room. He was wearing his player badge.

"I'm a player," he said. "I'm just walking over to the locker room, which is right there."

The guard—naturally—had no interest in hearing logic or common sense.

"No walk-ins," he said.

"So how do I get in?" Willett said.

The guard pointed to the end of the block. Willett was on his way to his pretournament press conference. He could have argued, lost his temper, demanded to see a supervisor, or waited for someone who knew what they were doing to come along. (Granted, that could have been a long wait.)

Instead, he shrugged and said, "I guess I'll have to drive tomorrow."

Willett had gone to college in the United States for two years. As a high school junior, he had paid about 2,500 pounds to a group called FirstPoint USA, which helped place overseas athletes in athletic programs in the U.S. James Hobbs, the longtime golf coach at Jacksonville State University in Alabama, often recruited players from overseas. He contacted the Willetts and sold Steve on the fact that Jacksonville was located in a small—read safe—town and that Danny wouldn't be the only non-American on the team. Sight unseen, Danny enrolled there in the fall of 2006.

"It worked out brilliantly," he said. "I loved the school, got along great with Coach Hobbs and the team. I learned a lot about responsibility—being on my own. At home, if I wasn't up in the morning, Mom came in and woke me. That doesn't happen at college. You have to behave like an adult. It was a great experience for me."

He stayed two years, winning the Ohio Valley Conference individual championship as a sophomore. He went home for the summer and played so well that he was the number-one-ranked amateur in the world early in 2008.

"At that point it didn't make any sense for me *not* to turn pro," he said. "I'd done about all I could do as an amateur. It was time to move on."

The only thing that had slowed his progression as a pro were some back issues that forced him to shut down at one point for eight months. Even now, he has to be careful not to overwork.

"It flares every once in a while if I'm not careful," he said. "There's really nothing I enjoy more than going off by myself on the range with some music and [teacher] Pete [Cowen] and just hitting lots of balls. Somedays I have to shut it down earlier than I'd like."

Willett had first gained notice in the U.S. when he had finished third in the World Match Play championships at Harding Park in San Francisco in May 2015. He had been seeded forty-eighth in the sixty-four-man field but went 3-0 in pool play—including a win over Patrick Reed—and beat Lee Westwood and Tommy Fleetwood to reach the semifinals before losing to Gary Woodland. He then beat Jim Furyk in the third-place match.

That finish gave him full status on the Tour for the rest of the year, but he chose to play in Europe most of the time and finished second to Rory McIlroy in the Race to Dubai. He came into 2016 wanting to prove that finish wasn't a fluke and to make the Ryder Cup team.

"I didn't want to be one of those guys who had one good year, finished second on the points list, and then never did much ever again," he said. "That sort of thing does happen.

"And I knew this was the time for me to play Ryder Cup. I'd thought about it since I was eleven, when I watched the matches at Brookline. I knew if I ever did anything in golf, *that* was something I wanted to do. Now I had a chance to make it real, not just a fantasy."

The fantasy became reality on a sparkling April Sunday at Augusta. As Spieth hit the wall and Willett took control, Willett's older brother Pete—also known as P.J.—began tweeting relentlessly and hilariously and quickly became a Twitter sensation. In real life, he's a high school drama teacher who, according to Danny, was just about as good a golfer as he was when the boys—two years apart—were young.

Pete began with digs at Spieth: "Spieth is lining up his putt. If I'm quick, I can get a beer, go to the toilet, and paint the spare room b4 he hits it." Later he referred to Spieth as "slowpoke"—perhaps a bit mean, but not inaccurate.

Then he took a shot at the crowd—whoops, patrons—a harbinger of future events, as it turned out. "Stand still you pricks," he railed at one point when he thought the crowd was moving around as his brother prepared to putt.

Then he began focusing on Danny. "If the boy does what he should, I will be able to say I shared a bath with a Masters winner . . ." And: "@DannyWillett you still owe me a birthday present. I'd like a jacket. A green one . . ." On the 18th green: "3 putt this and you might as well stay in America . . ." No pressure, right?

And, finally, when the deed was done: "Green makes you look fat, refuse the jacket."

It was clever, funny stuff. People—especially in England—wanted to hear more from Pete Willett. They would.

The win at Augusta took care of both of Willett's goals for 2016. Clearly, as a Masters champion he would never just be someone who had finished second one year in the Race to Dubai. More important, perhaps, the victory wrapped up his place on the Ryder Cup team.

"Clarkie [Darren Clarke] has been chatting with me all year about wanting me to be in the team," he said a few weeks after the Masters. "Now we can talk about who else we want on the team, who I might play with—all of that. It's a good feeling knowing I'll be there for certain."

He smiled. "I'm already preparing myself for those 1st tee nerves. I know I've won the Masters, but it will still be my first Ryder Cup. I'm sure it will be like nothing else I've ever experienced."

As it turned out, Willett was right about that—but not in the way he thought or hoped.

Eighteen

ON SATURDAY, SEPTEMBER 24, Davis Love flew to Minneapolis and checked into the Sheraton Bloomington. He was hoping to play golf the next day with Chandler Withington—his final respite before the grind of Ryder Cup week began—and then tape his announcement of the twelfth member of his team that was to air on NBC Sunday night.

There were two problems with the idea of playing golf on Sunday. First, the weather was awful: cold, windy, and rainy. Love was extremely glad Ryder Cup Sunday was still a week away because the playing conditions, had this been the last day of the matches, would have been miserable.

There was also the not-so-small matter of picking his last player. He still hadn't decided.

Love had hoped that one of the four candidates would play so well in the Tour Championship that his pick would be easy. The best-case scenario, from his point of view, was for Bubba Watson to find his game and make the pick academic. Watson was the logical pick. He was ranked seventh in the world, had finished ninth on the points list, and had played in three previous Ryder Cups.

Love also knew that Watson would be the perfect four-ball partner for J. B. Holmes. The two got along, and they were both bombers who would make a lot of birdies.

There was just one problem: Watson hadn't played well since early March. He had started the season fast, winning in Los Angeles and then following up two weeks later with a second-place finish in the WGC event at Doral. At that point, he was second on the points list, and Love had assigned Steve Stricker to make sure Watson's eclectic taste in food would be taken care of in Minnesota. "The good news is Bubba likes almost every flavor smoothie there is," Love said. "He and I are very different. He eats for fuel. I look at eating as a sport."

After Doral, though, Watson's game went south. He finished T-37 at the Masters, where he had won twice. He didn't do any better in the other majors: T-51, T-39, T-60. In fact, in the thirteen tournaments he played after Doral he had one top ten, a T-8 at the Olympics, which had a sixty-player field, many of them players from smaller countries who had no chance to seriously compete.

And so Love had a conundrum: he knew what Watson was capable of doing, but he also knew he hadn't done it for most of seven months.

There were some who thought that Love didn't want Watson on the team because he could be moody, could get down on himself very quickly, and might bring the whole room down if he wasn't playing well.

Love insisted that wasn't at all true.

"Look, I know Bubba *well*," Love said. "I've spent a lot of time with him. I know he gets anxious about things and he's an introvert by nature. But he gets along with the guys well. If I don't pick him, it won't be because of his personality. Not at all."

When Watson was comfortable, he was friendly and outgoing. When he wasn't, he could go into a shell. He did have anxiety problems, best exemplified, perhaps, by his belief that he, his wife, Angie, and their infant son, Caleb, were being followed as they left a charity concert in Columbus the week of the Memorial in 2012.

Making the team was very important to Watson—in fact, he was probably trying *too* hard. The last time his father had seen him play golf had been during the 2010 Ryder Cup as he lay in a hospital bed dying of throat cancer. Earlier in the year, after winning at Hartford for his first PGA Tour win, Bubba had cried talking about his father. "He taught me everything I know," he said. "It isn't much, but it's all I know."

Eleven days after the Ryder Cup ended, Gerry Watson died. That year had been the springboard to Bubba's stardom, culminating in his victory at the Masters in 2012 when he came from behind on Sunday to catch Louis Oosthuizen and then beat him in a playoff when he miraculously hooked a nine-iron around a tree and onto the 10th green.

That shot, that victory, and the fact that it came just two weeks after he and Angie had adopted Caleb made Watson an instant star. It was a spotlight he wasn't always comfortable with. He had a temper that showed up on the golf course—especially when he would yell at his longtime caddie, Ted Scott, who could apparently take anything and not lose his sense of humor.

Watson had won the Masters again in 2014 and had played well at Gleneagles for Tom Watson. "I've never been on a winning Ryder Cup team," he said in the spring. "I'd like to play on *one* winning Ryder Cup team before I'm done. I'm thirty-seven, I don't really know how many chances I have left."

With one week left to prove himself to Love, there was real doubt about whether he'd get another chance at Hazeltine. Love liked the idea of adding another young player—Justin Thomas or Daniel Berger—and the hot player coming down the stretch had been Ryan Moore. Still, he was leaning toward Watson when Sunday morning dawned so dreary and rainy.

The Tour Championship wasn't giving him a lot of help in finding a clear-cut pick. Going into the final round, Moore was in the best position among the four contenders, tied for second with Rory McIlroy—two shots behind leader Dustin Johnson. Thomas was four shots behind Moore, one shot ahead of Watson, and three ahead of Berger. Love wasn't going to pick either of the youngsters unless they won—which was very unlikely.

That left Watson and Moore.

"I was torn," Love said. "Ryan was playing the best golf and had been for a while. Bubba had the experience and the overall numbers. I went back and forth all day."

Having decided not to brave the elements to play golf, Love sat and watched the final round along with Zach Johnson—who hadn't made the Atlanta field and had flown up with Love—and Jim Furyk. At different times, Tiger Woods, Steve Stricker, and Tom Lehman were on the phone, telling Love what they thought. It was a very divided room—metaphorically, since not all of them were in the room.

Finally, Love decided he needed to stop hearing other voices and just hear his own. "I'm going to drive to the club," he said. "I have to get ready for the taping, and I've got to figure this out."

By this time, McIlroy had beaten Moore in a four-hole playoff to win both the tournament and the $10 million FedEx Cup bonus. He and Moore had both played brilliantly on Sunday, each shooting 64.

Adding Watson to the team wouldn't be very difficult for Love. Most of the players had been on teams with him before and understood his quirks. Stricker had the smoothies lined up.

Moore was a different story. He'd been on tour for eleven years and was a solid, respected player with five wins—including a victory six weeks earlier at the John Deere Classic. His record in major championships was less than sterling: he'd never finished higher than ninth in twenty-three starts and had only two top tens. On the other hand, he'd had a brilliant college career at UNLV, winning the U.S. Amateur, the Western Amateur, and the U.S. Public Links. You could not win those events without being very good at match play.

Love was pulling up to the clubhouse when he finally decided to go with what his gut was telling him: Moore. He wanted the guy who would come to town oozing confidence. He made the easy call first. When Moore answered, Love, trying to sound casual, said: "Really nice playing today. Where are you right now?"

"At the airport," Moore answered. "About to fly home [to Las Vegas] with my family."

Love paused for a second. "Okay, fine," he said. "But how'd you like to make a stop in Minnesota?"

For a moment there was silence on the other end of the phone.

"Wow," Moore said, an absolute outpouring of emotion coming from him. "Is it okay if I fly home tonight and to Minnesota tomorrow?"

"It's fine," Love said, smiling. Moore, as usual, was about as low-key as someone could be at a moment like that. "I'll get you hooked up with the PGA people, and they'll take care of your travel and everything."

They talked for another minute or two. As they were about to hang up, Moore said, "Hey, Davis?"

"Yeah, Ryan?"

"Thanks."

Love hung up with a grin on his face. It disappeared quickly, though. Now he had to make the hard call.

Bubba Watson answered on the first ring. He'd been waiting for the call, one way or the other. Love had made this kind of call before, in 2012, and he knew there was no way to soften the blow.

"Bubba, I'm sorry," he said. "I went with Ryan."

"Okay," Watson said. "Can you tell me why?"

Later, Love remembered that there was no anger in Watson's voice, that the question wasn't asked as if to say, "You better have an explanation for this."

"It was more like he wanted to understand it," Love said. "I told him it had been very close—because it had been—but in the end I went with the guy who was playing the best."

Watson listened. When Love finished he said, "Davis, I'd still like to come. Is there something I can do? I want to be part of this even if I'm not playing."

Love was stunned by the request. "I'll be honest with you," he said later. "I can't think of one other guy in that situation—myself included—who would have said that."

In fact, asked later, every one of Love's players agreed. Most used the same two words: "no way."

When he recovered his composure, Love said, "Well, we can still add one vice captain. If you want to come and do that, you're welcome. It's a lot of work, though, without much cheering at all. But if you come, you have to be all in. You can't just come and hang around."

"Can I call you back in five or ten minutes?" Watson said.

Love told him that would be fine. Five minutes later, Watson called back. "If you'll have me, I'm in," he said. "I just want to help any way I can."

Now Love had two guys he had to get to Minnesota. He would never have guessed that would be the case.

Having made his decision, Love had to tape his announcement. Once finished, he went to a prearranged PGA of America meet and greet with some of Hazeltine's members who would be working as volunteers.

Love walked out of the meeting room at about seven thirty Central time. He was going to head back to the hotel to watch himself making the Moore announcement at halftime of the Ravens-Jaguars game, which would probably come at about nine o'clock local time.

He looked at his phone and saw a text from his son, Dru. "Hearing that Mr. Palmer died," the text said. Mac Barnhardt, Love's agent, was waiting for him. He had the same bad news.

"There's word starting to spread on social media that Arnold died," he said quietly.

Both were referring, of course, to Arnold Palmer—not the greatest golfer of all time, but the most important. Palmer had made golf a TV sport and corporate America's sport in the late 1950s and the 1960s. If Tiger Woods made golfers multimillionaires, Palmer was the one who first made them millionaires.

More important, he had mentored just about any player who had spent more than fifteen minutes on tour, dating from the 1960s, when he'd taken Jack Nicklaus under his wing, to 2016, when he'd been a sounding board for—among many others—Rory McIlroy, Jordan Spieth, Rickie Fowler, and Jason Day.

"He had an amazing ability to make you feel as if you were the most important person in the world," McIlroy said. "I always felt like he had all day long to talk to me—even when I knew he didn't."

Love's father had been friends with Palmer, and Love had looked up to him since he was a boy. One of his fondest memories had come twenty years earlier when Palmer captained the second U.S. Presidents Cup team. The night before the matches began, Palmer talked to his players about what he expected of them, how important it was to represent their country and their tour with class, and giving everything they had to win the matches but always in the spirit of the game.

"He paused as he said that, and he pointed at me and said, 'Davis gets it,'" Love remembered. "'He understands that there's more to this than just making money and winning. You have to give back.'

"That was one of the coolest moments of my life," he added.

The next morning on Golf Channel, Love tried to retell the story. He couldn't get through it without breaking down.

Palmer's death wasn't a shock. He was eighty-seven and had been in failing health for a while. A number of players had changed their schedules earlier in the year to play in the Arnold Palmer Invitational at the Bay Hill Club and Lodge—which Palmer owned—because they suspected it might be the last one he'd be around to host.

"I just feel like I need to be there," Matt Kuchar had said in February, explaining his change in schedule.

Others did the same.

And yet, because he was such an iconic figure to everyone in golf, the players on both teams were stunned when they heard the news.

Jordan Spieth and Phil Mickelson had flown into Minneapolis from

Atlanta together. Shortly after they got off the plane, Spieth saw that his phone was blowing up with people letting him know that Palmer had died.

Stunned, he walked over to Mickelson, not knowing if he had heard the news.

"I wondered, if he hadn't heard, if it was my place to tell him," he said. "I knew how close he felt to Mr. Palmer."

Spieth asked Mickelson if he had heard the news. "What news?" Mickelson asked. He had apparently not yet checked his phone. Spieth told him.

"Honestly, I don't even remember Jordan telling me," Mickelson said, weeks later. "It was just a very sad thing for me. To be honest, I don't remember very much about the next twenty-four hours.

"There are a few players in golf I've always looked at as kind of mystical: Byron [Nelson]; [Ben] Hogan; Jack [Nicklaus]; and Arnold." He paused. "I guess I just thought he'd never die. And, in a sense, he never will."

Once they had confirmed the news that Palmer had passed away, Love and Barnhardt had to decide what to do next.

"Your announcement on Ryan can't air," Barnhardt said. "You can't be on TV tonight *not* talking about Arnold."

Love agreed and got in touch with Julius Mason. In the end, NBC pulled the tape Love had made and play-by-play man Mike Tirico simply announced that Moore had been selected as the twelfth American.

"It was a tough night," Love said. "But we couldn't just sit around and mourn. We had to figure out how we were going to honor Arnold during the week. Obviously, his death was going to cast a shadow over the first part of the week."

As the players from both teams began arriving late Sunday and early Monday, the story wasn't who would win the Ryder Cup—but Palmer and his impact on the game.

Golf Channel, which had an army of on-air talent, producers, and directors in town by Sunday to begin wall-to-wall coverage on Monday, abandoned Ryder Cup coverage completely and aired twenty-four straight hours of Palmer coverage—commercial free. The fact that Palmer had cofounded the network in 1995 was certainly one reason for the nonstop Palmer blitz, but his iconic status was a big part of it too.

Players arriving on Monday all did brief interviews, and the questions were all about Palmer. Love wasn't asked a single question all day about why he had chosen Ryan Moore over Bubba Watson. The announcement that Watson would be a vice captain for the U.S. went virtually unnoticed.

Only a few players ventured onto the golf course to get a look at it. The day was cold and windy, and the sense was—based on the weather report—that the conditions were likely to be entirely different by Friday, so practicing in the wind probably wouldn't have much value.

Monday afternoon, with everyone having arrived in town and gone to the golf course to at least hit some balls, several players gathered in the team room for a midafternoon drink and snack.

Love, exhausted from the whirlwind he had gone through in the previous twenty-four hours, walked in and collapsed in a chair. A waitress asked him what he wanted to drink.

"I'll take an ice tea," Love said.

She looked at Rickie Fowler, who was sitting next to Love. "I'd like an Arnold Palmer," Fowler said.

Love sat up straight in his chair. "Hang on," he said. "Make mine an Arnold Palmer too."

The waitress went around the table. Everyone ordered an Arnold Palmer. When the drinks arrived, Love picked up his glass and said quietly, "Let's make Arnold proud this week."

No one said anything in response, other than to hold their glasses up in the air.

By Tuesday, the Palmer talk had started to slow—though it hadn't stopped—and everyone began focusing on the task at hand. Naturally, there was already some controversy, and it had come—surprisingly—from Davis Love.

A week earlier, during a radio interview, Love had been asked what he might tell his team when they were alone in the team room before the matches began.

"I think I would tell them that I believe they might be one of the best teams ever assembled," Love answered.

Saying that sort of thing in private to his players was one thing; saying it in public a week prior to trying to break a string of eight losses in ten Ryder Cups was, to say the least, surprising.

Naturally, the Europeans had fun with it. When McIlroy was asked about the comment during a Tour Championship press conference, he grinned and said, "Well, they certainly have the best task force ever."

Later, McIlroy, who has a keen sense of the game's history, laughed and said, "I guess their team in '81 with nine Hall of Famers wasn't all that great."

Darren Clarke said he had no intention of pinning the quote to a wall in his team room because "all my players know about it already."

Earlier in September, Love had said half jokingly that he was channeling Bill Belichick by being cagey about who his captain's picks might be. The "best team" comment was about as anti-Belichick as could be imagined.

But it wasn't a mistake or a slip of the tongue, although Love did revert to the old "taken out of context" cop-out when the subject came up several seconds after his Tuesday press conference began.

In context, he'd been sending a very public message to his team: we are going to kick their butt. Not we're going to win, but we are going to *win*. Part of this made perfect sense: the last thing Love wanted was a down-to-the-wire finish on Sunday, because twenty-first-century history said that didn't work out too well for the Americans.

But it was more than that. He knew his team *should* win. It had every possible advantage, from the golf course setup to the home crowd to the inexperience on Europe's side, not to mention the motivation of having a team that *had* to win. Bob Sutton, the former Army football coach, always told his team the same thing before it played Navy: "All other things being equal, the most desperate team will win."

There was no doubt that the U.S. was desperate. Love had been setting a tone of "we're going to pound them" all summer.

In August, in Greensboro, he couldn't defend the Wyndham Championship title he'd won the previous year because he'd had hip surgery in June. He had been hoping to hold off on the surgery until the Ryder Cup was over, but he could barely swing a club by the time he got to Akron. He tried to hit balls on the range there on Wednesday but could not make a turn. The doctor told him it wasn't going to get any better, so he had the surgery.

He still came to Greensboro as a courtesy to Wyndham—the title sponsor—and on Wednesday night, he did a "fireside chat" in front of about a hundred people. The last question of the night was direct: "What will the score be at Hazeltine?"

Love didn't hedge even a little bit. "I want 20 points," he said, drawing a mixture of laughs and cheers.

"But you'll settle for 14½, right?" the questioner said.

This time Love was even more firm: "I want 20 points," he repeated.

That was the tone he wanted to set with his players. In fact, he took it a little further, telling them their goal should be simple: "Win every match."

That wasn't going to happen, but it was the mentality Love wanted from his players. They might not have been quite there when they arrived, but by the time Friday morning rolled around, that was exactly the way they were thinking.

The first funny moment of the week came on Tuesday morning, and it came at the expense of Tiger Woods.

The first task for the teams once they were all present and accounted for was to pose for a team photo. Love sat in the middle of the front row, holding the Palm Beach version of the Ryder Cup. The rest of the team assembled around him, five players sitting on chairs to either side of him, the rest standing behind them.

As the Americans lined up, Woods stood in the back row, to the far right, next to Rickie Fowler. Montana Pritchard, the PGA's photographer, waved at him to move. Thinking the back row was unbalanced, Woods walked to the other end and stood next to Ryan Moore.

Embarrassed, Pritchard told Woods the photo was only for the players and the captain. Woods backed away and joined the other vice captains. He was accustomed to being told he needed to be front row center— even when he preferred not to be there. Everyone—including Woods— cracked up.

Needless to say, the players needled him about the non-photo op for the rest of the day—nonstop. "You know what," Woods finally said that evening, "being a player is a lot easier than being an assistant captain."

Both captains had planned to bring in inspirational non-golfers to speak on Tuesday night. Clarke, the former rugby player, had invited Irish superstar Paul O'Connell to come and speak to his players.

O'Connell had captained Ireland's rugby team and had played in 108 international matches for Ireland. He was certainly an imposing figure—

six foot six and 245 pounds—and he spoke about Clarke's theme for his team, "shoulder to shoulder." This made sense since the Irish rugby team traditionally sang "Ireland's Call," which included the words "shoulder to shoulder," before every international match it played. It also didn't hurt that O'Connell was a single-digit-handicap player who loved the idea of helping Clarke get his team ready to play.

O'Connell talked emotionally about wearing the number five throughout his career and how he wanted to "walk away feeling like the number was in a better place historically than it had been before I wore it. I wanted there to be pride in the number five because I'd worn it."

Once Clarke had decided his team's order for the singles on Saturday, he presented each of them with a shirt with the number they were going off sewed into it.

"Paul was perfect," Clarke said later. "He pulled up a chair and sat close to everyone so he could look them right in the eye. By the time he was finished, the boys were ready to go out and do anything to win. He brought a lot of emotion to the room."

Love's non-golfer wasn't close to being a single-digit player, although he had improved considerably since making his Ryder Cup "debut" at Medinah in 2012.

That was Michael Phelps, who had hung out with the American team that week in Chicago a few weeks after the last swim meet of his remarkable career. Except, it hadn't been the last meet of his career. After an arrest for DUI, Phelps ended up in rehab before deciding to come back and swim in the Rio Olympics.

He had done so—brilliantly—adding five gold medals and a silver to his stunning total of twenty-two Olympic medals—eighteen of them gold. He was certainly someone who could talk to the American players about dealing with adversity and coming back from it.

He spoke at some length about why he loved being at the Ryder Cup, how much he enjoyed watching the players work together as a team in an individual sport. "I always loved relays," he said. "Because it was the only time in my sport you got to be part of a team. This is your chance to be part of a team in your sport and know how great it feels to win *together*."

There were only two team members in the room who had known that feeling: Phil Mickelson and J. B. Holmes.

Naturally, it was Kuchar who tried to bring some levity to the proceedings. "Maybe, since you and I are the only ones in this room with

Olympic medals [Kuchar had won the bronze in Rio], we can talk about what it feels like," he said to Phelps.

At that point, he pulled his medal from his pocket, put it around his neck, and walked to the front of the room to join Phelps.

"Classic Kuchar," Zach Johnson said.

For once, though, someone got the last word on Kuchar.

"Hey, Michael," Brandt Snedeker said. "Where do you keep your bronze medals?"

Phelps smiled. "Honestly," he said, "I have no idea where they are."

Kuchar was the king, but the king—at least for a moment—was dead. All hail Snedeker and Phelps.

That was the night of Love's unplanned event: the Duval-Chamblee face-off that set the tone for the week—exactly the tone Love wanted.

No one enjoyed it more than Phil Mickelson, who probably disliked Chamblee—or at least his on-air persona—more than anyone else on the team. He and Amy were in their room getting ready for dinner on Tuesday evening when the battle broke out. Mickelson was only half listening when it started, but within a couple of minutes, he was sitting in front of the TV drinking in every word.

"It meant a lot to all of us, but also to me personally, to have David [Duval] stand up for us like that," he said later. "A lot of us who have been directly involved with the team in the past—actually *played* on the team—have been shocked by how misinformed Chamblee's comments about the Ryder Cup have been. This was another example, but David was there to defend us. He was someone who actually knew what the Ryder Cup is like and who understood how many times we'd been blamed for losing when we had no control over what led up to the matches. [Frank] Nobilo did too because he's played on Presidents Cup teams."

One of the most oft-heard arguments from athletes when they are criticized is that the critics don't understand because they never *played*. Chamblee had played—but never in the Ryder Cup. For years, the most blunt ex-player on TV had been Johnny Miller, and many players truly despised Miller at least in part because they couldn't use the "he never played" defense. Miller had won twenty-five times on tour, including two major championships, and had played on two winning Ryder Cup teams.

But when it came to Ryder Cup, the players could roll out the "never played" argument on Chamblee. The reasons that players couldn't stand Chamblee were the exact same reasons viewers loved him: he wasn't afraid to call people out. Of course, he also spent plenty of time on-air praising players, but players didn't notice that.

The next morning, Chamblee got a text from Glenn Cohen, one of Mickelson's agents, asking, "What has Phil done to deserve the things you have said about him last night and in the past?"

Chamblee responded by noting that "about ninety-five percent of what I've said on-air about Phil over the years has been positive."

In truth, it was probably closer to 98 percent. Just not when it came to Ryder Cup. Chamblee had ripped Mickelson more bluntly than anyone else after his Watson tirade at Gleneagles. Mickelson hadn't forgotten.

Neither had Chamblee. Not surprisingly, he had heard about Duval's appearance in the American team room by the next morning. For two days, the two men didn't speak to each other. On Friday, when they finally talked, Chamblee asked Duval if it was true that he had gone into the room and received a standing ovation.

"Yes, it's true," Duval said.

"Well, the next time you go in there, you might point out to all those guys that, on their way to making the Ryder Cup team, they've won tournaments along the way and I've praised them at length on the air for their play, for their charity work, for being good guys. If they want to focus on my pointing out that the U.S. has lost eight of the last ten Ryder Cups, which is a *fact,* that's fine. But they should focus on *all* the facts."

Chamblee was frustrated—disappointed, to use his word.

"I have all the respect for David and his place in the game," he said months later. "And I have no problem with him disagreeing with a position I take on the air. I argue with Frank [Nobilo] and plenty of others all the time. What David did that night that made it different—at least in my mind—was that he made it personal. I've never made it personal with anyone else, and, honestly, no one had ever made it personal with me.

"Then, when I heard he'd gone into the team room, I was disappointed and I told him that. I told him I thought he should have politely declined Davis's invitation. I think when you are covering an event on television or radio or in print, you have to maintain a certain amount of objectivity. I thought David sacrificed that when he went into that room."

Not surprisingly, Duval disagreed.

"To begin with, the whole thing caught me off guard," he said. "I never expected anything like that to happen. I was just coming off the heels of a heated exchange, and it was still on my mind when I heard from Davis.

"But it never occurred to me to *not* go in the room and talk to the guys. I *do* think of myself as still being a Ryder Cupper even though it's years since I played. One of the things I tried to tell the guys was to savor the experience of playing in the event because it is an entirely different beast than anything else in golf, and they should enjoy being a part of it because a very tiny number of players get to do it. And you never know if this one will be the last one you play on. I thought I'd play again after '02 and I didn't.

"I don't think I sacrificed my objectivity going in there. Certainly no one said anything to me about lacking it during the next few days."

Duval admitted he was caught off guard by the standing ovation when he walked in.

"It was almost surreal," he said. "It's kind of a blur now. I never expected anything like it. But I guess they saw it as me standing up for them as being *one* of them. Which it was. To me it *was* personal. If you attack guys I played with in the Ryder Cup, then you're attacking me. That's why I reacted the way I did."

Chamblee didn't see it as personal. He saw it as doing his job. "To me it was about facts," he said. "When I went back and researched the last twenty years of the Ryder Cup, there was one common thread in all of it: Phil Mickelson. And, to a lesser degree, Tiger Woods. I didn't think they led the way the two best players in the world could have led or *played* the way the two best players in the world could have played. That's not personal, it's just facts."

Duval and Chamblee would sit down later and thrash out their differences in private. But that night, Duval's surprise appearance in the team room left everyone on a high—including Duval.

"It was pretty special for me," he said. "I told the guys being a *team* was what this was about: fighting for one another; watching each other's backs. Win together, lose together. That's what the Ryder Cup is all about."

After Duval finished and everyone was in a buoyant mood, Mickelson stopped to talk to Love before he went upstairs to bed. It was his turn to meet the media the next morning. It would be the first press conference he'd done at a Ryder Cup since Gleneagles.

"You sure you want me to go in there tomorrow?" Mickelson said. "You never know what I might say that will cause trouble."

He was joking. Twelve hours later, the joke had become serious.

Nineteen

THE MEDIA HAS less access to players at the Ryder Cup than at any other event in golf. Part of this is simple logistics: unlike at a regular tournament, where there are usually more than a hundred players involved, there are only twenty-four players. In 2016, the PGA of America accredited about nine hundred media members—a number that didn't include those working for NBC/Golf Channel.

If, as at other tournaments, credentialed media had locker room access, the players would have been overrun. For similar reasons, the media was also not allowed on the putting green or the driving range—although it was possible to stand at a corner of the range and try to grab a minute with players as they walked on and off before and after practice sessions.

Because access was so limited, the captains came into the media center to speak with the media every day, beginning on Monday—a day before the ticket-holding public was allowed onto the grounds. Each of the twenty-four players also had to make a pre-tournament appearance, and most lingered when they were finished to "scrum" with reporters on the terrace outside the interview room.

On Tuesday, three Americans and three Europeans had been marched through their interviews. On Wednesday, six Americans and three Europeans would be brought in, and on Thursday, the numbers would be reversed: six Euros and three Americans.

Phil Mickelson arrived late Wednesday morning, following Henrik Stenson and Justin Rose from team Europe and his teammates Jimmy Walker and Brandt Snedeker. He stuck to the script through most of the interview: how much it meant to him to make eleven straight Ryder Cup teams on points; how much he liked Hazeltine, having played in three major championships there (1991 U.S. Open, 2002 and 2009 PGAs); how much the crowd support would mean; what a good job he believed Love was doing.

Then, right near the end, came a simple but loaded question: "You've played for ten of them. How much difference can or does a captain make?"

Clearly, the thinking behind the question was to see if Mickelson would go after Watson again. He didn't. Instead, after talking about how important it was for the captain to have his players prepared to play, he said, "I'm getting looks. Let me give you a specific example, if I may."

John Dever, the PGA's press conference moderator, knowing that the question was rhetorical, said, "You may."

And then Mickelson went right off the high board, talking about Hal Sutton's decision to pair him with Tiger Woods at Oakland Hills in 2004. He explained in almost painful detail how the lack of notice to him and Woods—two days—had forced him to spend "four or five hours" each day off by himself testing Woods's golf ball. That, according to Mickelson, was the reason he and Woods had lost two matches on Friday.

"Starting with the captain, we were put in a position to fail, and we failed monumentally and absolutely."

Perhaps seeing different "looks," he added: "Now, I loved—I'm not trying to throw—to know anybody here because I actually loved how decisive Captain Sutton was."

It was too late—though Mickelson didn't know it . . . yet. He went on to (finally) take another shot at Watson: "But to say, well, you just need to play better, that is so misinformed, because you will play how you prepare."

There were a couple more questions, one about Jordan Spieth and one about the "ownership" in the team the American players felt—or didn't feel, since the European Tour ran team Europe but the PGA of America—not the PGA Tour—ran team USA.

"You're talking about financial ownership, I was talking about emotions," Mickelson said. He could have stopped there, but he didn't. "I got blamed for that decision twelve years ago," he added. "Even a month ago, I hear there was an analyst on the Golf Channel [Chamblee] who accuses me of being a non–team player for having to go off on an isolated hole away from my team to prepare."

Finally, he was done. Even though he hadn't mentioned Watson or Chamblee by name, everyone knew whom he was talking about. In this instance it didn't matter, though, because the story was Sutton.

"Honestly, I thought I'd done well," Mickelson said, laughing, a couple of months after the matches were over. "Julius Mason thought I'd done well too. So I walked out of there feeling pretty good."

Mason didn't think Mickelson had done well. He had known almost instantly there was going to be trouble when Mickelson started down the Sutton road. But when Mickelson, clearly pleased with himself, asked him as they left the room what he thought, Mason decided not to make the comments an issue until he was certain he had one: "Entertaining as always, Phil," he answered.

A few minutes later, Mason knew for certain he had an issue. Several reporters asked where they could find Sutton, who was in town as one of the past Ryder Cup captains.

"It didn't take long to know this was something that had to be dealt with," Mason said. "It had the potential to become a real distraction for our team."

Mickelson's good feeling lasted until he got back to the clubhouse and went into the team room. Most of the players were there eating lunch. They had all watched on television—much as they had watched Duval and Chamblee the night before.

"So, pretty good, huh?" Mickelson said, walking back into the room.

It was Brandt Snedeker who spoke up first. "Maybe not so good, Phil," he said.

Mickelson was stunned. Then, when everyone explained that he was already getting roasted on social media and on the Golf Channel for the Sutton comments, it sunk in.

All of a sudden, Mickelson—already the most scrutinized player on the grounds—had put the spotlight back on himself, and not in a way he had planned or wished for. Hoping for some damage control, he tried to call Sutton—several times. Sutton didn't answer or return the call. Clearly, he wasn't happy.

"The irony in it all was that I had been the one who had brought up in the task force meetings that we needed to make a point of inviting past Ryder Cup captains to be there and be part of the week," Mickelson said.

"In the past, for whatever reason, I don't think they'd felt welcome. I thought it was important to make sure they knew we wanted them there, we wanted them in the team room, we wanted them to feel as if they were part of the week because, as past captains—like with David Duval as a past player—they were *always* part of our team."

Love had invited all past Ryder Cup captains to be there during the week. Jack Nicklaus, Dave Stockton, Lanny Wadkins, Tom Kite; Ben Crenshaw, Curtis Strange, Hal Sutton, Paul Azinger, and Corey Pavin were all there for all or part of the week. Tom Watson was the only captain dating to 1991 who didn't attend.

Now, though, Sutton had gone from being welcomed back to the Ryder Cup "family" to being reminded in front of millions of his team's failure in 2004. That hadn't been Mickelson's intent, but it had been the result.

By that evening, Love felt the problem had to be dealt with head-on. He felt bad for Sutton and was concerned about Mickelson—who was once again taking a pounding from the media.

The two teams were scheduled to go to dinner together that night downtown at the University of Minnesota. This was another of the changes the task force had pushed for. In the past, Wednesday had been the night of the gala dinner, a black-tie event attended by about two thousand people. It had been at the gala dinner in 1993 that the Tom Watson–Sam Torrance "menu-gate" incident had occurred.

The night was exhausting for both teams. They were now less than twenty-four hours from the opening ceremony and were getting antsy—more than antsy—to stop talking and start playing. The evening involved getting into black tie (never fun) and taking what was usually a long bus ride to the gala site. Then they had to sit through speeches, be glad-handed by various sponsors and officials, and then make the long bus ride back to the hotel.

"It had just gotten to be too much," Love said. "There are a lot of off-course obligations Ryder Cup week, and that's tough during the most pressure-packed week you're ever going to face. We needed that to change."

And so, while officials and sponsors did have a dinner that night, they did so without the players and captains.

Before they left for dinner, though, Love and his vice captains felt they had to figure out the Mickelson-Sutton situation.

"I sent Phil a text because I knew he was in his room getting ready for dinner," Love said. "I was actually just letting him know we were trying to figure something out. He thought I wanted him downstairs with us to talk about it, so he came down."

Mickelson actually came down to let Love know that he thought he had things under control. Through Mason, he had been in contact with Golf Channel about making an on-air apology to Sutton the next day. Mason had spoken to both Courtney Holt—who coordinated most of the network's on-air interviews—and Tim Rosaforte, someone Mickelson trusted and frequently talked to when he had a specific agenda, to let them know Mickelson wanted some airtime the next morning.

Mickelson spoke off-air to Rosaforte that night, doing his mea culpa, saying how sorry he was and that he had reached out to Sutton to apologize.

In the meantime, arrangements had been made to have Steve Burkowski, one of Golf Channel's two "on the ground" reporters for the week (Todd Lewis was the other), "interview" Mickelson the next day. It would be not so much an interview as Burkowski teeing Mickelson up.

From there, Mickelson would deliver a prepared riff on how sorry he was. He had already rehearsed for the Burkowski interview by talking to Rosaforte—whom he had known for more than twenty years and was comfortable with. He was wrong, he said, for using an "extreme example" in trying to explain how a captain could help or hurt a team. The comments were "in bad taste," and he was truly sorry.

On the air, Mickelson went further, talking about how much he had wanted past captains to be part of this week and how great it had been to see them all in the team room. He said he "felt awful" for putting Sutton in such an "awkward" position. He repeated that and went on about how much the past captains were "part of the Ryder Cup family."

That had come after Love and the vice captains had told Mickelson they felt it important for the two men to talk to each other.

Several media members had tracked Sutton down Wednesday afternoon, and one of his comments had been "Phil needs to search his own soul a little bit."

Clearly, he was upset. That concerned Love.

"I suggested to Phil that, since Hal wasn't returning his calls, that Tiger, Steve [Stricker], and I would try to get in touch with him," Love said. "Things had been going so well, I didn't want anything to set us back."

Mickelson agreed with that strategy. The next morning, Sutton texted Love to say he was sorry he hadn't gotten back to him the night before, but "I'm old and I went to bed." He said he was okay with what had happened and held no hard feelings. That morning, Mickelson and Sutton talked and—at least publicly—agreed that all was well.

All wasn't exactly well—Sutton was just willing to take one for the team and not dwell on the story. "I talked to him that morning and he was still a little chippy about it," Stricker said. "I think we all felt badly, Phil most of all. It could have been a setback, but it turned out to be just a hiccup because Phil apologized and the rest of the guys had his back because they wanted to be sure he was going to be okay. And Hal handled it well, even if he was unhappy."

Months later, Mickelson said his mistake had been in thinking the media would understand that he was just trying to explain why preparation was so important before a Ryder Cup.

"The mistake I made was trying to give a specific example," he said. "Because it came across as me throwing Hal under the bus, which wasn't what I was trying to do. I thought if I explained to the guys [media] with something specific about the importance of a captain being sure his guys were prepared correctly, it would help.

"I was wrong. They took it as an attack on Hal. It wasn't where I meant to go with it."

Fortunately for Mickelson, Sutton took the high road, even though Mickelson's bringing up what he had said was one of the low moments in his golf career and clearly stung him.

The U.S. had dodged a potential bullet.

There was, however, a different bullet coming from overseas the same day that the Mickelson-Sutton drama unfolded, and it was headed right for the European team room.

Pete Willett, the third of the four Willett brothers, had become a minor celebrity in England in April in the wake of his live tweets that followed his brother from Augusta's back nine into the green jacket at the Masters.

As a drama teacher, he was clearly well read and literate. His writing style was clever and funny, and his connection to the Masters champion made him an in-demand writer, especially in golf circles.

He had been writing a column for something called *National Club*

Golfer and, naturally, wrote about the Ryder Cup and his brother's debut there for the online issue of the magazine that came out the week of the matches.

A lot of the piece was about how much he enjoyed the Ryder Cup and how thrilled he was that his brother was going to be part of it. He also broke the players down into six categories: beautiful, brilliant, bland, brainless, boisterous, and bastards. The last was described as "the type of student that will plan maliciously and destroy indiscriminately—the type of golfer that is a vice-captain for Team USA." That was a clear shot across the bow of Tiger Woods.

That was mild, though, compared with his thoughts on the American fans. It was here that Willett's razor-sharp humor—emphasis on the razor—came out.

"For the Americans to stand a chance of winning, they need their baying mob of imbeciles to caress their egos every step of the way.... They [Europe] need to silence the pudgy, basement-dwelling irritants stuffed on cookie dough and pissy beer, pausing between mouthfuls of hotdog so they can scream 'Baba booey' until their jelly faces turn red. They need to stun the angry, unwashed Make America Great Again swarm, desperately guarding their concealed-carry compensators and belting out a mini-erection inducing 'mashed potato,' hoping to impress their cousin."

There was more: "They need to smash the obnoxious dads with their shiny teeth, Lego man hair, medicated ex-wives, and resentful children. Squeezed into their cargo shirts and boating shoes, they'll bellow 'get in the hole' whilst high-fiving all the other members of the Dentists Big Game Hunt Society. Team Europe need to silence these cretins quickly."

There was clearly a lot of tongue-in-cheek here along with parody and hyperbole. Some of it was funny; some was accurate (see "get in the hole"), and some was pretty mean. But Willett wasn't quite finished.

"I'm realistic enough to admit that I will struggle to resist the occasional capitalized tweet (I'll keep the syllable count low for the sake of the dim Yanks).... I'll try to support gracefully by embracing the same sense of fair-mindedness that has permeated this unbiased article. If not, the Americans will claim their second victory this century... those fat, stupid, greedy, classless, bastards."

It was Wednesday afternoon when his story began making the rounds at Hazeltine. Players on the golf course could be seen showing one another phones as word about the piece spread.

"I knew as soon as I saw it that it was going to be trouble," Sergio García said. "It was an impossible situation for Danny. It was his brother, not someone he could just attack for writing it, even if a lot of it wasn't right."

Rory McIlroy felt much the same way. "We all felt for Danny," he said. "He was kind of an innocent bystander in it all. The worst thing was the timing—two days before the matches began."

The American reaction wasn't as sympathetic, although Mickelson, perhaps a bit relieved that his Sutton takedown was no longer the big story, said later it didn't bother him at all. "I barely paid any attention to it," he said. "People say things, people write things. It wasn't as if Danny or any of the European players said it. I didn't think it was a big deal."

Others did. "It was stupid and mean-spirited," Zach Johnson said. "It really made me angry."

"I know the guy is his brother," Brandt Snedeker said. "But what he should have said was 'My brother's an idiot.'"

The two people who had to figure out a way to deal with it right away were Darren Clarke and Willett.

Until that point, no one had been having a better time than Willett. He had wanted to play the Ryder Cup since he was a kid, and now the moment had finally arrived.

"It really hit me on Sunday night when we had a team dinner before we flew out of Heathrow in the morning," he said. "I looked around at all that had been done by staff and others to make everything as easy as possible for us to just focus on playing golf and realized how massive the whole thing really was.

"When we arrived, I was like a kid in a candy store. I loved wearing the uniforms; I loved practicing with the guys knowing we were all on the same side—which isn't the case, of course, week to week. I loved spending time with the lads in the team room. It was all great. Every bit of it."

And then it all changed. "I knew right away the rest of the week wasn't going to be the same," Willett said. "I tried to take the approach, 'It's done, nothing you can do. Say you're sorry because it's the right thing to do and try to move on.'" He paused. "Easy to say, not so easy to do."

Clarke was handed a copy of the story by European Tour media official Scott Crockett early on Wednesday afternoon.

"When I read it, my eyes rolled into the back of my head," Clarke said. "I knew right away this was a problem we were going to have to deal with. I had to go out on the golf course to talk to Danny about it right away."

The issue, more than anything, was the timing: two days before the matches started. "The story itself, looked at in a certain way, was funny," Clarke said. "I think we [British/Irish] tend to enjoy sarcasm in our humor more than Americans do."

Clarke was right about that. Willett knew his brother was writing with his tongue in his cheek and that there wasn't any *real* ill will in the piece. But he also knew it wouldn't be seen that way. Not in Middle America, and not two days before the Ryder Cup began.

"It was all about the timing," he agreed. "That's what I knew was going to be the problem right away."

As luck—good or bad, depending on your point of view—would have it, Willett's pre-Cup interview was scheduled for Thursday morning. He knew he was going to be bombarded with questions about Pete.

Willett spoke to Davis Love and several members of the American team on Wednesday night at the dinner for the two teams. He apologized, and they all said essentially the same thing: not your fault.

"You could see that he genuinely felt awful," Love said later. "I felt sorry for him."

Willett spoke to his brother on the phone twice that day, basically to say, "What were you thinking?" Pete said he was sorry. He had been trying to be funny—much of what he'd said *had* been funny—but the timing, for his brother's sake, was brutal.

Willett played a practice round Thursday morning before he met with the media in the early afternoon. At that point, the crowd response to him hadn't been too bad. But word was only beginning to spread, and many people weren't aware of it. Plus, there wasn't too much heckling going on in the practice rounds.

After moderator John Dever had asked the obligatory happy-talk, welcome-to-the-Ryder-Cup opening question, the floor was open to the media.

First question: "Danny, could you give us an idea of how the conversation went with your brother last night?"

"About the same as our conversation yesterday afternoon," Willett answered.

Before the press conference was over, Willett had been asked fourteen questions. The first twelve were about his brother in one form or another. Someone asked—jokingly—if this would affect the Christmas present he bought him.

Willett kept repeating he was sorry it had happened; that he'd apologized; and that he did not agree with what his brother had written. "Let's be honest," he said at one point. "If his last name wasn't Willett, we wouldn't be talking about this."

He was right. But Pete's last name was Willett, and his brother—and his parents and his wife, who were there walking inside the ropes—weren't going to escape what he had written until their plane was off the ground headed for home on Monday. That was a long way from Thursday afternoon.

Willett decided he needed to get away from the crowds, which were getting louder and more abusive as time went on. So, rather than go to the range, where the grandstand was packed, he and his caddie, Jonathan Smart, headed to a spot far from the clubhouse—the 5th tee—with a bag of range balls.

"I needed to work on some things with my driver," Willett said. "I wasn't very happy with the way I was driving the ball, but I really didn't want to go to the range. The 5th is a tight driving hole, and it was way out there where there weren't many people around since everyone was pretty much done playing and was getting ready for the [opening] ceremony. It was a good place to go for me, quiet, out of the way, so Jonny and I went there."

Willett had been hitting balls for a while when he saw a cart carrying Clarke and vice captain Thomas Björn heading in his direction. He suspected it wasn't a good thing.

Clarke had discussed the situation with his vice captains, in part because he wanted their input, and in part because he had decided before the matches began that he wouldn't make any important decision without hearing from them first.

"We talked it all around," Clarke said. "In the end it was pretty unanimous that we had to make a change. Friday morning at the Ryder Cup is always charged with emotion, regardless of circumstances. I just thought it would be better for Danny and for everyone if we held him out until the afternoon."

Willett had been scheduled to play in the morning foursomes with Lee Westwood. The decision was made to put Thomas Pieters into that slot.

Clarke told Willett what he had decided and why. He didn't expect Willett to be happy with the decision—and he wasn't.

"I'd worked fifteen years really to get to this moment," he said. "To hear my name called out onstage [at the opening ceremony] and on the 1st tee on Friday morning at the Ryder Cup. To feel that adrenaline. I felt like I'd earned it, and now it was being taken away from me because of something completely out of my control.

"Plus, Darren could have held me out until Sunday morning and I was still going to get shit from the fans. That was just a fact. So, if it was going to happen anyway, why change the lineup?"

Clarke didn't disagree. "Making that decision and then telling Danny was probably the hardest thing I did all week. He's right that he was going to get a going-over from the fans regardless of when he played. I just didn't think it should be Friday morning."

Willett wasn't going to argue, because he knew it was pointless and because arguing wasn't the right thing to do.

"You're part of a team, you do what the captain tells you to do," he said. "I knew Clarkie was doing what he thought was best for the team, and that was his job. But did I agree with the decision—no. Part of me knew it was coming but even so, it was gut-wrenching. My feeling was, we thought this was a good pairing, let's stick with it. The shit was going to come regardless.

"I'd actually started to hit the ball better just before Clarkie and Thomas came out there. When we finished talking, I just picked up the balls and we walked in. I didn't want to practice anymore. It was very difficult, to say the least. I was truly sad about it."

The opening ceremony was scheduled to start at four p.m. on the back of the driving range. There was seating for about 1,500 people, but many in the crowd—there were about forty-five thousand people on the grounds that day, and roughly thirty thousand stayed for the ceremony—stood in a sea of (mostly) red-white-and-blue surrounding the seating area and the giant stage set up at the front of where the seats were located.

The two captains had to submit their pairings for Friday morning's foursomes by three o'clock. Both had known for a while whom they would be sending out the first morning. Europe was going to lead off with Henrik Stenson and Justin Rose, their best team at Gleneagles. The Americans were going to counter with Jordan Spieth and Patrick Reed—

their best team in Scotland. No one was the least bit surprised that both captains were leading with strength.

Phil Mickelson and Rickie Fowler would play second for the Americans, going against McIlroy and Andrew Sullivan—Clarke hoping that Sullivan could lean on McIlroy's experience. Sergio García and Martin Kaymer, another seasoned team, would be next for Europe against Jimmy Walker and Zach Johnson. The U.S. would send Dustin Johnson—who had been the best player in the world all year—and Matt Kuchar out last. The one real surprise—to the fans anyway—was Europe's last duo: Lee Westwood and Thomas Pieters.

That hadn't been the plan. Clarke had to play at least two rookies in every session. His plan had been to pair Sullivan with McIlroy all along. Willett was supposed to be the other rookie in the morning session, paired with Westwood, who was a good friend and a mentor.

"Pete-gate" had changed that plan.

"It certainly wasn't what we wanted to do," Ian Poulter said. "But I think we all agreed that putting Danny out there the first morning when there's so much emotion on the 1st tee and in those first matches would be asking too much. On the one hand you can say, 'He's the Masters champion, he can handle pressure,' but on the other hand he's still a Ryder Cup rookie and nothing really prepares you for that feeling. You take all that and add what we knew some in the crowd were going to do to him, and it made sense to let him get the feel for the 1st tee in the morning and then play in the afternoon."

Golfers often use the phrase "black clouded" to describe a run of bad luck. Pete Willett's column had indeed put a black cloud over his brother's head . . . and there were plenty of Pete's "targets" who were ready to make sure the cloud followed Danny all weekend long.

Twenty

T HERE WERE NO dark clouds in the sky on Thursday as the players completed their final preparations and got ready for the opening ceremony.

There was no doubt that the European team—Danny Willett aside—was having more fun than the Americans. Which made sense, since they were the team playing with house money.

Most of the players played only nine holes on Thursday. By now they felt familiar with the golf course and wanted to be rested for Friday morning.

"Last thing you want to do is wear yourself out at that point," Henrik Stenson said. "Most weeks you're playing for real on Thursday."

Stenson, Justin Rose, Rory McIlroy, and Andy Sullivan were the first group out for Europe on Thursday. There was little doubt they were going to be two of the four Euro pairings the next morning: Stenson and Rose; McIlroy and Sullivan. The four of them were playing a friendly match and, when they got to the 8th green, after their real putts, they began trying putts from various spots on the green.

After Sullivan had missed a 10-footer, McIlroy tried it from the same spot. He missed too. Then he tried again. After another miss, a voice could be heard clearly from the crowd, "Hey, *I* could make that putt."

Stenson, never one to pass on a potential laugh, walked over to the ropes and motioned for the heckler to come out and see if he could make the putt. The heckler agreed. McIlroy handed him a putter and, "just to make it real for him," Rose put down a hundred-dollar bill next to the ball.

The guy's name was Dave Johnson, and he had come over from his home in North Dakota to see the matches. He was wearing a red pull-over, blue jeans, boat shoes, and sunglasses. He looked the putt over briefly, then stabbed it at the hole. "If it doesn't go in, he's chipping," Stenson said later.

Except that it went in—banging the back of the cup. The crowd went nuts; Johnson went nuts too with an old Tiger Woods fist pump, and the players and caddies hugged Johnson and high-fived him. Stenson picked up the hundred-dollar bill and handed it to Rose, who presented it to Johnson.

Johnson got Rose to sign the bill and then went off to have his fifteen minutes of fame as a wave of print reporters descended on him to find out who he was. The case could be made that Johnson had just made the most lucrative putt in Ryder Cup history, since he made $100 and none of the players are paid once the matches begin.

Now, though, the fun was over. It was time to get serious.

The opening ceremony of the Ryder Cup has become a TV show. In fact, the Golf Channel actually had a thirty-minute *pre*–opening ceremony show. Not exactly the endless all-day Super Bowl pregame shows, but somewhat mind-boggling nevertheless.

Once the various singing groups and bands had been introduced and had performed, Jack Nicklaus and Tony Jacklin came out for their scripted remembrance of the 1969 "concession" match.

Then, finally, came what the roughly thirty thousand people who had packed every inch of available space at the back of the driving range around the seating area and the stage had come to see.

The players and the captains.

They marched in, solemnly circling the seating area to get to the stage. The wives and partners didn't get to walk in with them. They simply stepped out from behind an onstage curtain and took their seats in the back row. This was a long way from the 1993 opening ceremony, when the wives had been introduced at the Belfry with as much fanfare as the players.

When the American wives marched in that day, two by two in their matching outfits, Lewine Mair, the talented longtime golf writer for the London *Daily Telegraph,* gasped and said, "My God, they've all married the same woman." It appeared the American wives were all five-foot-ten-inch blondes, except for Melissa Lehman, a five-foot-ten-inch brunette.

The teams came last. Then came the speeches from various golf officials and—finally—the captains. Both Darren Clarke and Davis Love were eloquent, talking about their respect for each other, for the traditions of the Ryder Cup, and about Arnold Palmer—an add-on at the start of the week to each man's speech. Then they introduced their players—many wearing sunglasses that seemed out of place but were necessary to block the direct blaze of the sun.

And finally, just when everyone was pretty much ready to go home, the Friday morning matchups were announced. The players knew before-hand whom they were playing with and in what order, but they didn't know who their opponents were until they were actually announced by NBC's Dan Hicks, the MC for the ceremony.

When Hicks announced the second match, McIlroy and Sullivan against Mickelson and Fowler, McIlroy jumped from his seat, put his fists in the air, and high-fived Sullivan.

"I was hoping to play against Phil," he said later. "We'd played twice before [in four-ball/foursomes but never in singles] and he'd won both. I wanted a crack at him right out of the gate. Plus, I wanted to show the guys I was ready to go emotionally, that if they wanted to look to me to lead, I was ready to go."

Mickelson was far more controlled. In fact, when Love had intro-duced him, he had stood up quickly, keeping his sunglasses on, waved briefly, and sat back down.

"The opening ceremony is the moment when your stomach really begins to churn," he said later. "The talk's over. It's time to get serious. You know the golf course and now you know who your opponents are going to be. For me, this time around especially, I was feeling the pres-sure that I knew was coming the next day. I'd put myself in a position where I was going to be the guy looked at and examined and either praised or criticized when the matches were over.

"I wasn't afraid of it. I'd done a lot of it on purpose. But I would have been crazy to not be aware of it."

The two U.S. rookies—Brooks Koepka and Ryan Moore—would sit

out in the morning. Europe would play all six of its veterans and two rookies—Sullivan and Pieters. The other four would get their first taste of the Ryder Cup later.

One person who was convinced the Americans were ready to play was Butch Harmon. He had three of his pupils—Brandt Snedeker, Jimmy Walker, and Rickie Fowler—on the U.S. team, in addition to Mickelson, with whom he had worked for almost nine years.

"I first went to the Ryder Cup as a kid in 1959," he said. "I've done the last eleven on TV [for Sky, the U.K. carrier of the matches], and I've always had the chance to be around the guys. The whole week felt different this time.

"I don't think there's ever been a U.S. team under the pressure these guys were under because of everything that had happened dating to Gleneagles, and you know what, I think they *liked* it. They thrived on the pressure. They all said the same thing to me on Wednesday and Thursday: can't wait to get started."

There was one other thing Harmon sensed. "This really *was* a team. It wasn't twelve guys playing golf, it was one team playing golf. That was different."

Harmon and others noticed one other thing: almost no one was playing Ping-Pong in the team room and *no one* was talking about it. In the past, the Ping-Pong table and talk about who won and who lost were about the only thing all the American players seemed to have in common. Now the two tables stood empty most of the time. Everyone was genuinely enjoying themselves with one another.

That night, after everyone was finished eating dinner in the team room, Jordan Spieth stood up and asked for everybody's attention.

Even though he was playing in his second Ryder Cup and his fourth international match (two Presidents Cups) as a pro, Spieth was still the youngest player on the team, having just turned twenty-three at the end of July. Patrick Reed, who was twenty-six and whose birthday was in August, and Brooks Koepka, twenty-six in May, were the next youngest.

And yet Spieth understood that, because of his place in the game and his past experiences, he needed to be one of this team's leaders. Others had played more often—Mickelson was in his eleventh Ryder Cup, Zach Johnson was in his fifth, and no one else had played in more than three—but Spieth knew that he and Reed were being looked at by their teammates as leaders on this team.

Mickelson was still the grand old man, but he was forty-six and was a lot closer to being a captain than he was to being the pissed-off rookie of 1995 who couldn't believe that Lanny Wadkins sat him down on Friday morning.

Now Spieth was standing in front of his teammates and basically saying, "I get it, I know I have to be one of *the* guys, not just *a* guy, this time around and in the future."

He would never describe what he said that night as "taking leadership" in the team, but that was the way the others took it—and wanted to take it.

Spieth is not a spur-of-the-moment kind of guy. Unlike McIlroy, who often transfers his thoughts to his mouth quickly, he thinks most things out before acting. He knew that both Mickelson and Love wanted him to put himself into a leadership role, and he had been thinking about it during the week, even voicing to his girlfriend, Annie Verrett, that he felt he should say something at some point.

The question was, when?

"I waited a couple of days because I wanted to get a feel for the mood of the team, for the golf course, for everything going on around us," he said. "I'd heard all the talk about how the Americans *had* to win this time and the pressure we were all under. I wanted to say something that might relieve the pressure a little bit, maybe give the guys some confidence.

"Things had gotten quiet in the team room on Thursday, and we were all going to bed early since we had such an early start, so I decided, 'This is the time,' and I just stood up."

Spieth wanted his teammates to know how much confidence he had in them—"because I really did," he said. "I wasn't trying to give anyone a pep talk. I was just telling them how I felt."

Long after the matches had ended, he could repeat most of what he had said, almost verbatim: partly because it meant a good deal to him, partly because he has a steel-trap memory, especially when the subject is golf.

"I just want you guys to know that even though this is only my second Ryder Cup, I've played with all you guys quite a bit," he began. "And I've played with everyone on the European team a good deal too. I feel like I know your games and I know their games, and here's what I think: We're better than they are. We're just better players. I believe we can win *all* the matches, not just win the Cup, win *all* the matches. There's no reason why we can't go out tomorrow morning and sweep them, 4–0. Patrick and I will get out there and set the pace, and the rest of you guys follow us. And when we're up 4–0, there's no reason to stop. Just keep on going, keep on winning."

He reminded them of something Tiger Woods had said to him before the week. "Tiger told me when he was playing his best golf, he always played every hole backward in his mind, from green back to the tee. He could see his putts going in the hole every time. If Tiger says that works, it gets my attention. We all know this golf course now, and we know if we play with them from tee to green, we're better than they are on the greens.

"We should go out there with the mind-set that we're going to kick their ass, because there's no reason not to. We should think we're going to be perfect against these guys—perfect. Don't be scared to sweep them in any session; in every session. They don't have to win *any* matches."

Spieth had everyone's attention before he finished. "I'd heard all the noise all week," he said. "I knew some of it was rhetoric, but I really wanted everyone to be thinking, 'Let's go out there and *trounce* these guys.' If I had thought we weren't good enough to do that, if I had doubts about the team, I'd have said something different. I'd have talked about being patient and not getting down if things went wrong.

"But I didn't feel that way. I really thought we were ready to go out and beat them, and I wanted them to know I felt that way. I wasn't trying to insult the Europeans at all. I knew they had great players—we all knew that. But I honestly believed we were *better,* that there wasn't one match we couldn't stand up on the 1st tee and not have a chance to win. So why not go ahead and win each one?"

When Spieth finished, his teammates came up to tell him how much they appreciated what he'd said and the way he'd said it.

Mickelson put an arm around him and said, "That was perfect. Absolutely perfect."

Later, Mickelson said there was no moment that meant more to him during the week than Spieth's Thursday night talk.

"It wasn't so much what he said but how he said it," Mickelson said. "In many ways it was typical of Jordan—wise and understanding beyond his years. He'd clearly thought about what he was going to say, and the message was 'Follow me. We're all in this together, but I can handle being the leader.'

"It was important for someone who wasn't me to stand up and say that. It was important it be one of the younger guys because, let's face it, we older guys only have so much time left in Ryder Cup. It was *best* that it was Jordan because, regardless of how old he is, he's already a great player, an important player, and a guy everyone looks up to.

"Of all the moments I remember about the week—and there were a lot of them—that's the one that stands out the most. It was like a passing of the torch. And it came at exactly the right moment."

Love and Mickelson had both been pushing Spieth all week to say something to the team. They both knew that, in spite of his youth, the other players already looked up to him because of his play and because of his smarts and maturity.

There were no more speeches when Spieth finished. It was time to get some sleep and go play golf.

Sunrise on Friday morning in Chaska, Minnesota, was at 7:12 a.m. Hazeltine National Golf Club was alive with noise and nerves long before the sun showed up.

Spieth and Reed were the first two players to arrive, both on the putting green an hour before their 7:35 tee time. The forecast was for more perfect weather, including an afternoon high of about seventy, but with the sun not yet up and the practice areas lit only by temporary lights put in for the week, it was quite brisk—to put it mildly—when the two players ventured outside. Spieth was bundled up. Reed was in short sleeves.

He had adopted this approach in Scotland, partly because he just didn't feel right wearing extra clothing, partly because he knew it had a psychological effect on his opponents. Much like the pitcher who shows up on a forty-five-degree day in April in short sleeves or the football player who goes bare-armed in subfreezing temperatures, Reed wanted his opponents to know that he was tougher than they were.

"I actually tried wearing a sweater for about two holes at Gleneagles," he said. "I didn't like it, so I just pulled it off and went from there. It was freezing most of the time there, but I was actually hot a lot of the time in my short sleeves. I never really felt the cold."

Reed and Spieth were the perfect pairing for a lot of reasons. They'd known each other since junior golf in spite of the three-year age difference, because Spieth had been so precocious as a young player. They were both intense on the course, though in different ways. And their off-course personas were perfect fodder for the media.

"He's the golden child," Reed said, laughing. "I'm the villain."

Reed's "villain" persona had changed in the eyes of many after Gleneagles. He'd gone 3-0-1, and a lot of players on the team had come away with a different feeling about him, having spent time with him in the team room. There was never much doubt in anyone's mind that he and Spieth should lead off for the U.S. As Mickelson said, in many ways this needed to be their team.

When Reed and Spieth appeared on the putting green, they were cheered lustily by the fans who were already beginning to pack the grandstands around the 1st tee. The gates had been opened at six thirty, and many fans had sprinted in the direction of the 1st tee as soon as they cleared security and were on the property. This wasn't Augusta. There were no rules against running, and a lot of people set off at a dead run to grab a spot.

Jeff Hintz's music—complete with a DJ—was already cranking up. When there was a break, fans from both sides burst into song on their own. The Americans far outnumbered the Europeans, but the "Olé" song was getting a good workout from the Euro fans before a ball had been put into the air.

The fans could actually see Reed and Spieth even though they were behind the grandstands, because there was a giant screen showing them as they arrived to start warming up—literally and figuratively. The other players began making their way to the practice areas soon afterward—McIlroy the last of the eight players in the first two groups to show up, not because he didn't know what time zone he was in but because he's never been big on lengthy warm-ups.

"Especially when it's cold," he said.

Shortly before seven thirty, the four players scheduled to play first began the most stressful walk in golf: from the practice area to the 1st tee on the first day of the Ryder Cup. It was 114 steps from the edge of the putting green, across the range, and down the path to the fifteen steps that led up to the tee. The PGA of America's new slogan for the Ryder Cup—"Where Legends Are Forged"—was emblazoned on each step.

Reed remembered feeling as if all the oxygen had been sucked out of the air on the 1st tee at Gleneagles. One of the reasons for feeling that way at Hazeltine might have been how packed the teeing ground was with people. The captains were there; vice captains too. Officials from the PGA of America and the European Tour were there, as were the eight players sitting out the morning matches, who were there to observe and feel the atmosphere. TV crews were everywhere.

The sun had been up for only a few minutes and the chill was still very much in the air. No one seemed to feel it—especially the players.

The only time the tee got quiet was for a moment of silence in honor of Arnold Palmer. On the back of the tee, where everyone could see it, was Palmer's bag from the 1975 Ryder Cup when he had been the U.S. captain at Laurel Valley.

Both teams loved seeing Palmer's bag. Ian Poulter was the first to cross the tee to take a picture of it. Others—not those playing—followed suit.

"I was just drinking it all in," Spieth said. "Arnold's golf bag being there was so cool. The whole thing was cool. I actually felt bad for Patrick because he had to get ready to hit. I could just kind of take it all in."

Finally, the four players were introduced and Rose, teeing off on the odd holes for Europe, hit the opening tee shot of the competition. Reed followed for the U.S. Rose just missed the fairway, Reed found it. Spieth and Stenson both hit solid second shots onto the green.

The 1st was a long par-4—490 yards—but fairly straightforward with an uphill second shot to the green. Spieth's shot drifted about 15 feet left of the hole; Stenson's was 10 feet behind it. Birdie chances for both teams.

Reed missed, the putt drifting just low on the right side of the hole. That left Rose with a chance to give Europe a quick lead, exactly the kind of crowd-quieting start that Pete Willett had said was imperative.

He missed, the putt veering right at the last possible second. A huge cheer, more of relief than anything else, went up from the crowd.

At the 2nd, a shorter, easier par-4, Reed hit his second shot to 10 feet. After Stenson had failed to make his long birdie putt, it was Spieth's turn; the best putter in the world had a makeable birdie putt. The Ryder Cup had been under way for twenty minutes and already the crowd was holding its breath.

It was one of those "every hole is like the back nine of a major" moments. Or, as Spieth might describe it, one of those "knock that shit in" moments.

Spieth knocked it in.

"I really didn't think that much of it at the time," Spieth said. "It was nice to see red go up on the board early like that. I knew that would be good for the guys behind us to see."

The early birdie set a tone for the morning, one that the U.S. desperately needed. After all the talk about the "best team ever assembled" and how the task force and Love had given the players the input they needed to be prepared to succeed, a quick European start might have deflated everyone on the American side.

Instead, it was Europe that struggled all morning. Mickelson, clearly tight, had trouble finding fairways throughout, but Sullivan wasn't much better. Mickelson and Fowler, 2 down through fourteen holes, rallied to win one up. Sullivan had actually played solidly the first fourteen holes. He'd holed a 12-foot par putt at the 11th hole for a halve and set McIlroy up for a birdie at the par-3 13th.

But he hit a poor chip on 15 that led to a door-opening bogey. After the Americans birdied the 16th to tie the match, Sullivan's tee shot found the water on 17. That gave the Americans the lead. When McIlroy missed a long birdie putt at 18, Mickelson and Fowler had a surprising win.

That was the only match that went to 18. Spieth and Reed never let up on Stenson and Rose and won 3 and 2. Sergio García and Martin Kaymer were one up on Zach Johnson and Jimmy Walker through eleven holes before they bogeyed the 12th to open the door for the U.S. to win five straight holes and close out the match on 16. The fourth match was a virtual walkover. Westwood and Pieters bogeyed the first two holes and never got into the match, getting whipped, 5 and 4, by Dustin Johnson and Matt Kuchar.

Not surprisingly, Pieters was fighting first-time Ryder Cup nerves. But he really had no chance, because Westwood couldn't find the planet. Neither player hit a *fairway* on the front nine. The Americans probably could have both played left-handed and had a decent chance to win.

Since it was the only match to go the distance, Mickelson-Fowler versus McIlroy-Sullivan was the last match to finish. As McIlroy was lining up the birdie putt he needed to make at 18 to steal a halve, he heard someone yell out, "Get an American."

After missing the putt and shaking hands, McIlroy bolted quickly to the team room to cool down a little.

"I wasn't that upset about the heckler," he said later. "It was annoying, but a hostile crowd is part of playing on the road in the Ryder Cup.

What I was really upset was that we let that match get away from us. Honestly, the way Phil played, the places he hit some shots, we never should have lost. Rickie did it for them."

That match was a huge boost for the Americans: they'd won even though Mickelson didn't play very well, Fowler had won his first full point in nine Ryder Cup matches, and—most important—they had a 4–0 lead.

No one was more thrilled with the morning matches than Fowler. "Finally," he told Butch Harmon later. "Finally I won a full point. It felt *so* good to do that."

What's more, Fowler had been largely responsible for winning that point—which Harmon pointed out to him.

It was the first time the U.S. had led 4–0 since 1975, when their captain had been Arnold Palmer.

Karma?

"I think wanting to win for Seve's memory gave us a boost in 2012," Ian Poulter said. "I think, as much as all of us on both teams loved Arnold Palmer, his death gave the Americans a little something extra to play for."

Not long after the last of the four morning matches had teed off, Mark Windschitl, having watched the opening shots on the 1st tee, walked inside for a cup of coffee. He was scheduled to head to the 6th hole later in the morning to work there as a marshal.

In a sense, Windschitl was the host for everyone on the grounds at Hazeltine, since he was the mayor of Chaska, Minnesota. Chaska, as a sign on I-12 East told people, had a population of 23,770 as of the 2010 census. "Probably closer to twenty-five thousand now," Windschitl said. "We've grown since the census."

Windschitl had become mayor in 2010. He had just retired after working for twenty-seven years as a firefighter in nearby St. Louis Park. "Never been in politics in my life," he said, laughing. "I'm not a Democrat or a Republican. Don't get into the partisan stuff at all. Just threw my hat in the ring because I'd retired [as a chief] and figured why not? I've lived here almost my entire life."

Four years later, Windschitl and several members of the city council had flown to Gleneagles to get a feel for the Ryder Cup and to let people know about Chaska—and Minnesota. They'd set up an information booth and had been stunned at the number of people who thought the nearest major city to the golf course was Chicago—six hours away by car.

"People kept saying, 'Really, Minneapolis has an airport?'" Windschitl said with a smile. "I think we were actually pretty helpful to quite a few people."

Windschitl and his four-member council wanted people to remember that Chaska was where Hazeltine was located and for it not to be, as he put it, "a forgotten city."

So they came up with an idea to remind people coming to the golf course exactly where they were: painting a sign on the footbridge across I-12 just before the exit for the course. The problem was, the Minnesota Department of Transportation wanted nothing to do with the idea.

"They said, 'If we give you a permit, we'll have to give one to everyone who wants one,'" Windschitl said. "We said, 'How many other towns in Minnesota are likely to host the Ryder Cup?!'"

Just when it appeared the idea would die on the vine—or in red tape—Windschitl attended the "year out" event in downtown Minneapolis.

"We were standing there before everything started and someone said to me, 'Look, there's the governor,'" Windschitl said. "I turned around and, sure enough, there he was—standing by himself. I figured I had nothing to lose."

And so Windschitl walked over to Governor Mark Dayton, introduced himself, and told him about what he and the Chaska council wanted to do.

"That's a great idea," Dayton said. "You should do it."

Windschitl explained the problem with the Minnesota DOT.

"Within a couple of days, the permit was in the works," Windschitl said. "Not sure it would have gotten done if I hadn't run into the governor."

The sign went up about two months before the matches began. It read, "Welcome to Chaska, Host of the 2016 Ryder Cup."

The permit the Minnesota DOT issued was a temporary one, meaning the sign was supposed to come down when the matches were over.

"We'll deal with that when the time comes," Windschitl said. "It should be permanent."

In the meantime, he was marshaling, helping out in the "Welcome to Minnesota" booth, and watching as a fan. Best of all, at the last possible moment, the PGA had come through with a coveted parking pass.

"A ticket I could get, no problem," he said with a grin. "The parking pass was gold."

By the end of the morning, the U.S. team was brimming with confidence, which was understandable. But there was no panic in the European team room during the lunch break, only some frustration at letting at least a point or two get away that could have been—should have been—winnable.

As soon as Westwood and Pieters shook hands with Johnson and Kuchar, Westwood sought Clarke out and told him he shouldn't put him back out to play in the afternoon.

"I needed to get on the range with [teacher] Pete [Cowen] and figure out what was going on with my swing. I didn't want to go back out there until I had found something that would work. I told Darren I'd let him know when I thought I could help by being back in the team."

A number of players wondered how Clarke would react to the poor start. They knew how important the captaincy was to him. And they'd all been witness to his temper at different times.

"I was, honestly, pleasantly surprised," McIlroy said. "Darren has a temper, everyone knows that. And there we were after the first morning down 4–0, at least in part because we hadn't played well. I thought he might lose it—which, actually, would have been justified.

"But he was completely calm during the lunch break. Maybe it helped that there isn't much time before you have to turn around and go play again, but he just said, 'Early days, boys. Okay, we've dug ourselves a hole, but there's a lot of golf yet. Let's just try to win each session and work our back into this. And, in truth, that's what we did.'"

With Westwood out of the picture, Clarke decided to pair Pieters with McIlroy. He put Rose and Stenson back out as his leadoff team, convinced they would play better in the four-ball than they had in the morning foursomes. Both were capable of making a lot of birdies. He decided to pair García with countryman Rafael Cabrera-Bello, the most experienced—at thirty-two—of his rookies, and get Willett onto the golf course partnering Kaymer. His hope was that Willett's enthusiasm would get Kaymer going.

Love might have been tempted to stick with what was working, but he knew that four-ball was a very different game than foursomes and he wanted to be sure that all twelve of his players had a match under their belts by sundown on the first day.

Having won his gamble by putting Mickelson and Fowler out in four-somes, he decided not to push his luck and gave them the afternoon off. This wasn't a huge surprise, since Love and Mickelson had talked often about Mickelson not playing five times—perhaps not even playing four times, depending on how the matches were going. At forty-six, he was six years older than anyone else on the U.S. team and twenty-three years older than Spieth.

Love also decided to rest Zach Johnson and Jimmy Walker in order to make sure all four players who had watched in the morning—J. B. Holmes, Ryan Moore, Brandt Snedeker, and Brooks Koepka—would play. He paired Holmes and Moore, the strong, silent types, with each other—and sent Snedeker, who could relax almost anyone, out with Koepka.

Clarke's calm demeanor at lunch paid off for Europe in the afternoon. The opening match was the same as it had been in the morning: Spieth and Reed against Stenson and Rose.

Spieth and Reed played well—they were a combined six under par. But they had no chance. Stenson and Rose combined to make ten bird-ies in fourteen holes, made no mistakes, and turned the tables from the morning with a 5-and-4 win.

Seeing the blue up on the board early had much the same effect on the Europeans that the red had on the Americans in the morning.

"We knew we hadn't played well in the morning—none of us really," Stenson said. "We knew though that we were good enough to come back. It isn't as if we hadn't had to come from behind in the past."

With Cabrera-Bello playing very well, he and García built a big lead on Holmes and Moore and held on for a 3-and-2 win.

The only match that went well for the Americans was the last one. Snedeker and Koepka were brilliant; Kaymer and Willett were not. Willett didn't play especially well, but he played better than Kaymer, who failed to make a single birdie.

Not surprisingly, the match was sullied by the behavior of a few fans. Willett was booed on the 1st tee—which he'd expected—and promptly pumped his opening drive down the middle.

"That was a good moment," he said later. "One of the few."

But the "one percenters," as Jordan Spieth later dubbed them, wouldn't let up. They yelled profanities at Willett's family—his wife Nicole and his parents were walking inside the ropes—and often yelled things like "Put it in the bunker" or "Go home, Danny, we hate you" at Willett while he was trying to address his ball. Finally, on the 6th tee, Snedeker and Koepka turned to the fans to try to quiet them. They did—briefly. When Willett duck-hooked his drive a moment later, a huge cheer went up.

The shame of it was that the heckling overshadowed how well Snedeker and Koepka played en route to an easy 5-and-4 win. Their victory gave the U.S. a 5–2 lead with one match still on the golf course.

That was McIlroy and Pieters versus Dustin Johnson and Kuchar. Pieters had gotten past his rookie jitters and was clearly a lot more comfortable playing with a hot McIlroy than a cold-as-ice Westwood. Both men poured in one birdie after another and built a 4-up lead after thirteen holes. But Johnson and Kuchar hung in and won the next two holes to close the gap to 2 up with three holes to play.

By now, all the other players, the captains, the vice captains, and the wives and partners were following the match. If the Americans could rally to pull out a halve, it would be huge psychologically and would give them a solid 5½–2½ lead. If Europe hung on to win, the margin would be just 5–3 and the momentum going into Saturday would be on their side.

McIlroy made certain his team went home Friday night feeling good about itself.

The 16th—normally the 7th pre–Ryder Cup—is a 572-yard par-5, a true risk/reward hole, with water down the left side of the fairway and left of the green. McIlroy, perhaps the only player in the world who can come close to matching Dustin Johnson off the tee, hit a massive drive and—unlike Johnson—found the fairway. After Johnson and Kuchar both failed to find the green, McIlroy, with 228 yards to the hole (meaning his drive had traveled almost 350 yards), hit a four-iron to 18 feet, making him the only player in the group with a chance to make eagle.

Worst case, he'd make a birdie and the Americans would have to come up with a birdie themselves to get a halve and keep the match alive. McIlroy removed any suspense by draining the eagle putt.

Match over; U.S. lead down to 5–3. But McIlroy wasn't finished.

As soon as the putt went into the hole he let out a primal scream, both arms in the air. He turned and bowed to the crowd. Then he did it again, clearly mouthing a not-nice word as he did so.

"We'd been hearing from them all day—certainly not all of them— but some of them," he said later. "I wanted to let them know we weren't going to be intimidated, that we were here to compete regardless. I was a little bit wired, sure, but I also wanted my teammates to feed a little bit off my emotion."

They did, charging McIlroy and Pieters to congratulate them.

"I'd rather be ahead 5–3 than behind 5–3," Clarke said. "But this feels like a pretty good 5–3, even though we're behind."

Love knew exactly what he meant. He pointed out to the media that a 5–3 lead was a good start for his team. He also knew that Clarke's words to his team at lunch had been accurate: there was a lot of golf left to be played and a lot more work still to be done.

Twenty-One

MANY PEOPLE WERE surprised by Rory McIlroy's reaction to the last putt of the day. They had seen McIlroy wound up at critical moments in major championships, but had never seen him direct hostility toward fans.

"I think part of it was I just wasn't used to hearing people say some of the things they were saying to us," he said. "I'm accustomed to being supported in the U.S. because most of the time that's the way golf fans are. They root *for* players, not against them.

"The Ryder Cup's different. There are times in Europe when fans cheer for bad shots or missed putts by Americans who they normally want to see play well. I get that. It's part of what makes the event unique.

"Overall, the fans that weekend were great. They were four, five times louder than Medinah. I think we all loved that. But there were a few that were over-the-top—way over-the-top. To me, that's a concern going forward. The Ryder Cup gets bigger and bigger all the time, and there needs to be some way to keep things from getting out of hand.

"I understand that when you're letting fans in at six thirty in the morning and selling beer, that some of them aren't going to be in great shape by the afternoon. Maybe they need to limit that somehow in the future.

"Golf isn't like other sports because the fans are so close to the players. In football, if fans are yelling profanities at the players, they never hear it. They never see faces. There's a distance that makes it safe to yell pretty much whatever you want. That's just not the case in golf."

McIlroy has never been one to go "PC," as Jordan Spieth calls it. He answers questions honestly and isn't afraid to express his opinions or share his emotions. That had gotten him into trouble at the British Open that summer when he had been asked about his decision not to play in the Rio Olympics.

McIlroy was one of twenty-one players who qualified for the Olympics but chose not to go. None of the top four players in the world rankings—Dustin Johnson, Jason Day, Spieth, and McIlroy—opted to go. All four were nervous about the Zika virus, security, and the ridiculously compressed golf schedule for 2016. What's more, while all were intrigued by the idea of being Olympians, none had grown up with the Olympics as a dream, since golf hadn't been played in the Olympics since 1904.

Spieth had met with the media on the Tuesday before the Open began at Troon and had been asked to explain his decision not to go. He said all the right things about how much he hoped to play in the future, how it was the most difficult decision he'd ever made, how he knew he'd regret not being there.

"I meant what I said," Spieth said. "But I was also being PC, which I know I do at times." He smiled. "Unlike Rory."

McIlroy came in not long after Spieth. The subject of the Olympics came up, and someone asked in a self-righteous tone if the argument could be made that McIlroy and the other stars who had chosen to skip the Olympics were "letting the game down, since so many non–golf fans will be watching in Rio?"

McIlroy usually thinks before he answers a question, takes a deep breath, and then gives an honest answer. This time there was no pause and no deep breath. They weren't needed. The question annoyed him.

"I don't feel I've let the game down at all," he said. "I didn't get into golf to try and grow the game. I got into golf to try and win major championships . . . I got into golf to win. I didn't get into golf to get other people into the game.

"But look, I get where different people have different opinions. I'm very happy with the decision, and I have no regrets about it. I'll probably watch the Olympics, but I'm not sure golf will be one of the events I'll watch."

Someone asked which events he thought he'd watch.

"Probably events like track and field, swimming, diving. The stuff that matters."

Later, McIlroy would wish he'd left out the last four words or said "the more traditional Olympic sports" instead of "the stuff that matters."

Everything else he'd said was refreshingly honest—and was also guaranteed to get him buried by some in the media.

Spieth had gone back to the house near the golf course that he was sharing for the week of the Open with Zach Johnson, Daniel Berger, Smylie Kaufman, and Justin Thomas. He was watching McIlroy's interview with his roomies and a number of others.

"When it was over, someone turned to me and said, 'You need to send Rory a really nice bottle of wine,'" Spieth said. "Because *no one* is going to be talking about you withdrawing from the Olympics after that."

It was true. As soon as the McIlroy press conference concluded, Brandel Chamblee—someone who likes and admires McIlroy greatly—jumped on him with both feet.

"When Rory McIlroy's career is over, I think he will look back on that press conference as perhaps his lowest moment," Chamblee said.

Chamblee is one of golf's smartest people. That was one of his least smart comments. Even if McIlroy regretted more than the last four words—which he didn't—blowing a four-shot lead on the last day of the Masters would certainly rank well ahead of any press conference on the low moments list. So would walking off the golf course in 2013 at the Honda Classic in a snit and tossing a club into the water at Doral two years later.

Among many other moments.

"I like Brandel, I really do," McIlroy said, laughing. "I think he's smart and well prepared. But that one really surprised me."

At that point in time, McIlroy was far more concerned with a consistently balky putter than with people tsk-tsking over his decision not to play in the Olympics. It also helped that a number of star players— notably Jack Nicklaus—jumped in to defend him.

"I never thought about growing the game when I was playing," Nicklaus said. "That came *after* I wasn't playing anymore."

No athlete thinks about "growing the game" while he's competing. The two men who grew golf the most were Arnold Palmer and Tiger Woods. Palmer, as it happened, enjoyed interacting with people and did what came naturally to him when he wasn't on the golf course. His looks and charm, along with his bold playing style, grew the game.

Woods was 180 degrees different. It wasn't an accident that he named his yacht *Privacy* and did everything he could to stay away from the public and the media when he wasn't between the ropes or pitching a product.

But both grew the game. McIlroy has grown the game too by being a brilliant player and an approachable guy. Neither he nor any of the other players who decided against going to Rio had any obligation to play there, no matter how much the media or the people running the game—who were invested in the Olympics being successful both financially and emotionally—screamed.

The summer of 2016 was disappointing for McIlroy. He played well at Troon, finishing tied for fifth, but then missed the cut at the PGA on a golf course he thought a perfect fit for him.

"I honestly thought going into Thursday I had a real chance to win," he said. "Baltusrol seemed to be set up for my game—lot of long par-4s, two par-5s at the end. I felt great in the practice rounds. Then I got out there Thursday and couldn't buy a putt all day. Short ones, long ones—I was consistent. I missed them all."

He ended up shooting a four-over-par 74, which put him well outside the projected cut. He fought back the next day with a one-under-par 69, but missed the cut by one shot. That meant he had missed two cuts in majors in 2016—he'd also missed by one shot at the U.S. Open.

McIlroy's problem was evident to everyone in golf: his putter. He had never been a *great* putter, but because he was such a brilliant ball striker, he was often plenty good enough to win. And when he got hot with the putter, he was virtually unbeatable. That was what had led to him twice winning majors—the 2011 U.S. Open and the 2012 PGA—by eight shots.

Now, though, McIlroy was a mess. He kept trying to change his grip, his stance, his mental approach. Nothing was working. He was baffled and frustrated.

Then, in early August, he caught a break—although he didn't really know it at the time. Nike announced it was getting out of the golf equipment business. That meant that a number of players—most notably McIlroy and Tiger Woods—had to look for new equipment deals.

McIlroy had signed a huge deal with Nike at the beginning of 2013 and had needed a full year to get the hang of the new clubs. There had been other issues that year, but the new Nike clubs were certainly a factor working against him.

He had come back to win two majors in 2014 but, as with Woods, most players believed he won in spite of the Nike equipment, not because of it. The quality of the Nike clubs was one reason why the company was losing money even though it had Woods and McIlroy as its out-front promoters and had spent millions on advertising.

After Baltusrol, McIlroy decided that the demise of Nike's equipment division might be an opportunity for him. It wasn't that he was looking for any sort of lucrative new deal—that would come in time—it was that he thought it was time to go back to square one with his putting.

The week after the PGA, he flew to San Diego and went to Scotty Cameron's factory to try out new putters. "I figured since I wasn't committed to any company that I had an opportunity to just go and pick a putter I felt comfortable with—any putter," he said. He smiled. "I thought maybe it was some kind of a sign."

Since he was trying a new putter, he thought perhaps this was the time to try a new putting coach. He had worked with Dave Stockton for several years and, at times, had a good deal of success with him. But, as most players will do when they are struggling, he decided he needed a new voice in his ear, a different approach to solving the same problem.

"It's the nature of sports," said Butch Harmon, arguably golf's best swing coach ever. "I've been fired by the best: Greg Norman, Tiger Woods, Phil Mickelson among them. I think I helped all of them when I worked with them, and I think they all got to a point where they felt they needed a change. I get it. I don't think I stopped being a good teacher, but maybe they stopped hearing me after a while."

McIlroy felt that way about his putting. Like everything else in today's sports, golf coaching/teaching has become hyper-specialized. Most top players have a swing coach, a short-game coach, and a putting coach. There are exceptions: Jim Furyk has had one teacher/coach his entire life—his dad.

Mickelson had changed coaches in 2016, leaving Harmon after nine years to work with Andrew Getson. His play improved measurably in 2016, although it was worth noting that most of that improvement—statistically anyway—came in his short game, not necessarily because of the "new" swing he talked about loving so much.

McIlroy had pretty much decided he needed a change after the PGA. "If almost any other player had hit the ball where I did that week, he'd have probably won the tournament," he said. "But the way I was putting I didn't even make the cut.

"I was having one good week, then one bad week—or two bad weeks. I was frustrated. I figured changing things couldn't possibly hurt."

McIlroy chose Phil Kenyon as his new putting coach. Kenyon wasn't that well known in the U.S. but was something of a putting icon in Europe, having worked at various times with players like Justin Rose, Martin Kaymer, Lee Westwood, and Colin Montgomerie. Kenyon was also working at the time with Henrik Stenson (who had just won the British Open with the best putting performance of his career), Louis Oosthuizen, and Danny Willett.

A pretty good group, to say the least.

Working with Kenyon, McIlroy discovered he had a couple of serious technical problems with his grip and his stance. Those are the two basics in golf that have to be correct—whether one has a driver or a putter or anything in between in one's hands. McIlroy was either cutting across the ball with his stroke—causing the ball to go right—or overcompensating so much that the ball was going left.

This is what's called a two-way miss. Off the tee, it means you have no idea where the ball is going—left or right. On the putting green, for the same reason, it means you aren't likely to make very many putts.

When McIlroy arrived on Long Island in August for the Barclays, the first PGA Tour playoff event, he decided to wake up early Tuesday morning and get to the golf course before it was overrun with players, media, and fans. He was up at dawn and on the putting green in front of the clubhouse by seven a.m. Any other day of the week, the place would have been buzzing with activity. But Tuesday is arrival day on tour, and it is usually midmorning before most people start showing up.

McIlroy had ninety minutes to himself on the putting green, along with his longtime caddie, J. P. Fitzgerald.

"It was actually a very good session," he said later that day. "Kind of fun too, just working out there with no one around. I haven't got it yet, but I feel like I'm finally pointed in the right direction. I know what was wrong, now I have to correct it. Easier said than done, I know, but I think I'll get it done. I just don't know how soon."

It turned out to be sooner rather than later. After finishing T-31 at the Barclays, McIlroy went to Boston and won the second playoff event. After a not that surprising letdown in Indianapolis, he came back to win the Tour Championship with a final-round 64 that got him into a playoff—which he won on the fourth playoff hole against Ryan Moore.

"Obviously winning and winning that way was great," he said. "I'd never won the FedEx Cup and I was happy to get that done. But playing that way allowed me to go to Hazeltine with a kind of swagger because I knew I was playing well and my teammates knew I was playing well.

"Paul McGinley had pushed me to take more of a leadership role in 2014. I was still only twenty-five and one of the younger guys on the team [only Victor Dubuisson was younger], but Paul emphasized to me my standing in the golf world because I'd already won four majors. He said the other guys were going to look to me and it was up to me to take on that role as a leader.

"I still wasn't entirely comfortable with it to be honest, not with [Lee] Westwood, [Henrik] Stenson, G-Mac [Graeme McDowell], and [Ian] Poulter still on the team with their Ryder Cup records. But I understood where he was coming from, and I tried to work on it—be more verbal—be a guy who took the lead at times in the team room.

"This time, I knew I had to be the leader. G-Mac wasn't on the team and neither was Poults or Luke Donald. Henrik, Rosey, and Lee were all there, but they're quieter by nature." He smiled. "Of course, we're all quieter by nature than Poults. But I knew this was the time I had to step forward."

He also had probably made the most eloquent statement of the week when Arnold Palmer's name came up. "It's a loss for all of us on both teams," he said. "I think the best thing we can do to honor him is to play the Ryder Cup in the spirit he would have wanted to see it played."

But McIlroy had also made it clear before the matches started that he wasn't going to make any attempts at being politically correct or trying to win the crowd—which he knew he couldn't do under any circumstances. So when his team needed a jolt on Friday afternoon, he was more than willing to provide it.

Darren Clarke hadn't gotten all twelve of his players onto the golf course on Friday. Davis Love had. That meant that Chris Wood and Matthew Fitzpatrick got to finally make their Ryder Cup debuts on Saturday morning after watching all day on Friday.

Surprisingly, Clarke opted to break up Henrik Stenson and Justin

Rose after their sizzling Friday afternoon performance. Rather than put the two rookies out together, he put Stenson with Fitzpatrick and Rose with Wood, hoping at least one of the rookies would play well.

He got his wish when Rose and Wood, playing in the third match, managed a one-up victory over Jimmy Walker and Zach Johnson. That was a surprise. And a boost for Europe. Clarke had sent McIlroy and Pieters out first, hoping they could maintain their momentum from Friday afternoon, and they did, easily beating Mickelson and Fowler, 4 and 2.

"Phil reminded me I needed four cracks at him to get a win," McIlroy said. "It was nice to get that done but more important got us off to a good start in the morning. We were doing just what Darren had hoped we'd do, chipping away at the lead."

The hot American team from Friday afternoon was Brandt Snedeker and Brooks Koepka—who had won the only U.S. point in the four-balls. Love kept them together and was rewarded when they beat Stenson and Fitzpatrick, 3 and 2.

Clarke's decision to break up Stenson and Rose ended up being a wash: Stenson and Fitzpatrick losing, Rose and Wood winning.

That left one match on the golf course, the newly formed Spanish team of Sergio García and Rafael Cabrera-Bello taking on the Captain America team of Patrick Reed and Jordan Spieth.

The American players had put Captain America on Reed earlier in the week, and it had quickly gone public and viral. Reed loved it. If there was ever a stage built for him, the Ryder Cup was it.

"Every time I hear a 'USA' chant, I get chills," he said.

That meant he was getting a lot of chills, because there were approximately 8,458 "USA" chants . . . per day.

On Saturday morning, wanting to make amends after their loss to Stenson and Rose on Friday, the Captains America bolted out of the gate with four birdies in five holes. That sort of thing wasn't too surprising in four-ball play, where each team had two chances on every hole. But it was almost unheard-of in foursomes play.

By the time they reached the 9th hole, the Americans were five under par and had a 3-up lead on the shell-shocked Spaniards. As they walked onto the green, the crowd was so wound up that it burst into an impromptu version of the national anthem, causing Spieth and Reed to whip their caps off, Reed putting his hand over his heart.

At the very least, it was different from the "USA" chant.

On the 11th, García had a two-foot par putt to halve the hole. Normally the putt would have been conceded, but García had made Spieth putt an equally short putt on the 5th—bringing to mind the days of Seve Ballesteros's gamesmanship.

In the opening match of the 1993 Ryder Cup at the Belfry, Tom Kite and Davis Love had faced Ballesteros and José-María Olazábal. On the first hole, Love rolled a long birdie putt to about two feet. Standing nearby, Ballesteros said, "That's good, Davis."

Fortunately for the Americans, Kite had played against Ballesteros on numerous occasions. He turned to Ballesteros and said, "Did you say 'That's good,' Seve?"

Ballesteros grinned. "I said it was a good putt," he answered. Then, as Kite started to get over the putt he said, "Come on, Tom, it's good. Just kidding."

Kite didn't think for one second that he'd been kidding.

García simply said nothing on the 5th green. After Spieth tapped in, he and García shared a few words walking to the 6th tee.

"No big deal," Spieth said later.

Six holes later, with the putter on the other foot, Spieth and Reed said nothing. García missed and the Americans were 4 up.

But just when it looked like the match would be a rout, the Americans cooled and the Spaniards warmed up. Both teams birdied the 12th, but then the Americans bogeyed 13 and 15. On 15, Reed hooked his drive and Spieth attempted what he later called a "hero shot," trying to skip the ball across the water since there wasn't room to fly it over the water. The ball drowned, and so did the U.S.—on that hole.

With the margin down to 2 up, the Europeans birdied both 16 and 17. Reed's tee shot at the par-3 17th left Spieth with a 30-footer, the kind of putt he made more than anyone else on the Tour.

He missed by less than an inch. In fact, the putt was so close to hanging on the lip that Reed waited the full ten seconds allowed by the rules before tapping it in, hoping it might just slide over the rim and into the cup.

"I honestly thought I'd made it," said Spieth, who went to his knees when the putt stopped a quarter roll short of going in. "Something in my gut told me Rafa was going to make his once mine didn't go in."

Spieth's gut was right. García had hit his tee shot to 10 feet, and

Cabrera-Bello's birdie putt was dead center. Suddenly—stunningly—the match was all square.

By then, the other morning matches were all over. The Americans' lead was now down to 6–5, and for the first time in two days, the fans weren't quite as loud—except for the European fans, who were starting to break out an occasional round of the "Olé" song.

Everyone from both teams was standing around the 18th green as the four players came up the fairway. Love and Clarke had been required to turn in their lineup cards for the afternoon almost an hour earlier. Love had agonized for so long over his pairings that Kerry Haigh had sent him a text saying, "Need your lineup NOW."

"I was stalling," Love said. "I was waiting for Phil to finish his match because I wanted to talk to him before I sent my pairings in. Plus, we were going back and forth about what to do with Jordan and Patrick."

The Mickelson issue was about whom he should play with in the afternoon. After sitting out Friday afternoon, Mickelson had played better on Saturday morning—even as part of a losing team.

"Phil had actually started to play well on the back nine on Friday morning," Love said. "He played well Saturday morning. I wanted him out in the afternoon, but I wasn't sure who to put him out there with."

Sitting on his cart with his son, Dru—who had replaced George W. Bush as Love's driver four years after Medinah—Love listened to his vice captains on the radio giving him updates on how his players were playing. All were suggesting lineups.

"I had the number-one player in the world [Dustin Johnson] sitting in the clubhouse; I had Kooch, who had played great Friday afternoon sitting out, and I had J.B. and Ryan dying to get back out there.

"They had to play. I couldn't sit them out the whole day. I honestly think if I hadn't put Kooch out there as well as he'd played, I would have hurt not only his morale but the whole team's morale."

As all the proposed pairings came in, Love had an idea: Mickelson and Kuchar. The two were friends and had talked in the past about perhaps playing together. That's why Love was stalling—he didn't want to surprise Mickelson with a pairing that hadn't really been discussed.

Fortunately for Love, McIlroy and Pieters closed Mickelson and

Fowler out on 16. Love was waiting for Mickelson. He laid out his idea to him.

Mickelson thought it over for about fifteen seconds, then nodded. "I love it," he said. "I think that's a great idea."

Love now had one decision left to make: what to do with Reed and Spieth. There was no way Reed wasn't playing in the afternoon. The question was Spieth.

"You could see Jordan was tiring a little bit," Love said. "Patrick's a bull. He can play and play and play. The plan had been to get everyone out at least twice the first two days and no one out four times. But Patrick had to play. The question was who to play him with."

Love thought about pairing him with Dustin Johnson—two guys who would make a lot of birdies in four-ball. He also considered Snedeker, who was making just about every putt he looked at on every green.

It was Woods, while out walking with Spieth and Reed, who finally convinced him to stick with the Captain America team. "He sent me a text that said, 'Jordan might be a little tired, but he's a big boy,'" Love said. "There was also another issue though, and that was how Patrick might react to *not* playing with Jordan. He'd never played a Ryder Cup match [seven of them] with anyone but Jordan. Ultimately, I decided Jordan was tough enough to hang in and that Patrick needed him out there."

With the Reed-Spieth/García–Cabrera-Bello match headed to the 16th hole with Reed and Spieth 2 up, Love took a deep breath and sent Haigh his lineup.

Thirty minutes later, he stood behind the 18th green watching the four players come up the fairway with the match even. With his arms folded, his eyes hidden by sunglasses, Love looked impassive. But his stomach was churning.

"That morning, making those decisions and watching the last match play out after I'd already submitted the lineup was the toughest few minutes of the entire weekend," he said later. "I believed in my team. I thought we'd be okay."

If he had any doubts, though, this was the moment when they were bound to creep in. It was Saturday afternoon, and the pressure was ratcheting up by the minute.

Twenty-Two

DARREN CLARKE HAD fewer options than Davis Love—which made his job both more difficult and simpler at the same time.

There was no way he was breaking up the team of Rory McIlroy and Thomas Pieters or moving them out of the leadoff spot after the way they had played in the morning. They would face Dustin Johnson and Brooks Koepka, creating what had to be the longest-hitting foursome to ever be on a golf course together anywhere, much less in a Ryder Cup.

Clarke also knew that Stenson and Rose had to be put back together, and he wanted them anchoring, since the last match on Saturday turned out to be crucial on so many occasions. Love, once he had decided to put Reed and Spieth back out together, almost *had* to play them last since they had been on the course until after noon and needed at least some down time before venturing out again.

It was the middle matches that were difficult for Clarke. Westwood had told him that he thought he'd fixed his swing problems and was ready to go. There was no doubt he had to play, and it made sense to pair him with Willett—since that had been the idea in the first place.

He actually felt good about that pairing because Willett, in spite of the abuse he was taking from the crowd, hadn't played badly on Friday afternoon. The problem had been Martin Kaymer, whose game was nowhere to be found all day on Friday.

The question for Clarke was whether to get Kaymer back on the golf course on Saturday afternoon or have him sit out the whole day. Sergio García was going to play. He had been involved in thirty-seven Ryder

Cup sessions and had played in thirty-five of them. He had played well—again—in the morning, and Europe was still chasing the U.S.'s Friday morning lead.

"I knew going in I had several guys who had to play five times," Clarke said. "Rory, Stenson, Rose, and Sergio."

What Clarke had to decide was whether to continue to pair García with fellow Spaniard Rafael Cabrera-Bello or to put him out with Kaymer.

Like Love, Clarke had to make his decision before the final match of the morning was over. At the moment when the lineups were due, García and Cabrera-Bello were still 3 down to Spieth and Reed. Based on that, Clarke decided to go with Kaymer, hoping that he'd find enough of his game on Saturday afternoon to win a point or a half point *and* might get some confidence for the singles.

"If I had known what was going to happen the last four holes of that match, there's not a prayer that I'd have pulled Rafa for the afternoon," Clarke said. "Not a prayer, no way. But at the moment I had to submit the lineups they were getting beaten pretty soundly. I wasn't pulling Sergio. I thought it would be good to get Martin back out there. But if I'd submitted the lineup an hour later, Rafa would have been playing."

From 3 down, García and Cabrera-Bello rallied to pull out the halve. García was certain that he and Cabrera-Bello would be back out together in the afternoon. They had beaten Holmes and Moore handily in fourballs on Friday and had just rallied to steal a half point from the Americans' best team.

Walking off the 18th green, García found Ian Poulter waiting for him.

"It's you and Kaymer third off this afternoon," Poulter said.

García was stunned. "I said, 'What—Kaymer, not Rafa?'" García remembered. "Rafa was playing very well. I thought we had a good thing going together. I went to talk to Darren about it and he told me we'd been 3 down when he had to put in the pairings. We could have lost 4 and 3 for all he knew, and he wanted to get Kaymer out in the afternoon. After that I understood his thinking."

The score was now 6½–5½. Europe had done exactly what Clarke had suggested at lunch on Friday: chip away each session. They had won Friday afternoon, 3–1, and Saturday morning, 2 ½–1½.

Clarke figured nerves had to be getting a little bit frayed in the U.S. team room. If he had been in the lead, he might have thought—briefly—

about resting Stenson, Rose, García, McIlroy, or Pieters, all of whom had played all three sessions. He would have especially liked to have given Stenson a break, since his surgically repaired knee was still a little bit gimpy—especially walking thirty-six holes on back-to-back days.

But he didn't have a choice. Only Cabrera-Bello—with García—and Chris Wood—with Rose—had scored for Europe outside the iron five. The U.S. had gotten points from ten players at that moment.

Even a split in the afternoon matches would leave Europe just a point behind going into the singles. "We knew if it was close on Sunday we'd have an advantage because of what had happened in the past," McIlroy said. "If it came down to the last few matches, that was about all we could ask, playing on the road with all the rookies and starting off down 4–0. We knew going into Saturday afternoon those four matches were going to be crucial."

No one was more nervous at that stage than Phil Mickelson. As soon as he and Love had agreed that he would play with Kuchar, he went looking for his new partner. Kuchar had come in from the range after warming up and was relaxing in the team room when Mickelson found him. He had already been told by Love that he was going to play with Mickelson and was pleased to hear it.

"I just wanted to play," Kuchar said. "I'd never played with Phil before, but it was something I'd always wanted to do. I hadn't thought it was going to happen this time around, but when Davis told me he wanted to do it, I thought it was a great idea."

Mickelson sat down with Kuchar and told him exactly what he was thinking.

"Listen, I need something that we can do out there to help us get loose, actually help *me* get loose," Mickelson said. "Have you got any ideas?"

Kuchar thought about it for a moment. He remembered high fives he and Woods had done at past Presidents Cups. He needed something different. Then it came to him.

"How about a Steph Curry shimmy?" he said, talking about the Golden State Warriors star guard.

"Show me," Mickelson said.

Kuchar stood up and demonstrated. "When we make a big putt, we stand opposite one another and do this," he said.

He wanted to put positive thoughts into Mickelson's head, as in: *when* we make a big putt, not *if* we make a big putt.

Mickelson liked it. "Let's practice," he said—not kidding. So, for the next ten minutes, they practiced.

"We did it like four or five times," Mickelson said later. "That's why I nailed it."

"Nailed" being a relative word.

While the players were on their lunch break, Dan Jenkins, who had covered sixteen Ryder Cups during his illustrious career as, arguably, the greatest golf writer of this or any generation, sat down at his desk in the media center. He had just walked outside to smoke a cigarette— something he had been forbidden to do by his doctors, his family, and all his friends, but still did anyway.

"I'm almost eighty-seven," he liked to say. "They haven't killed me yet."

Jenkins was rarely serious about anything—whether in the words he wrote or the words that came out of his mouth. Now, though, as he sat down, none of the usual Jenkins wisecracks were anywhere to be found or heard.

He leaned forward in his chair and pulled the nameplate that said "Dan Jenkins, Golf Digest" off the small riser in front of his desk. Each desk had a nameplate on it. He looked at his seatmate and said, "My last Ryder Cup. I thought I'd keep this one."

"Your last Ryder Cup?" his seatmate said. "Perish the thought."

Jenkins just smiled—wistfully—and tucked the nameplate away.

The afternoon didn't start especially well for the Americans. Hazeltine was now officially overrun with people. In all, counting fans, media, officials, volunteers, marshals, and the teams and their support people, there were close to sixty thousand people on the property Saturday afternoon.

Even though adjustments had been made to try to get people through concession lines and portajohn lines as fast as possible, the lines between the morning and afternoon sessions were extremely long.

There was tension in the air. The exuberance created by the Friday morning U.S. sweep had worn off. People were beginning to get a little bit of a "not again" feeling. When McIlroy and Pieters bolted to an early lead on Johnson and Koepka, there was an almost eerie quiet around the golf course.

The combination of Europe's charge—America's retreat?—and all the beer and the warm weather was starting to turn some in the crowd truly ugly.

"When it was really loud, it was tougher to hear the fans who were yelling bad things," Henrik Stenson said. "When it got quieter, you could hear more."

Stenson had undergone knee surgery a year earlier and, playing his fourth match in four sessions, was feeling a little bit sore. "Nothing I couldn't handle," he insisted.

But on a couple of occasions when he had to walk into a bunker, some fans yelled at Stenson that maybe his knee might give way and he could fall. Or, maybe he *should* fall. Stenson wasn't bothered by it. Jordan Spieth was.

"Look, they were the one percenters," he said. "We all knew that. Most of the fans were just having a great time and pulling for us to win—the way it should be. But there were a few who were just flat out of line. After a while, it got to *me*."

So much so that Spieth began yelling at a handful of fans after some of them had become quite profane and were yelling as the Europeans started their backswings. "Jordan, it's okay," Stenson said. "Don't let it affect you. We're okay."

Later, Spieth remembered that moment fondly. "That's what the Ryder Cup should be about," he said. "I was upset because I didn't want them affecting the way those guys were playing. I didn't want to win because someone yelled in Henrik or Justin's backswing or because they wore them out with profanity. And Henrik didn't want *me* getting upset worrying about how the fans were affecting them."

The worst moment came as McIlroy was walking between the ropes from the 7th green to the 8th tee. He had been hearing from the one percenters for two days, even more so on Saturday after his victory double-bow on Friday afternoon. Now, as he passed through the crowds on either side of him, he very clearly heard a man who was a few feet in front of him screaming (repeatedly), "Hey, Rory, why don't you just suck my ———."

"Normally you just put your head down and keep walking," McIlroy said weeks later. "There's absolutely nothing to be gained by responding in any way at all. It's what they want. But this was different, not just because of what he was saying but because I happened to make eye contact with him while he was saying it. I looked right at him. I can still see him in my mind's eye now: he had kind of a weathered face, was wearing a stripy sweater, and he had a can of Stella Artois in each hand.

"Remember, this had been going on for two days at that point. Honestly, I almost went over the rope after him. If I hadn't turned to security and told them to get him out, I might have done it—which would not have been a very good idea. But I was wound up, running on a lot of adrenaline.

"The closeness of fans in golf is one of the great things about the sport. Normally, I love it. But normally, wherever I am, I'm being cheered on. The Ryder Cup is only going to get bigger with time. This is something that needs to be dealt with. Unfortunately, it only takes a few drunks to ruin a great atmosphere."

The fact that McIlroy and Pieters were already 2 up no doubt fueled both the angst and the anger among the American fans. Once again, Europe was putting blue on the board early, and with the other matches behind them all close, Hazeltine was as quiet as it had been since the gates had opened on Friday morning.

Chandler Withington felt it as he drove around in his cart, trying to put out logistical fires and see a little bit of golf whenever he could. He had driven out to an area near the 6th hole where some of the TV trailers were located. He found Billy Kratzert, the five-time PGA Tour winner who was working on the PGA of America's streaming feed, standing outside one of the trailers.

"I don't like the way this is going," Kratzert said. "They've got the momentum now. McIlroy and Pieters put up a point [the match was now heading to the back nine and McIlroy and Pieters were 4 up], that means it's tied."

Withington nodded. "We need something big to happen, something to turn it back around, get the crowd going again, pump up the guys."

Kratzert was about to answer when the two men heard a huge roar from not far away.

"Sixth hole," Withington said instantly, knowing the lay of the land as he did.

"Reed and Spieth?" Kratzert said. He smiled. "That doesn't sound like a birdie roar, it sounds like a hole-out roar."

He was right.

The 6th hole was the longest par-5 on the golf course, playing 642 yards stretched out. Before the captain's blackout had begun, Love had suggested to Kerry Haigh that playing the par-5s from the back as often as possible was a good idea. Why? Because the stats guys from Scouts Inc. had told him that the U.S. was statistically better with wedges in their hands than the Europeans.

The U.S. was one up in the match after Reed birdied the short par-4 5th hole. On the 6th, Reed's second shot finished 79 yards from the pin. From there, he hit a lob wedge that landed 15 feet behind the hole and spun back—as he had planned—into the hole, which he had not planned. When Reed heard the thunderous roar from the crowd and realized the shot had gone in, he threw his arms into the air and began jumping up and down in celebration.

Spieth, a few yards away, raced over to him, thinking he was going to chest-bump him. As he got closer, he decided it wasn't a great idea.

"The way Patrick was jumping up and down, I thought if we chest-bumped he might knock me on my back," he said later. "For a second I thought high five. For some reason we ended up doing a sort of medium five."

The hand slap was waist-high. Spieth was right to be concerned about Reed's adrenaline. Reed slapped him so hard that Spieth felt pain instantly in his right hand, not the kind of pain that goes away with a quick shake or two, but real pain.

"We walked directly to the 7th tee, and we were up since we'd won the hole," he said. "I turned to [caddie] Michael [Greller] on the tee and said, 'I'm not sure I can grip the club.' It was only a stinger, but it hurt a lot at that moment."

The crowd was still going nuts as the four players walked onto the tee, so no one really noticed that Spieth was shaking his hand, trying to work the pain out of it. Half gripping his three-wood, he more or less bunted his tee shot at the 402-yard hole—and found the water.

"The pain went away gradually," he said. "I mean, I could still feel it a little bit, but it wasn't anything serious. I did learn a lesson though. Next time I might just point my finger at him and say, 'Great shot, partner!'"

Somehow, a rumor got started after play was over that day that Spieth was seriously hurt—so much so that there was talk Sunday morning that he might not be able to play.

"I was walking to the range and Jim [Furyk] said to me, 'You okay? Are you going to be able to play?'" Spieth said. "I told him I was fine."

Reed's hole-out seemed to change the atmosphere everywhere on the golf course—just as Withington had thought it might. Dustin Johnson birdied 11, 12, and 15 to cut the McIlroy-Pieters lead to 2 up, but Pieters birdied 17 to close out that match.

The other three matches were all tight. As well as Reed played in the afternoon, making six birdies in addition to the eagle at 6, Stenson and Rose stayed in the match, largely because Stenson made six birdies and Rose chipped in with a couple of his own on holes where Stenson was out of the hole. Reed and Spieth were just a little better, Spieth contributing his two birdies at just the right moments, allowing the U.S. to beat a team that shot a combined eight under par, the match ending on 17 with one last Reed birdie.

"It was amazing to be part of that match," Reed said later. "I was just brimming with so much confidence at that point. When I holed the shot at 6, that was the loudest roar I'd ever heard in my life. I felt like my feet weren't even touching the ground the rest of the afternoon."

Spieth joked later that it was the first time he'd ever been injured on any kind of "five"—high, low, or medium. Reed joked that he'd been injured too: "My back hurt from carrying him all afternoon."

That was the magic of the Reed-Spieth pairing. Entirely different personalities, but they jelled perfectly. "Tiger said to us, 'You two guys just want to beat the crap out of each other—and it works,'" Spieth said. "He was right."

Too bad that Woods and Mickelson couldn't have taken that approach in 2004. It would have saved Hal Sutton a lot of angst.

The match directly in front of Spieth-Reed/Stenson-Rose was also high quality; not the birdie fest the last match turned out to be, but very good golf nonetheless. Kuchar's presence did for Mickelson exactly what Love had hoped it would do—calm him to the point where he could focus on playing good golf and not worrying about the consequences of the dwindling American lead.

Clarke wasn't as lucky with his lineup change. García was still sizzling, but Kaymer was still searching. The Americans were 2 up through nine holes, but García dropped a 25-footer on the 11th hole and Europe was only one down. Both teams birdied 12 and then, on the long par-3 (248 yards) 13th, both Kuchar and Mickelson found the green. Mickelson had about a 15-footer, and Kuchar was about 25 feet away. There would be two chances to take the lead to 2 up, after both García and Kaymer failed to make birdie.

"A lot of the time Phil likes to have the guy who is closer putt first," Kuchar said. "This time I went first and, as it turned out, it was the right thing to do."

Kuchar's putt was perfect, breaking right to left and going right to the bottom of the hole. This was the moment. Kuchar, a broad grin on his face, started to shimmy. Mickelson walked over, stood directly opposite him, and did the same.

It was truly awful. The crowd went nuts.

On television, Johnny Miller exclaimed, "Where in the world did they learn that?"

"At a task force meeting?" Dan Hicks answered—easily the funniest TV line of the week.

"Ryder Cup committee," Miller corrected, and they both cracked up.

"Have to admit it was funny," García said. "You'd never see something like that anywhere except in the Ryder Cup." He paused for a moment. "Which is a good thing."

The putt and the shimmy were the turning point in the match. García was playing, more or less, one on two and simply couldn't keep pace. Mickelson and Kuchar closed the match out on 17. When Spieth and Reed took a 3-up lead through 15, it looked like the Americans were going to push their lead back to 8½–6½ with—one match—Westwood-Willett and Holmes-Moore playing 17, all square.

Even though they were not technically the last match of Saturday afternoon, they had become the last match on the course still in serious doubt. A win for Europe would mean the margin for the U.S. going into Sunday was one point—which was almost exactly what Europe had been hoping for from the beginning of the week. A halve would mean a two-point margin, still close enough to make the U.S. nervous on Saturday night. A U.S. win would make the margin three points and, even though both teams would have Medinah on their minds, would give the clearly deeper U.S. team some real breathing room.

Westwood had played superbly all afternoon, having gotten the swing fix he needed from instructor Pete Cowen while sitting out two sessions.

He had birdied 5, 6, and 7—the last on a 40-footer across the green. That gave Europe the first lead of the match. Holmes tied it with a birdie on the 9th, but another Westwood birdie, this on the 10th, put Europe one up again before Holmes—who made seven birdies in the match—tied things up again at the 13th.

Willett also played better than he had on the first day. He chipped in at the 2nd to save a halve and birdied the 4th. It seemed as if most of the one percenters had turned their attention to McIlroy and García, who was serenaded the entire weekend with screams of "You're a choker" and "no majors"—a reference to his lack of victories in major championships.

García took it all in good humor, although his girlfriend, Angela Akins, a born-and-raised Texan, told Jordan Spieth at one point that the constant screams made her feel embarrassed to be an American.

When the subject came up in the closing press conference on Sunday evening, García shrugged it off with a great one-liner. "Well, after this weekend, I know for sure that I've never won a major," he said. "I'd like to come back in four years and have them yell, 'You've only won one major.'"

Later, García amended the comment: "Maybe two," he said.

All four players in the Westwood-Willett/Holmes-Moore match understood the import of their duel. Both teams produced birdies on the 16th hole, and they went to the 17th still all square. It was there that Westwood's lifelong bugaboo, the one thing that has kept him from being a multiple major champion, reared its head again at an awful time for him and for Europe.

His putter.

Players will tell you that, at his best, Westwood is one of the most talented iron players of his time. It is his ball-striking ability that made him the number-one player in the world briefly and a top-ten player consistently for many years. But in the biggest moments, when he was leading or contending in majors, his putter failed him.

On 17, Holmes's tee shot found the water, but Moore hit the green and made a two-putt par. Willett flew the green with his tee shot, chipped to 10 feet, and missed. That left Westwood with a five-foot par putt to keep the match even going to the final hole.

He also missed.

That was, as Willett would put it, "massive," because it meant the worst the Americans could do was halve the match and take a two-point lead into Sunday. But both hit poor tee shots and had no chance to make birdie on the 18th. That left the door open for Willett and Westwood, and both hit excellent second shots: Willett to 10 feet, Westwood stuffing a brilliant seven-iron to just inside three feet. It looked almost certain that the match would be halved.

As he walked to the green and looked at the two putts, Ian Poulter, whom Clarke had assigned to walk with the match, had a thought: let Westwood putt first.

"It crossed my mind," he said later. "It's one of those things where if the guy with the short putt goes first, mentally, he's got a little backup knowing the other guy has a decent chance to make his even if he misses. Looking back, I kick myself for not just saying to Lee, 'You putt first.' He's been around the block, he'd have understood where I was going."

Up ahead, Clarke was standing behind the green, arms folded, face hidden by sunglasses. He had the same thought as Poulter.

"If I'd been partnering Lee, I'd have gone to him and said, 'Why don't you putt first?'" he said. "I think it does help a little, when you've got a little putt that might be a bit tricky, to know your partner's still got a makeable putt backing you up.

"But as I was standing there watching them, I remembered my first Ryder Cup in 1997 when Seve [Ballesteros] was everywhere. I mean, he'd jump out from behind trees to tell you what to do. He was all over the place, involved in every match, which is just the way he was. He couldn't really control anything, so he was trying to control everything he could—or thought he could. That was just his personality.

"I told myself then, 'If I'm ever Ryder Cup captain, I'm not going to do that because it's distracting.' So even though my thought was that Lee should putt first, I didn't want to go over there and insert myself into it at that moment. I thought, 'If they think it's the best thing, they'll do it.'"

And so, neither Poulter nor Clarke said anything. Willett and Westwood took the traditional approach, Willett putting first. The putt slid just right of the hole. Westwood's putt was short enough that it was almost gimme range. But it was too important, and Holmes noticed there was shadow on the hole, which made it just a little bit more difficult than it looked.

Earlier in the match, when Willett had a long eagle putt, he'd had

Westwood try his much shorter birdie putt first. "That way, if he makes his, I can make a real run at the eagle," he said. Westwood missed, and Willett had to lag his eagle putt to be certain he'd make birdie. Maybe that was in the back of both their minds before Willett putted.

Willett's putt died just right of the hole. That left it up to Westwood— with no backup.

Westwood took his time, lined the putt up—and missed.

It was a gasp-worthy moment, especially given what it meant.

Stenson had kept the final match alive on 16 by chipping in for an eagle, but the Americans were about to halve the 17th hole and win that match. Westwood's miss meant the U.S. would be up 9½–6½ going into singles. Beyond that, though, was what it did emotionally to both sides.

"We actually weren't as far behind as we had been at Medinah," McIlroy said. "But this time was different. We were trying to be optimistic, but we were also realistic."

García agreed. "The last two games [matches] at Medinah definitely set the tone for that night and the next day," he said. "The tone this time was different. We knew we could still win, but we knew they were feeling good about themselves."

They were. But Love was taking no chances on letting the momentum slip even a little bit.

"At Medinah, I never really had a chance to talk to the guys on Saturday night," he said. "I was tied up talking to the vice captains about our lineup. Then I had to do media. By the time I got back to the hotel, both Presidents Bush had already spoken to the team and I'd missed a lot of the night. Everything felt rushed, and I didn't feel as if I got to get my message across to them in a calm, deliberate way—which I needed to do after the way the matches ended that day."

The two former presidents had spent the week at the matches (when Bush 43 had been Love's cart driver most of the time).

This time, Saturday night was a lot different. Love sent his five vice captains into the locker room to sit at a round table in the middle of the room and started working through Sunday's lineups. Then he sent word out that he wanted all the players in the team room—normally the club's main dining room—pronto.

"They were all dressed the same, so they weren't hard to find," Love said. "I put out the word that the last guy in the room was going to be the guy in the envelope."

"The envelope" is—literally—an envelope in which each captain puts the name of one player on Saturday night. If someone on one team is injured or sick and can't play Sunday for some reason, the player on the opposition whose name is in the envelope sits out, the match is declared a draw, and each team gets a half point.

The envelope had come into play twice. In 1991, Steve Pate had injured his ribs in a car accident while being driven to the gala dinner. He had sat out all day Friday, but played Saturday afternoon with Corey Pavin. The two played respectably, losing 2 and 1 to Colin Montgomerie and Bernhard Langer, but Pate had said afterward that he was too sore to play on Sunday.

That meant he and David Gilford, who was in the envelope for Europe, both received a half point. The matches were tied 8–8 starting play on Sunday. When the Americans won 14½–13½, there were murmurs on the European side that U.S. captain Dave Stockton had decided his chances of getting a half point in that match were better if Pate sat out. If the match had been played and Gilford had won, Europe would have retained the Cup with a 14–14 tie.

It's worth remembering that this was during the "War by the Shore," when there was considerable enmity between the two teams.

Two years later, at the Belfry, Tom Watson was told early Saturday evening by Bernard Gallacher that Sam Torrance had an injured toe that made it too painful for him to walk eighteen holes the next day. Torrance had played in the morning foursomes on Friday—losing 4 and 3 with partner Mark James—and hadn't played since then, so there was (as with Pate's accident) reason to believe he was legitimately hurt. Watson was going to put one of his four rookies into the envelope when Lanny Wadkins pulled him aside and said, "Put me in the envelope. They earned their way onto the team on points, I didn't. Raymond is playing too well to sit."

Wadkins and Raymond Floyd had been the captain's picks. Watson went along, and the U.S. rallied from 9–7 down the next day to win.

There was no reason on Saturday night at Hazeltine to believe anyone wasn't going to play Sunday. And yet, no one wanted to be in the envelope. Plus, there really wasn't anyone on the U.S. team playing poorly enough to be an obvious choice. So Love played the old "last one in is a rotten egg"—or in the envelope—game.

It was Ryan Moore. Ever the workaholic, Moore had gone to the range after he and Holmes had won their match, not happy with himself since Holmes had carried the team most of the afternoon. He was the last to get word that Love wanted everyone in the team room and the last to walk in.

"Guess you're in the envelope," Love said when Moore walked in. Moore had no idea what he was talking about. Later, Love told Moore he wasn't necessarily in the envelope, that he hadn't decided yet.

"I just figured as long as it wasn't needed, no one needed to know who was in it," he said later, conceding that "maybe" Moore had been in the envelope.

In fact, Kerry Haigh, who received the two envelopes, insisted he never opened them. "No need," he said. "I only open them if they're needed. If not, I destroy them."

Ever cagey, Haigh shares with no one—even other members of the PGA staff—exactly how the envelopes are destroyed. Ritual burning might be a reasonable guess.

Once Love had his players in the room and had their attention, he laid out his plan for the final day.

"Our goal isn't to get to 14½ points," he said. "I don't want you guys scoreboard watching and thinking, 'Okay, we need four more points, three more points . . .' We need to win every match. You need to go out and win *your* match. You need to think your match is going to decide the Ryder Cup.

"We've done our job so far, but tomorrow's the most important day. Twelve points out there. Our goal is to get all of them."

Love knew his team wasn't going to win 12 points, just as he had known it wasn't going to score 20 when he'd made that declaration six weeks earlier in Greensboro. But that mentality had worked for two days; he wasn't backing away from it on the third.

"I wanted to talk to them before we went back to the hotel because Saturday night at the hotel has gotten a little formal through the years with wives and caddies and speakers," he said. "I wanted it to be me in there having that talk right away, when everyone was still wound up, just me and them—no one else. Even the vice captains, although I really did need them working on the pairings.

"I knew we were close, especially when we won those last three points. *We* had the momentum, unlike Medinah. I didn't want to take any chances on losing it."

Twenty-Three

D ARREN CLARKE ALSO wanted to meet with his players as soon as
possible. And so, while Love was talking to his team, Clarke gathered his players in the European locker room—normally the women's
locker room at Hazeltine. It was just about the only time all week when
Clarke didn't ask his players to sit in a circle.

"I stood in the front of the room," he said. "The players all sat or stood
or stretched out after a long day so they could be comfortable."

Clarke had already spoken to Westwood as he came off the 18th green.
"There's not much you can say at a moment like that," he said. "I tried
to talk to him as his captain, as his friend, and as his former partner. I
reminded him how well he'd played most of the day and said what was
important now was to be ready to go on Sunday. What was done was
done."

Of course what had been done was that the Americans now had the
momentum back. While Clarke was trying to pep-talk his team, Love
was making jokes about who would go into the envelope.

"It wasn't as if it was grim," Rory McIlroy said. "But it wasn't upbeat
the way it had been at Medinah."

How the Saturday afternoon session ends is always critical to the
mind-set of both teams. Since 1995, when the U.S. had won the Saturday afternoon session 3–1, only to lose the singles resoundingly the
next day, only one team that had lost the final team session had won the
Ryder Cup: that was Europe in 2002, and even then, Paul McGinley
had won the final hole of the final match to tie the overall score at 8–8,

meaning Europe still felt good at the end of the day even though the U.S. won the session 2½–1½.

Now the U.S. had won the Saturday afternoon session, 3–1. It had won the last three matches, and the last critical putt of the day had been Westwood's three-footer.

"A lot of us in the room had been at Medinah," Clarke said. "There, we'd been further behind, but I know I'm dealing with smart guys and they know we don't *feel* the same as we did back then. But I pointed out to them how close we'd been to sitting in here feeling like we had all the momentum and if we could put some blue on the board early the next day, we'd have the momentum back and we'd be feeling good about ourselves and they'd start to wonder, 'Is this happening again?'"

After he had finished meeting with the team, Clarke pulled McIlroy aside. He knew he had to front-load his lineup because the U.S. had the lead, but he wanted to know where McIlroy wanted to play before he submitted his lineup. The captains had one hour from the conclusion of play to submit their lineups to Kerry Haigh.

McIlroy traditionally had played third in the past. In fact, in 2014, he had let Jordan Spieth know he was going to play third in case Spieth wanted to let Tom Watson know so that they could face each other. Watson had slotted Rickie Fowler against McIlroy—probably a break for Spieth, since McIlroy made four birdies and an eagle the first six holes.

McIlroy and Clarke were both pretty convinced that Love, knowing that the Euros were going to "load the boat," as Love put it, would put Reed and Spieth at the top of their lineup. McIlroy wanted a crack at Captain America.

"It was kind of up to me to go out there and try to take him down," McIlroy said. "I mean, he was playing so well. He was their emotional leader, at least out on the golf course. I thought if I could beat him, maybe it would set a tone for the day; maybe it would give our guys a boost and deflate them a little bit."

Clarke felt exactly that way, but was glad to hear McIlroy say it. If McIlroy had asked to play third again, he would have played him third because he thought he deserved to play where he wanted to play. But McIlroy, who took great pride in the fact that he hadn't lost a singles match, was willing to put that record on the line against the U.S.'s number-one guy.

"I went out of my way all week to not single anyone out on my team,"

Clarke said. "That's why I had everyone sit in a circle. Everyone was equal—shoulder to shoulder. I preached that all week. But I was *so* proud of Rory. I mean, I've known him since he was a kid and he completely took on the mantle of leading the team in every possible way. He played brilliantly almost the entire week; put everything into it as emotionally as you could possibly ask from him. When he said, 'Let me go first because I think it will be Reed,' I practically glowed because that's what I wanted to hear. By then, to be honest, I'd have been shocked if he said anything else."

Clarke wanted Stenson, who had been both good and gutty all week even on his gimpy knee, to follow McIlroy. Pieters, who had won three straight matches paired with McIlroy, would go next, followed by Rose, Cabrera-Bello, and García. That meant the only player in Europe's back six who had won a point was Chris Wood. The only veterans in that group were Westwood and Kaymer, who had combined to go 0-5. Clarke had, as Love put it, "loaded the boat."

Love had both the lead and a clear depth advantage. By the time Saturday's matches were over, every American had scored at least one point. It was the first time since 1975—when Arnold Palmer had been the captain—that all twelve U.S. players had scored. Europe still had five players who hadn't gotten on the board yet.

And Love had the lead. So he didn't have to put *all* his best players at the front of the lineup. Even so, he wasn't taking any chances on Europe getting off to a fast start, putting blue on the board, and getting on the kind of roll it had gotten on at Medinah.

When Love sat down with his vice captains after he'd finished talking to the players, there was some division about who should play in the crucial first two spots.

"Rory always told people he liked to play third," Love said. "We knew we wanted Patrick against him, and there was no doubt that Patrick wanted to play him. But we also thought that maybe Rory had been saying third when he planned to play first."

The six men went back and forth for a few minutes until Love finally said, "Let's not overthink this. We're in the lead. Let's put together what we think is our best lineup, regardless of where we think Rory or anybody else is going to play."

Earlier, Reed and Spieth had told Love they wanted to go out 3 and 4, in part because they thought that's where McIlroy and Stenson might be, but also because they were thinking they could sleep a little later if they didn't go out in the leadoff positions.

"We totally forgot how much later the tee times were on Sunday," Spieth said, laughing. "We'd been up at four thirty two mornings in a row and we were thinking another thirty minutes of sleep would be nice. Then Davis reminded us the first tee time wasn't until after eleven [11:04] and we could sleep regardless. At that point, we were both saying, 'Bring it on.'"

So Love granted them their wish: Reed would lead off, followed by Spieth. Then Love would begin to mix and match so there would be experience at the back of the lineup if things went awry early and the late matches became crucial.

He put Holmes, who had made seven birdies on Saturday afternoon, in the third spot. Rickie Fowler, who hadn't played in the afternoon and was rested, would go fourth, followed by Jimmy Walker. Phil Mickelson would, in effect, anchor the top half of the lineup, going sixth.

Matt Kuchar and Zach Johnson, the team's two most experienced Ryder Cuppers outside of Mickelson, would be Love's safety net, going off eleventh and twelfth.

When Love and Clarke finally went to the media center to announce their pairings, the lineups looked like this:

McIlroy vs. Reed
Stenson vs. Spieth
Pieters vs. Holmes
Rose vs. Fowler
Cabrera-Bello vs. Walker
García vs. Mickelson
Westwood vs. Moore
Sullivan vs. Snedeker
Wood vs. Dustin Johnson
Willett vs. Koepka
Kaymer vs. Kuchar
Fitzpatrick vs. Zach Johnson

Based on the way play had gone for two days, the first six matches looked like toss-ups.

The sixth match, between García and Mickelson, was especially intriguing because the two men weren't exactly best friends. Even though there hadn't been public blowups as with García and Tiger Woods, there had always been a simmering coolness between them.

"Let's just say we have different personalities," García said later.

"We've had moments," Mickelson said.

They would have a critical moment together on Sunday.

The lower half of the draw clearly favored the U.S. Even though Westwood had played well most of Saturday afternoon, his putting meltdown was bound to affect him in his match against Moore—who had been solid—especially if it was tight in the final holes. Sullivan hadn't played since Friday morning, and Snedeker had been as good as anyone on the U.S. team.

And so on. If the last two matches turned out to be decisive, the U.S. would have Kuchar, the shimmy master, against Kaymer, who had been mostly awful, and, finally, Zach Johnson against Fitzpatrick, who had also played only once—and lost.

The players were still in their team rooms when the lineups were handed out to them while Clarke and Love were speaking to the media. When McIlroy saw the lineups, he knew his team would have to dominate the top half and hope for a couple of upsets in the lower half to win. He also knew his teammates would figure that out pretty quickly. So he decided it would be a good idea to loosen the mood a little.

He grabbed a lineup sheet and said, "Okay, everyone, listen up, here's the lineup for tomorrow."

Then he went through the matches one by one.

"First point for Europe," he said. "McIlroy over Reed. He's good, McIlroy's better."

Everyone cheered.

"Second point for Europe, Stenson over Spieth. Sorry, Jordan, you picked the wrong guy to play this weekend."

"Third point for Europe, Pieters against Holmes. J.B., I honestly feel sorry for you."

He went on like that through all twelve matches. García would beat Mickelson because Sergio would make every putt the way he always did in Ryder Cup. Willett was getting better each day and would take care of Brooks Koepka.

He finished with Matthew Fitpatrick against Zach Johnson. "Sorry, Zach, move over for the young guys!" McIlroy declared.

Everyone was laughing and cheering at once.

"Europe 12, U.S. zero; Europe dominates and wins again!" McIlroy finished.

There was no disrespect in his comments for any of the American players. It was a good old-fashioned pep talk—spiced with humor.

Now they felt better. They all knew what McIlroy was doing, but it didn't matter. They needed a boost and he'd given them one. They needed only 7½ points the next day to retain the Cup. Based on McIlroy's slightly tongue-in-cheek analysis of the matches, that shouldn't be a problem.

There was only one interruption to Love's team meeting. Julius Mason came in to tell everyone that the PGA of America had decided that something needed to be said publicly about some of the fan behavior that had taken place that afternoon. Apparently the McIlroy incident and the continued harassment of Danny Willett and his family had made it imperative that the PGA say something publicly—regardless of whether it was one rotten egg, one hundred, or fifty thousand.

Mason read Love and the players the statement that the PGA was about to put out and told them that there would be an announcement made on the 1st tee in the morning asking for all fans to be respectful to the players on both teams. The announcement would also be posted on the message boards around the grounds on Sunday. Everyone understood. It didn't matter if it was only 1 percent of the fans. They had all witnessed ugly moments.

"It really was a small percentage of the fans," Kerry Haigh said later. "The vast majority of fans really enjoyed the atmosphere. But there were isolated incidents that appeared to increase as the match days progressed. We decided during the day Saturday we had to take additional action and limit alcohol sales and the hours of alcohol sales."

In other words, the fewer people confronting players with a Stella Artois in each hand, the better.

A number of fans had been removed on both days, more on Saturday than on Friday. No one wanted those sorts of incidents to be the lasting memory people had of the Ryder Cup.

—

Just before the meeting broke up, Kuchar announced to his captains and teammates that he had "something special planned for tonight," once they were back at the hotel. Everyone was convinced this was another Kuchar prank. Only it wasn't.

"I'm going to ask you all to give me two things you're thankful for, and it can't be friends, family, or health," he said. "So start thinking about it."

The idea had come to Kuchar after a birthday dinner he had attended eight years earlier at the home of Seth Waugh, the former CEO of Deutsche Bank, a longtime PGA Tour sponsor. "He just said, 'Okay, this is a family tradition,' and started going around the room," Kuchar remembered. "It really made you think. It was actually pretty cool."

Kuchar had made the idea a part of his Thanksgiving family dinner. Now he wanted it to be part of Saturday night at the Ryder Cup.

"Saturday is usually a fun night," he said. "Everyone gets up and talks and a lot of different things come up. I just thought for my turn I'd try to get everybody focused on some things that they felt good about."

Love had planned a relatively informal evening that would include a lot of non–team members. That was why he wanted to talk to the players alone before they left the golf course.

"Once you're back at the hotel, you kind of come out of the zone," he said. "Which is a good thing. You can't sit around all night thinking about what may or may not happen the next day. It will wear you out."

Mike Eruzione, the captain of the 1980 Miracle on Ice U.S. Olympic hockey team at Lake Placid, would be there. Darius Rucker, a huge golf fan whom all the players knew, would sing a few songs. The ex-captains would be around, and as always the wives/partners and caddies would be in the room too.

No one was completely certain just how serious Kuchar was about his plan.

"I'm not sure we wanted to know," Zach Johnson said, laughing.

Johnson also had something planned, something he'd been working on all week.

Clarke didn't have any special guests joining his team. The Irish rugby player Paul O'Connell—Europe's answer to Michael Phelps—had spoken to the team Tuesday. Neither team had brought in anyone else formally, but Love had encouraged the various celebrities and ex-captains to make themselves at home in the team room.

"I wanted things to happen spontaneously," he said. "I didn't want it to be like, 'Okay, at eight o'clock on Thursday Jack Nicklaus is going to speak.' About the only thing that happened—other than Phelps—that wasn't entirely spontaneous on the part of the speaker was Jordan on Thursday night. And that wasn't Jordan as much as it was Phil pushing Jordan to get up and say something because he and I had agreed it was important."

Eruzione brought hockey jerseys for all the players to the team room Saturday night. They all said "USA" on the front and had the players' names on the back. Then he spoke about the importance of understanding the moment, reminding the players what U.S. coach Herb Brooks had told his team before it played the Soviet Union in the most important hockey game ever played, on February 22, 1980: "You were all born for this moment."

Love laughed remembering Eruzione's talk. "He was great because he's such a pro," he said. "He's been doing it for years—whether talking to a Ryder Cup golf team or the top executives at IBM. He knew just what notes to hit."

Rucker got up and told the players how much their friendship meant to him and how much he enjoyed being around them. "I want you to know," he said, "that anytime any of you need me to come and play in one of your charity events, I'm there. Anytime, anyplace. I'll play golf, I'll play music, whatever you want or need."

He paused. "But if you lose tomorrow, I'm charging you full price."

Then it was Zach Johnson's turn. He passed out shirts that said simply: "Make Tiger Great Again." He had spotted them online a few weeks earlier and had bought them for everyone on the team. Every player and vice captain put one on. Love had told Woods earlier in the week that there would come a moment for him to talk to the team—but that it shouldn't be forced.

"It'll just happen," he said. "You'll know when it's time."

With everyone in the room yelling "speech," Woods knew it was time.

He told the players how much it had meant to him to be part of the team, how much he had enjoyed everything that had gone into the week, and how close he now felt to each of them.

"It was a cool thing," Mickelson said later. "I think Tiger had been heading in the direction of being one of the guys for a while, but the week at Hazeltine really put it over the top.

"Of course I wish he didn't have that fourteen/seventy-nine thing going. It makes it a lot harder to get into a zing thing with him."

Earlier in the week, in a car going from the golf course to the hotel, Mickelson and Woods had engaged in the sort of shit-giving exchange no one had ever dreamed they would witness.

"Can't wait to see you back on tour," Mickelson said at one point. "I just hope you can find the planet off the tee again sometime soon."

"Found it enough to win fourteen and seventy-nine, didn't I?" Woods answered.

Zing.

Mickelson also had a gift to give to his teammates: dog tags. Each had the player's name on it and the word "Beginning." Mickelson had always maintained that Hazeltine would be the beginning of a new era for the U.S. Ryder Cup team. He wanted to give the other players one more reminder of that.

Finally, after the celebrity speeches and the gift giving, it was Kuchar's turn. He'd brought in a whiteboard and placed it in front of the room. He stood before his teammates and, with none of the usual Kuchar "gotcha" in his voice or his demeanor, told everyone what he wanted from them.

"I want each of you to tell me two things in your life that you're really grateful for," he said. "You aren't allowed to say friends, family, or health. We're all grateful for those things, and we all understand how important they are. I want other things. I want things you're thinking about right now sitting in this room tonight."

It took a moment for everyone in the room to realize Kuchar was serious. If there was any doubt, he proved it by starting.

"I talked about how much I loved golf and how grateful I was I could play golf for a living," he said. "I'd also thought about something Phil had said at the Presidents Cup in Korea. He talked about how cool it was that the captains and vice captains thought enough of him to make him a captain's pick even though he hadn't made the team on points. That resonated with me—especially after Davis made me a captain's pick."

They went from there. Some guys were brief. Others, notably Bubba Watson, were not. Watson talked at length about why it was so important for him to be part of the team as a vice captain after *not* getting picked and went on emotionally about how much it meant to him that his father had lived long enough to see him play in the Ryder Cup in 2010.

"It was actually a challenge," Brandt Snedeker said. "I think it made all of us stop and realize how lucky we were to be sitting there getting ready to try and win the Ryder Cup the next day. It was really pretty cool."

Snedeker followed Watson. He began by thanking him for all the input and support he'd given him all week. Then he talked about how fortunate he felt to be in this moment and how important it was to him to make sure not to let anyone down the next day: Love, Mickelson, the other players and captains—past captains.

"I kind of went on a while too," Snedeker said.

Then Snedeker pulled out his phone. A hockey fan, he had read a book a few years earlier by Mike Babcock about coaching the Canadian Olympic team in 2010 under nearly unbearable pressure because the Games were in Vancouver.

The book was called *Leave No Doubt,* and in it Babcock had referenced a quote his coaching mentor, Scotty Bowman, had passed on to him. It came from a pastor/radio talk show host named Chuck Swindoll.

"I keep it in my phone," Snedeker explained, "because it helps me to pull it out and read it again when I really feel like I'm under pressure."

He began to read: "'The longer I live the more I realize the impact of attitude on life. Attitude, to me, is more important than facts. It is more important than the past, than education, than money, than circumstances, than successes, than what other people think or say or do. It will make or break a company, a church, a home.'"

Here, Snedeker added three of his own words: "or a team."

"That's when I started to lose it," he said.

He tried to continue. "'The remarkable thing is we have a choice every day regarding the attitude we will embrace for that day. We cannot change our past. . . . We cannot change the fact that people will act in a certain way.'"

By now, Snedeker had lost it completely. He handed the phone to his wife, Mandy, and she finished for him.

"'We cannot change the inevitable. The only thing we can do is play on the one string we have, and that is our attitude. I am convinced that life is ten percent what happens to me and ninety percent how I react to it. And so it is with you. . . . We are in charge of our attitudes.'"

Mandy's voice was quavering too at the finish, but she got through it. Unlike her husband.

By now, many in the room were crying. Steve Stricker was next. He was already crying when he stood up. He said about four words and broke down completely.

"Because that's what I do," Stricker said, laughing. "By the time they got to me, half the room—at least—was crying. I got up, started to talk, and lost it. Not only am I not sure what I said, I'm not sure anyone *understood* what I said. But the whole thing was great."

Watson, Snedeker, and Stricker were all sitting close to one another. When Stricker finished, someone yelled, "Let's try the other side of the room."

"I think they were hoping someone would get up and *not* cry by then," Snedeker said.

"The coolest thing about it was we all ended up sitting there thinking how lucky we were to be exactly where we were," Zach Johnson said. "Instead of feeling the pressure that we knew was coming the next day, we all felt great. I think that's exactly what Kooch was going for."

Kuchar stood at the easel throughout, writing down what each person was thankful for until he'd filled several pages. At one point, Jack Nicklaus poked his head in the door, saw what was going on, and said, "Just keep doing what you're doing—in here and on the golf course."

"It worked out perfectly," Love said later. "After Kooch was done, we all went around the room and everyone said a few words about the week—including the wives."

He smiled. "Robin had to do her 'Take dead aim' thing, so I let her go last."

In the famous Saturday night meeting at Brookline prior to the Sunday rally there, Robin Love had quoted Harvey Penick's famous line about the key to competing in golf: "Take dead aim." She hadn't done it at Medinah on Saturday night, so she had told her husband he had *better* give her the chance to use it this time around if he wanted his team to win on Sunday.

The European get-together on Saturday didn't take as long and didn't involve as many people. Some of the more experienced players— Westwood, McIlroy, and García spoke—reminded everyone about what had happened at Medinah. Even though Clarke understood the circumstances were very different, the theme was the same: put blue on the board early, and *they* will start remembering Medinah.

Five of the American players—Mickelson, Snedeker, Dustin and Zach Johnson, and Kuchar—had played at Medinah. Four of the vice captains—Woods, Furyk, Stricker, and Watson—had also played there, and Love had been the captain then, as now.

Clarke saved Poulter for last because he knew the kind of fire Poulter would bring to the room. When Poulter had finished, Clarke showed a video from the last day at Medinah.

"I think by the time the video was over, we felt very good about what was to come," Clarke said. "We knew the key would be a good start, and we had our best guys up front."

He also knew they would have to dominate those matches to have any chance at all to win. There was really nothing more to be said. Everyone could sleep in Sunday morning. That didn't mean very many of them would.

Twenty-Four

D AVIS LOVE WENT to bed before midnight, expecting a restless night. The lineups were in; the speeches had been given. The tears had been shed. All that was left to do was hope his players had one more good day of golf left in them.

He woke up at some point after midnight and found a new text in his cue. It had been sent at 11:51 p.m. and said, "Can't sleep. Lineups are done. Nothing left for me to think about."

It was from Tiger Woods. Love laughed.

"Tiger had been obsessing about our lineup, especially the singles, since July," Love said. "Now it was done and he couldn't sleep. I cracked up."

Love knew it was probably going to be his last funny moment for a while.

Sunday dawned exactly the way the first two days had: cold and sunny, the temperature at sunrise barely reaching fifty. The difference was, there were no players in sight, since the first tee time was at 11:04 and everyone had a chance to sleep in.

"*Sort* of sleep in," Jordan Spieth said. "I don't think anyone slept too soundly that night."

Spieth was actually receiving more attention from those arriving at the golf course early than any of the other players. The rumor that he had hurt himself mid-fiving with Patrick Reed after Reed's hole-out Saturday afternoon had gone near viral, and there were whispers that he was going to sit out, meaning he and whoever was in Darren Clarke's envelope would split a point.

"I know the rumor was around," Spieth said, laughing, several weeks later. "But I was fine. It *did* hurt when it first happened, but by the time we finished Saturday, I was pretty much pain-free. It certainly wasn't anywhere near close to me giving any thought at all to not playing."

Spieth was actually one of the first players to arrive Sunday morning. He drove to the golf course with his caddie, Michael Greller, and left Greller to park the car while he jogged up to the clubhouse. Spieth rarely walks when going from one place to another. On the golf course, when there's a lengthy distance between a green and the next tee, he runs. When there are stairs, he runs up, then he runs down. This time, though, he wasn't running (a fast jog) just because it's what he does.

"I actually wanted to get inside without cameras recording my arrival the way TV likes to do with guys, especially on Sunday at a major," he said. "So I figured if I kept moving, they wouldn't find me. I just wanted to go to work."

There was little doubt that this was a workday for everyone. Even though play started much later, the gates were opened at seven thirty with the music from the 1st tee blaring all over the golf course. As soon as the gates opened, fans began stampeding in different directions to find ideal places to watch. If it had been Augusta, all fifty-five thousand of them probably would have been removed for committing the seminal crime of running. But this wasn't Augusta.

Nick Faldo was walking behind the 1st tee to a TV set a few minutes after the gates opened, and he saw people sprinting to line up to get into the grandstands there.

"Don't these people know there's no golf for another three and a half hours?" he asked rhetorically.

They knew. They didn't care.

The weather warmed quickly once the sun was up, and the players going off first began arriving. Some of those playing later stayed back at the hotel to try as best they could to relax.

When Spieth got to the range, he was pleased to find he could swing pain-free.

"You okay?" Jim Furyk asked, having heard about the Spieth-Reed slap.

"Fine, all good," Spieth said, not wanting anyone to doubt for a second that he was ready to go.

Patrick Reed was more nervous than he had ever been. The spotlight was firmly on him, and he knew it. He was, after all, Captain America, and in that role it was his job to slay Captain Europe—Rory McIlroy.

"I was tight on the range," he said later. "Really tight. I didn't like the way I was hitting the ball, and I knew it was nerves. I was telling myself to calm down and just get ready to play, but it wasn't working."

Tiger Woods was on the range, watching Reed and Spieth—whom he had taken to describing as "my guys," since they had been in his pod and in his care all week—warm up. He could see that Reed wasn't quite himself.

"Hey, Patrick," he said. "Come here a minute."

Reed walked over to where Woods was standing. As had been the case all week, Woods's eyes were covered by sunglasses and his cap was pulled down tight. If not for the goatee he was sporting, he could have been a Secret Service agent watching President Obama play a round of golf. He even had the earpiece for the radio all the vice captains carried.

"I thought sure he was going to give me a pep talk, say something about my swing or about just relaxing and not trying too hard," Reed said. "I walked over there. He had his arms folded. I waited. He looked really serious.

"And then he told me a dirty joke."

Woods is well known among the players for telling and enjoying dirty jokes. Athletes in general like so-called locker room humor. It is not, however, limited to male athletes. One of the all-time-best dirty-joke tellers among the jock set was Chris Evert, the girl-next-door tennis immortal. No one looked more demure or proper than Evert. No one loved a good down-and-dirty joke more than Evert.

Woods is similar—he just looks a lot different from Evert. When he told Reed the joke, his face never changing expression, Reed broke up.

"It was actually the perfect thing to do," Reed said later. "It just broke the tension. I went back to hitting balls, and all of a sudden I was loose as could be. I was ready."

So was McIlroy. He knew exactly what was at stake in the leadoff match, that it was about far more than one point.

"I needed to get out there in front and put that blue in front of everybody—on both teams," he said. "It wasn't just about closing the gap by winning the first point. It was also about taking Reed down and making everyone think, 'We can do this. We've done it before, we can do it again.'

"Reed was playing so well, and he's so passionate about the Ryder Cup. I just felt if I could find a way to beat him, it might crack the Americans' confidence a little bit."

McIlroy certainly gave it his best shot. But every time he threw a punch, Reed had an answer.

Not surprisingly, both men were a little tight on 1: Reed hooked his drive left into the trees; McIlroy missed the fairway right. Both missed the green, but McIlroy pitched to three feet. Reed had to pitch out of the trees and had a 20-footer for par. He nailed it. That set the tone for the day.

"Getting out of that hole with a halve *and* making a long putt to do it got me pumped all over again," he said. "I kind of looked at Rory, saw how intense he was, and thought, 'This is on.'"

It was. McIlroy was one up through four holes before the two men played, arguably, the four greatest holes in Ryder Cup history.

McIlroy made four straight birdies on 5 through 8. And lost ground.

Kerry Haigh had moved the tee up on the short par-4 5th hole. On the scorecard, the hole was listed as 352 yards—from the back tee. In fact, the shortest it was listed was 310 yards. Haigh had it set up at 303 yards, a risk/reward tee shot through a narrow chute to what was a reachable green.

McIlroy laid up and pitched to three feet. He never got to putt, though, because Reed laced a driver to eight feet and rolled in the eagle putt.

"That was a wow moment," McIlroy said. "He gambled and just hit a brilliant shot. Then he made the putt."

They both birdied the par-5 6th and the 7th. That brought them to the par-3 8th, all square. Both found the green, but neither really had a makeable birdie putt. McIlroy was on the front of the green, 40 feet shy of the pin; Reed was about 25 feet left of the flag.

And then, McIlroy made the putt of the week, draining his birdie putt from the front of the green. When the putt went in, McIlroy was as pumped as he could ever remember being. He shook his fists, then his entire body in a sort of solo shimmy. Then he held his hand to his ear in an "I can't hear you" gesture, clearly saying, "I can't hear you!" to the crowd.

"Part of it was just pure adrenaline, raw emotion; the putt going in, the importance of it," McIlroy said. "But part of it was just *fun*. I was having a great time out there. The Ryder Cup is the only event in golf where you would even think to act that way. It's the only event where you're going to get a crowd response—one way or the other—like that.

"It was all just very cool. The quality of the golf at that point was off the charts, and I was just, as they say, in the moment." He laughed. "Very much in the moment."

Reed was just as in the moment. He calmly stepped up to his putt and, just as McIlroy had done, rolled it dead center. He turned to McIlroy, pointed, and wagged his finger at him as if to say, "Not so fast."

All McIlroy could do was laugh as the crowd went absolutely crazy.

"The roar on 6 on Saturday when I made the eagle was, without doubt, the loudest I'd ever heard," Reed said. "The roar on 8 on Sunday had to be four or five times louder. It was beyond belief. There was no point in even trying to talk. No way could you hear anything."

Matt Kuchar, who didn't tee off until after one o'clock in the eleventh match, was sitting in the team room watching all this unfold. For a moment, what was happening on the 8th green made him a little nervous.

"When Rory made his putt, I thought he might rip his shirt off and do the Hulk thing," he said. "Then Patrick makes his and he's pointing his finger at Rory. I thought, 'Whoa, this is getting really tense.' Then Rory went over and bumped fists with him and they both smiled. I kind of breathed a sigh of relief when he did that."

McIlroy had started to walk off the green, then stopped, turned, and held up a fist to Reed. They fist-bumped, patted each other on the back, and began the long walk to the 9th tee together.

"You realize, don't you, that imitation is the most sincere form of flattery," McIlroy said to Reed as they walked to the tee. He was remembering Reed's Sunday act at Gleneagles.

Reed grinned. "This is fun, isn't it?" he answered.

Behind Reed and McIlroy, Europe had gotten off to the kind of start that Clarke had hoped for. The first seven matches were all close, but Europe had a slim lead in Stenson-Spieth, Pieters-Holmes, and Cabrera-Bello-Walker. Mickelson and García were throwing birdies at each other, and Rose and Fowler—in match four—were dueling back and forth. There wasn't much daylight between leader and trailer in any match.

Which was why both McIlroy and Reed understood how important the outcome of their match was going to be.

Almost inevitably, both lost a little bit of steam after the stunning exchange on the 8th green.

"I think we were both a little drained at that point," McIlroy said. "We were both playing in our fifth match, we'd both been trying to kind of carry our teams emotionally. The intensity of the first eight holes was off the charts. I definitely felt it on the back nine. Unfortunately, he felt it just a little less."

McIlroy was still riding a little bit of a high from the 8th green theatrics when he walked onto the 10th tee. Among those standing there was Courtney Holt, the senior director of player relations and booking at Golf Channel. In English, that means she coordinates almost every major interview Golf Channel does with a player. Which means she knows McIlroy well.

Spotting her, McIlroy walked over to the ropes, grabbed her shoulder, and said, "How great is this? I mean, how great is *this*?"

McIlroy was riding on adrenaline and exhaustion at the same time. He simply couldn't stay at that level playing his fifth match in a little more than fifty hours. Reed was tired too, but just a tad less tired, as it turned out.

Reed took the lead on the long par-4 12th hole when both players missed the green but he got up and down, making a 10-foot par putt, and McIlroy failed to match him, making his first bogey of the day. By now, all the players were on the golf course and could all see the red "1" on the scoreboard in between Reed's and McIlroy's names.

"Seeing that was a huge boost," said Brandt Snedeker, who had gone off ninth in Love's lineup. "We knew how much they were counting on Rory, and we were counting on Patrick just as much."

Phil Mickelson, playing sixth, agreed. "Honestly, I wasn't looking that closely at the boards because I had my hands full," he said. "But when I saw that Patrick had taken the lead, I definitely felt a little chill go through me."

By now, the two players were like Rocky and Apollo Creed in the final rounds: reeling with exhaustion but refusing to go down. Reed birdied 16 and was 2 up with two to play. McIlroy, though, wasn't finished. He won the 17th and came to 18 knowing he had to make birdie to steal a half point.

"By then, a halve would have been a victory," McIlroy said. "I'd given Patrick everything I had on the front nine, and he stayed with me. Then he outplayed me on the back nine, even though he was tired."

The 18th hole at Hazeltine—normally the 9th—is a not-too-difficult 432-yard par-4. Kerry Haigh had the pin—as with most of the pins that day—in a relatively easy spot, toward the back of the green but not tucked near any of the bunkers.

McIlroy, with the honor, hit a perfect drive down the middle. Reed did the same.

Davis Love was now following the match, knowing how crucial it was. After Reed's tee shot, he walked quickly onto the tee and scooped up Reed's tee, which Reed had not picked up. "I just wanted to have it," Love said. "Either way, it had been one of the great Ryder Cup matches in history."

Reed, charging up the fairway with the crowd screaming, happened to look over his shoulder as Love was picking up the tee and saw him do it. "Put a big smile on my face," he said.

Later, Love was stunned when Reed told him he'd seen him pick up the tee, since Reed was already 30 or 40 yards up the fairway when he did it. "Eyes in the back of my head," Reed told him.

Love believed him.

When Reed got to his ball, he wasn't at all surprised to find himself 140 yards from the flag, which was 24 feet from the front edge of the green and eight feet from the right edge. He was, however, a little surprised to see McIlroy's ball 30 yards past where he was standing. "Trust me, I hit mine great," he said later, laughing. "Fair to say he was a little pumped up."

McIlroy was pumped up. He also knew he *had* to make birdie to give himself a chance. But when he saw Reed's second shot—a pitching wedge—flying at the flag, he knew birdie might not be good enough. "I figured if he got it anywhere inside 20 feet, he'd probably make it the way he'd putted under pressure all week," he said. "I actually stood over mine, thinking if I wanted a halve in the match, I might have to hole it."

He didn't, although he hit a superb shot, right over to the flag, the ball stopping eight feet behind the hole. Reed had 10 feet left for birdie.

"I knew I had to make it," Reed said. "And I knew I was *going* to make it."

Sure enough, his putt rolled dead center, just as so many others had in the previous three days. McIlroy wasn't surprised even a little. He congratulated Reed, saying simply, "I enjoyed the match. Great playing."

He walked away feeling miserable. He knew that his loss was going to make it very difficult for his team to rally. He was also saddened because one of his career goals—one he hadn't talked about publicly—had been to retire having never lost a Ryder Cup singles match.

"I had a selfish moment there," he said. "I did think about that. I think in a way I was looking at that as a consolation prize in case we didn't win the Cup. Then I realized that, in the big picture, it didn't mean that much. I had played about as well as I could have hoped for three days; I'd done some good things, but it wasn't quite good enough.

"Patrick was unbelievable. The passion and energy he brings to the Ryder Cup is incredible. I really believe if he cut his schedule to twenty or so events and focused that energy on winning majors, he'd win multiple times—he's that talented."

Three weeks later, Reed played in Malaysia. McIlroy checked the leaderboard on Sunday night and saw that he had finished tied for fifty-first. "How can that be the same guy I played at Hazeltine?" he wondered. "Hardest thing in golf is to keep your energy level high. We all have down weeks. When he's up, he's as good as it gets."

Reed was as up as it gets at Hazeltine. His win was critical—especially given the timing. Just behind him, Stenson and Pieters were both winning against Speith and Holmes; Rose and Fowler were deadlocked; and Cabrera-Bello was leading Walker.

"I think it gave us all a boost to see Patrick's win go on the board," Mickelson said. "We knew the back half of our lineup was very strong and if we even came close to holding our own on the front half, we were going to win. That first point meant a lot."

The second point, as it turned out, came from Fowler. Neither he nor Rose played especially well, combining for a total of five birdies—as opposed to Mickelson and García, who would combine for *nineteen* birdies—but Fowler made the last one, on the par-5 16th, to take a one-up lead that he hung on to as both players parred the last two holes.

"I guess you could say it wasn't pretty," Fowler said. "But I'd never won a singles match [0-1-1], so it was nice to chip in a point when we needed it."

Rose has a temper, which shows up occasionally on the golf course and in private moments right after a round. But he's a genuinely nice man, one who rarely says anything controversial in public. But after a less than sterling weekend, capped off by less than sterling play in the singles, Rose showed his frustration later in the day during Europe's press conference, calling Kerry Haigh's hole locations "ridiculously easy."

The hole locations were not very difficult—the 18th, with plenty of room to the left of the flag and far enough back that the players could, to quote Harvey Penick and Robin Love, take dead aim. That was the way Love wanted it because the stats people had said to him, "Your guys are better putters than their guys are. The more you make this a putting contest, the better."

"If we know we're better putters than they are, why wouldn't we set the golf course up to give ourselves a chance to make some putts?" Mickelson said again, after hearing Rose's comments. "It would be stupid to do otherwise. They like tighter fairways and more rough. They like tucked pins that require more precise iron shots because they're great iron players. So why would we set up the golf course to *their* advantage and not ours? What's the point of being the home team if you don't give yourself the best possible chance of winning?"

The Europeans didn't disagree with that way of thinking. "When we get to Paris [in 2018], you'll see tighter fairways, more rough, tougher pin positions, and slower greens," Clarke said. "That's the way the Ryder Cup is."

His players got that. They knew even before they landed in Minneapolis that Haigh's definition of "Ryder Cup" green speeds would be in the 13-to-14 range on the Stimpmeter, give or take a half foot—as long as the golf course was dry. In Europe, the greens would be closer to 11 and the pins harder to attack. Rose—no doubt upset with his performance—just thought it went too far.

"The golf course was set up that way to one degree or another all week," he said. "But I just think on a Sunday in any major event, you want to test the players. You've got twenty-four of the best players in the world here, don't you want to try to bring out their best, especially the last few holes? Force them to perform under pressure? See what great golf they can produce when the most is at stake?"

The answer, from the Americans' point of view, was no. They wanted to win. Period. If putting every flagstick dead in the middle of the green would help them win, they were all for it.

Rose is one of the best ball strikers in the world, and he had beaten Mickelson to win the 2013 U.S. Open at Merion with a classic display of remarkable play, tee to green. The irony, though, was that he had also made one of the great putts in Ryder Cup history: the 50-footer on the 17th green at Medinah on Sunday, leading to his critical victory that day.

Fowler's win made the match score 11½–9½. Stenson, Pieters, and Cabrera-Bello had all wrapped up their matches on the 16th hole, each of them winning 3 and 2. The Stenson-Spieth match had a fairly bizarre ending. Two down playing 16, Spieth had to take a shot at reaching the green in two after Stenson found the green with his second shot. He pulled the ball a little and ended up in the water to the left of the green.

The water was just shallow enough to allow Spieth to at least think about taking a swing from there. He took off his shoes and socks, rolled up his pants leg, and stepped into the muddy water.

But as he addressed the ball, he saw it move under the water. He had to penalize himself. Realizing that, even if he could somehow get a club on the ball without it moving again, holing out was an impossibility. He pulled himself out of the water, walked over to Stenson, took off his cap, and shook his hand.

"I actually played well," Spieth said later. "I think I would have won against most guys that day. But Henrik was finishing off an amazing year. I think he had seven or eight one-putts in a row at one point. I said that to him, 'What'd you have, seven, eight one-putts?' He laughed and said, 'Talk about the pot calling the kettle black.' I had to laugh at that. I did make some putts on him in the past."

Spieth knew that Stenson had won the match far more than he had lost it. Still, he felt as if he had let his teammates down. "If I back Patrick's win up with a win, it's just about over," he said. "At that point, I thought to myself, 'Okay, you didn't win, find a way to go help the guys still playing.'"

Spieth was tempted to circle back to give Fowler—two matches behind him—encouragement, but he decided to stay out of sight and wait for the match to finish.

"Rickie doesn't really like to see people following him like that when he's playing," Spieth said. "A lot of guys want a vice captain or guys who are done playing to be out there with them. Rickie doesn't."

In fact, Love had specifically *not* assigned a vice captain to walk with the Fowler-Rose match for just that reason.

The best-played match of the day for all 18 holes was Mickelson and García. Although there was plenty of very public negative history in the García-Woods relationship, he and Mickelson weren't exactly buddies either. Their match was played with very little talk or "nice shots" between them, even though there were plenty of nice shots.

Mickelson had found his swing while partnering with Kuchar during the Saturday afternoon match and was driving the ball about as well as he ever had. García was still smarting from his loss with Kaymer the previous afternoon and matched Mickelson shot for shot, putt for putt.

"I'd been upset Saturday because I thought Martin and I losing and then what happened with Lee at the end really killed our momentum," García said. "I knew we had to have every point possible, and I could see the board was pretty mixed and that wasn't good enough.

"I was playing really well by then. But so was Phil; I had seen that Saturday afternoon. We didn't talk much because of what was at stake, but it's true, we've never really been friends. Different personalities. Some personalities just don't match up. It's as simple as that."

Like Rose and the other Europeans, García was surprised by how easy the pin placements were.

"On the one hand, you understand it, of course," he said. "But you would think the last few holes they'd want to challenge you a little. It was fun to make all those birdies, it's always fun to make birdies. But I was a little bit surprised."

Mickelson and García made a jaw-dropping *nineteen* birdies between them: ten by Mickelson and nine by García. Mickelson made the only bogey, three-putting the par-5 11th. That gave García a one-up lead, but Mickelson promptly birdied the 12th and the 15th to go back into the lead. Neither player ever held more than a one-up advantage.

García drew even again with a birdie at the par-5 16th. Remarkably, Mickelson shot 63 while playing the four par-5s in even par. With the match tied again, both men birdied the last two holes. When Mickelson rolled in a 22-footer for birdie on 18, he performed a leap reminiscent of his gravity-challenged jump after he made his birdie putt to win the Masters in 2004.

"I think I got a little higher in '04," he said, laughing. "I was a lot younger. But this one felt just about as good."

The putt meant that the best García could do was halve the match, and he had to make a 15-footer of his own to do so. He rolled it in coolly, and the two men shook hands and—briefly—congratulated each other on their sterling play.

"It was kind of heartbreaking, to tell you the truth," García said. "I threw everything I had at Phil, and he kept making putts. It was a great match, but what you remember is that you didn't get the point."

Mickelson admitted it was "probably" the best Ryder Cup match he'd ever been involved in but didn't want to go much further than that. He didn't want to give García credit for pushing him the way he had.

Mickelson's half point gave the U.S. a 13–10 lead. A few minutes before he and García shook hands, Brooks Koepka had closed out Danny Willett, 5 and 4, ending a dreamlike Ryder Cup debut for Koepka (3-1 record) and an absolute nightmare (0-3 and "Pete-gate") for Willett.

The board was now filled with red: Brandt Snedeker was leading Andrew Sullivan; Dustin Johnson had a comfortable lead on Chris Wood; and Zach Johnson was well ahead of Matthew Fitzpatrick. The U.S. needed to win only one and a half of those three points to clinch the Cup before the final matches played out.

By now, Love wasn't thinking about winning all twelve matches or getting to 20 points. Clinching the cup was all that was on his mind.

"Once Brooks won and Phil and Sergio halved, it was obvious we were in pretty good shape," he said. "But I didn't want to relax, didn't feel like I could relax until it was actually done."

Love was sending various vice captains out to pick up the later matches as they neared conclusion. No one had been with Zach Johnson—playing the last match—all day, so Love sent Jim Furyk out to follow him. By then, Johnson was 3 up with four to play.

Snedeker, who had played wonderfully all weekend, came to the 17th hole 2 up on Sullivan. He had lost two of the first three holes at the start of the match, but had come back to take control. His charge had started when Bubba Watson came out to check on him on the 5th tee.

"I birdied that hole," Snedeker said. "I turned to Bubba and said, 'You aren't going anywhere. Stay with me.' He did—until the end of the match."

Snedeker birdied four of five holes to take a 2-up lead. That was still the margin with two holes to play.

Standing on the 17th tee, hearing the roars all around the golf course, Snedeker knew victory was at hand. A chill went through him and he thought about Arnold Palmer.

He had 173 yards to the flag and 165 yards to make sure he covered the hazard to the right of the green. He had an eight-iron in his hands. He looked at Scott Vail, his caddie.

"What do you think?" he asked.

Knowing how pumped up his player was, Vail said, "I think it's a nine-iron."

At that moment Snedeker thought, "What would Arnold Palmer do right now?"

He knew the answer. He grabbed his nine-iron, did everything Palmer would do except hitch up his pants, and hit a "sling-hook" that flew over the hazard and ended up six feet from the flag. "Maybe the best shot of my life," he said later.

Sullivan had to make birdie to have any chance at all. He missed the green right, then tried to chip in, the ball sliding 10 feet past the hole. Unless Snedeker, one of the best putters in the world, three-putted from six feet, the match was over. Sullivan took his cap off and offered his hand.

The U.S. led 14–10. The only question left was who would have the honor of clinching the Cup. Both Johnsons—Zach and Dustin—were closing in on wins. But just as he had come more or less out of nowhere to make the team, here came Ryan Moore.

Lee Westwood had played well again, not letting his late-Saturday failures affect him on Sunday. Through fifteen holes, he was 2 up, and it looked as if he would score a consolation point and leave the clinching to one of the Johnsons.

Except that Moore hit two excellent shots to reach the 16th green in two and then made the putt for eagle. He was one down. Then he hit an eight-iron to 15 feet on the 17th and drained that putt for a birdie. The match was even.

"I was back on 16, thinking Dustin was going to get the clincher," Jim Furyk said. "All of a sudden I looked up and Ryan had birdied 16 and 17, and all he needed to do was halve the 18th for us to win. I began sprinting in the direction of 18."

Most of the players on both teams who had finished their matches and the captains and vice captains were doing the same thing.

Moore, pumped up perhaps as he never had been, drilled his tee shot at 18 down the middle. Westwood's shot drifted right, into the fairway bunker. His second shot found the bunker to the right of the green. Moore's pitching wedge found the green, about 20 feet short of the flag.

It was ten minutes after four o'clock Central time on what was now a crisp, spectacular early fall day. Westwood had to hole his bunker shot for a birdie and hope Moore missed his putt, or the Ryder Cup would be over.

Westwood didn't come close. The only way for Moore to lose was to three-putt from 20 feet. That wasn't going to happen. He cozied the putt to within a foot of the flag. Westwood walked over, took his cap off, and put out his hand.

It was 4:11 p.m. The Ryder Cup was coming back to the United States.

Twenty-Five

AFTER DAVIS LOVE had walked onto the green to shake hands with Lee Westwood and wrap Ryan Moore in a lengthy hug, he noticed that Moore hadn't picked up his golf ball. He flashed back to 1993—his first Ryder Cup as a player—when he had made the six-foot putt on the 18th green at the Belfry to, in the words of Lanny Wadkins, put the Cup on the Concorde.

"I never picked that ball out of the cup that day because everyone stampeded me when the putt went in," he said. "All I was thinking about at that moment was that I hadn't shaken hands with Costantino [Rocca] and I had to get to him. I finally got free and caught him going off the green. But I never went back to get the ball."

As with Moore, there were still matches on the golf course that day at Belfry, so someone had removed the ball from the cup, but Love had no idea who it was and he'd never seen the ball again.

"I've always regretted it," Love said. "I wish I had that golf ball. So when I saw Ryan's ball lying there, I went over and picked it up. I tried to hand it to him, to tell him this was one he should keep. He shook his head and said, 'No, Captain, I want you to have it.' That was when I first started tearing up."

There were more tears to come, in spite of the quiet around the green. Jordan Spieth had been whooping it up with Phil Mickelson, Jim Mackay, and Rickie Fowler when he noticed that the thunderous noise he'd been hearing for three days had quieted—relatively speaking.

"For a minute I thought, 'Is the board wrong?'" he said. "Or maybe people don't know that we've won? It was confusing because it had been *so* loud for three days. But then I looked around and all our guys were hugging and all the Europeans were congratulating us."

Darren Clarke and Rory McIlroy were the first two Europeans to reach Love once he had completed his lengthy, tear-filled hug with Bubba Watson.

"It was a tough moment for me," Clarke said later. "All the work that had gone into it and, bottom line, we'd failed. My first goal as captain was to feel as if I had represented my team, my country, and my continent well. I believe I did that. But anytime you lose, especially on a stage that big, it's disappointing.

"That said, I was happy for Davis and I told him that. I knew how much Medinah had hurt him. It was a difficult moment for me, but it was softened by knowing how much it meant to my friend to win."

There were still three matches on the golf course, although two of them were quickly wrapping up. Zach Johnson closed out Matthew Fitzpatrick on 15, and soon after that, Dustin Johnson held off Chris Wood—who had quietly played well for Europe—to win one up. That made the score 17–10. It wasn't 20 points, but it was the most lopsided American victory since 1981—the second time all of Europe had been part of the matches—when the U.S. won 18½–9½.

Dustin Johnson's win left one match on the course: Matt Kuchar and Martin Kaymer. The latter had finally figured out what was wrong with his swing and played extremely well on the final day—not making a single bogey. Kuchar was actually 3 up after eight holes, but Kaymer rallied, winning three of the last five holes to win one up. Kuchar could certainly be forgiven for losing a little bit of steam once the Cup had been clinched.

"You start the day knowing your job is to win your point," Kaymer said. "It's tough to play when you know your team has lost, but you just keep grinding. It was probably tough for Matt too."

Kuchar wasn't going to make excuses. He didn't need to. The final score was 17–11. The U.S. had won the singles 7½–4½—which was the exact score Europe would have needed to win by in order to retain the Cup.

It took a while to get everyone to the back of the range for the trophy presentation. Until 2014, the final official moment of the Ryder Cup had been called the closing ceremony. But after the devastated American players had to sit through forty-five minutes of speeches at Medinah, the two sides had agreed to shorten the ceremony and to allow the losers to leave the podium when the winners' celebration began.

The Europeans were ready to make the walk to the back of the range almost as soon as Kuchar and Kaymer shook hands, but they had to wait for the Americans, who were standing on the bridge between the clubhouse and the range, pouring champagne on one another and on the adoring fans beneath them.

At one point, Phil Mickelson poured a huge swallow of champagne straight from the bottle down Jordan Spieth's throat.

"I saw it on tape later," Brandt Snedeker said. "It was almost as if Phil was passing the mantle on to Jordan at that moment. I can't imagine the joy and relief Phil was feeling. I know how I felt, but the way he'd put himself on the line, it had to be right up there with those five majors he keeps reminding all of us about."

Mickelson readily admitted that he felt complete joy—but not relief.

"No relief," he said. "I knew—*knew*—we were going to win. I never doubted it. I thought we had the better team; we were at home and Davis did a phenomenal job of making sure we were prepared to play our best. You're going to have ups and downs during those three days. Don't misunderstand me—they were good and they played some very good golf too. But I knew we were going to win.

"I plan to play more Ryder Cups. Jim [Furyk] and Tiger [Woods] may play in more of them too. But the time has come for the young guys to take leadership of this team. That's why it meant so much for Jordan to get up and speak to everyone the way he did on Thursday night."

The trophy presentation wasn't short—but it *was* shorter—and the Europeans didn't have to stay until the end. When the American team walked in, the European players and captains were the first ones to stand and applaud them. When the Europeans left, the Americans led the ovation.

It was, in all, very sweet.

"Can't wait till Paris," Rory McIlroy said later. "Even though we lost, I'm not sure I've enjoyed a week at a Ryder Cup more. It was just fun. I hated losing to Patrick [Reed], but I loved being part of the match. You get to feel things at Ryder Cup you don't get to feel anywhere else in golf."

While the Americans were still down on the range giving speeches, the Europeans came to the media center en masse.

They dealt with their defeat with grace and humor—lots of humor. Naturally the behavior of the fans—Spieth's one percenters—came up.

García threw out his line about knowing for sure now that he'd never won a major. Lee Westwood jumped in and said, "Look, the good news is, someone out there called me a turd yesterday. I haven't been called that since I was twelve. Made me feel young again."

It was left to Willett, though, to steal the show with four words. Asked if he could describe the experience of playing in his first Ryder Cup, Willett said, "Shit."

Asked if he could expand on that comment, Willett said, "Sure. Really shit."

"Pretty good summation, I'd say," Ian Poulter said later. "I thought it was brilliant."

So did everyone else. The entire European press conference was filled with warmth, humor, and grace. Everyone, from Clarke on down, made a point of saying the poor fan behavior had been a distinct minority and that the American players had gone out of their way on numerous occasions to try to stop it.

Appropriately, it was left to Love, after formally accepting the Cup from PGA president Derek Sprague, to have the final word—words—on the week.

"To quote Bobby Jones," he said, "'if I can take all the events of my life and have them this week in Minnesota, I'd be happy." Jones had won the third leg of his 1930 Grand Slam at Interlachen, seventeen miles east of where Love was standing.

He talked about how magical the week had been: the weather, the golf course, the fans, the people putting on the event, the Europeans, but most of all, his team.

And finally, he said: "I have a pretty good guess what Arnold Palmer would say about the 2016 Ryder Cup. And so, we all leave here with our heads held high and will gather again in twenty-four months."

Then he introduced the players who had allowed him to hold the seventeen-inch trophy he was gripping tightly as he spoke.

The sun was setting as the American team marched out—heading for a long night of celebration.

On to Paris.

Epilogue

B OTH TEAMS PARTIED deep into Sunday night and until close to dawn on Monday morning.

The Americans began with a gathering at the hotel in their upstairs team room that included only players and captains. They eventually moved downstairs to the larger team room and a much larger party.

"The place was really packed," Steve Stricker remembered. "It got to the point where it felt like there were a lot of people in the room who weren't part of the team."

That was when Robin Love politely asked those who really weren't part of the team—anyone who wasn't a player, a caddie, a captain or vice captain, or a wife or partner—to leave. Right to the end, even with the trophy in hand, you were either *us* or *them,* with no in between.

There was, to say the least, a lot of drinking in both team rooms.

At one point, Dustin Johnson and Phil Mickelson got into an argument about whether Mickelson could get out of a D.J. headlock

"No chance, dude," Johnson said, finding the notion almost laughable.

"Let's find out," Mickelson insisted.

Everyone gathered around and Mickelson tried to get loose. No luck. He insisted on trying again. No luck. Then, again. Same result.

"By the time it was over," Stricker said, "Phil looked pretty beat up. He had no shot."

That didn't deter Mickelson. Fueled by alcohol and ego, he kept insisting that *this* time he'd get loose.

"What can I tell you," Mickelson said. "I thought I could do it."

He couldn't.

Shortly after ten o'clock, Tiger Woods waved several players over for a chat. All week, he had worked closely with Jordan Spieth, Patrick Reed, Matt Kuchar, and Dustin Johnson. He had been their "pod captain." The four of them and Brandt Snedeker walked over to where Woods stood.

Standing in a corner of the room, he had a few outgoing words for them. None of the players remembered his exact words later, but they remembered the gist of the message and many, if not most, of the words. And the emotion in them.

"I want you guys to be sure to savor this," Woods said quietly, gesturing at the party going on around them. "Savor this night because no matter how many Ryder Cups you may play in or you may win, you'll never have a night quite like this.

"You will never be with this exact same group of people this way again. You need to enjoy every second of it and savor the memories."

Then he paused and got a little bit emotional. "After we won in '99 at Brookline, I was exhausted. I left the party at about ten thirty and went up to my room to bed. At about midnight, someone started pounding on my door. It was Payne [Stewart]. He said, 'You need to get your butt back downstairs.' I told him I was tired and he said to hell with that. You never know if you'll ever have a night like this again, and I *know* you'll never have another night like this with this group of people.

"He wasn't leaving without me. I went back downstairs. I can't tell you how glad I am that I did."

He didn't have to finish the rest of the story: a month later, Stewart was killed in a plane crash.

They all listened. It was later that they realized that Woods hadn't been a part of a winning Ryder Cup team since that year. Or part of a celebration like this one since that night.

It was closing in on eleven o'clock when Rory McIlroy suggested to Darren Clarke that it was time to go and pay tribute to the winners—to congratulate them and raise a glass with them.

Clarke and McIlroy led the way across the lobby to where the Americans were partying. When they walked in, Clarke found Love and said, "Your team room is a *lot* nicer than ours."

"Home-court advantage," Love said.

The first thing McIlroy noticed was what Love was wearing: a onesie that said "USA" on it. Rickie Fowler had brought a number of onesies for himself and the "USA" ones for the rest of the team. In victory—fueled by the alcohol—Love had agreed to wear one.

The second thing McIlroy noticed was the T-shirt Snedeker was wearing. "We'd all been given shirts at the beginning of the week that said 'Beat Europe' on them," Snedeker said. "When we got back to the hotel, I took mine, found a Sharpie, and wrote 'WE' on top of the 'Beat Europe.' Then I put it on."

When McIlroy saw the T-shirt, he reached into his pocket for a Sharpie of his own—golfers almost always carry a Sharpie in their pocket to be prepared to sign autographs—walked over to Snedeker, and, under the "WE Beat Europe," wrote, "For the first time in a decade!"

Ian Poulter was right behind him. He turned Snedeker around and, on the back of the shirt wrote, "I didn't hit a f—— shot!"

"I promise you that T-shirt is in a safe place," Snedeker said.

Someone found a microphone, and Clarke told everyone in the room what a great week it had been and how honored he had been to lead Europe and to compete with the U.S. Then everyone broke into small groups and the toasts and the alcohol flowed.

"I'm sure I had a great time," Lee Westwood said. "But I don't remember much about it."

McIlroy found Woods near the bar, and the two began to give each other putting lessons. Stricker and Furyk stood watching, enjoying the victory that they had all put so much work into.

"There was such a feeling of pride," Stricker said. "It wasn't just that we had won, although that was a big part of it, it was also the fact that we were genuinely close as a team. I've always been bothered by the fact that people said we didn't get along in the team room in the past and Europe did and that's why they won.

"I never felt that way. But the younger guys on this team were really friends—close friends. You could see that even before we got to Hazeltine, and it was such an important part of the week."

Woods and McIlroy gave up on trying to teach the other how to putt, and McIlroy found himself at the bar drinking shots with Sybi Kuchar.

"I lost, as best I can remember," McIlroy said. "The girl can drink."

Matt Kuchar, watching his wife and McIlroy, had his Kuchar grin firmly in place. "It was just nice to see Sybi so relaxed and to see the camaraderie between the two teams," he said. "I was loving it."

Midnight came and went. On one side of the patio, Snedeker, Dustin Johnson, Brooks Koepka, Spieth, Woods, and Notah Begay were smoking victory cigars.

"It was kind of funny to see Jordan smoking a cigar," Snedeker said.

At the other end of the patio, Mickelson, Clarke, and Love sat, drinks in hand, reliving past Ryder Cups. As Love listened to Mickelson and Clarke—two men bonded by far more than golf—he couldn't help but enjoy the moment.

"*That* might have been the highlight of the whole week for me," Love said. "Look, I'm a little corny sometimes, but I sat there listening to the two of them and I honestly thought to myself, '*This* is what Sam Ryder had in mind all those years ago,' a competition where the two teams fight like crazy to win and, when it's over, they go raise a pint to one another and share the experience.

"Think about it. Think about what Darren and Phil had been through together. Phil and Amy were there for Darren back in '06, and he was there for them when Amy got sick. There's a bond between them that no golf match can ever break.

"Of all the moments that week—and there were a lot of them—sitting there with the two of them is the memory I'll cherish the most."

Mickelson and Clarke felt pretty much the same way. "I don't think there are two men I respect more than I respect Davis and Phil," Clarke said. "They're very different, but all three of us share a lot in common.

"I remember at Medinah, when we got word the American players just couldn't deal with seeing all of us that night, we all understood completely. Then I looked up and there was Davis, coming to the room because he felt, as the captain, he had to come in and congratulate us. He's such a class act—in victory, in defeat—all the time. Of all the people I've known, no one has ever put others ahead of himself more than Davis.

"He stood up and talked to all of us briefly that night—which is what inspired me to do the same at Hazeltine. When he was finished [on that

Sunday night at Medinah], I walked over to him, put my arm around him, and said, 'What the hell were you thinking today with that lineup?'

"He looked at me for a second, and then he realized I was joking and he started to laugh. That's what I wanted that night—to see him laugh. I knew how devastated he was. I wanted to try to lighten the load a little bit."

Now, four years later, they all laughed well into the night, and at last the Europeans made their final rounds to say congratulations again and headed back to their own (smaller) team room.

The players had planned one final surprise for Clarke.

One of the many images he had brought to Hazeltine for inspiration was a ten-foot-by-five-foot poster he had found in an Irish dance hall. It depicted a dozen men with their arms linked—shoulder to shoulder—Clarke's theme for the entire week.

The players had taken it down after the matches, and all twelve of them and the five vice captains had signed it, each with a little message of gratitude for their captain. Now when they returned, with dawn only a few hours away, they presented it to Clarke.

The vice captains made the presentation, and McIlroy spoke for the team, telling Clarke how much they appreciated the work he'd done for two years and the leadership he'd provided throughout the week.

Clarke had very little to say when he was handed the poster—because he was too choked up. Then his players surrounded him, locked arms—shoulder to shoulder—and sang: "Olé, Olé, Olé—Olé, Olé, O-oh-lé."

Their voices echoed into the early morning—all singing at the top of their lungs—as the losing captain in the 2016 Ryder Cup wept . . . for joy.

Acknowledgments

Once again I have written a book that requires acknowledgments almost as long as the book itself. This happens often and for very good reason: without the people listed in the next few pages, there would be no book.

Let me begin with those who willingly gave me not just time but the kind of insight I was looking for when I began my research, fourteen months out from the start of the 2016 Ryder Cup.

I have to start with the two captains: it's not a coincidence that the introduction of this book begins with a Davis Love III anecdote. Davis has been both a resource and a friend since the early days of my research for *A Good Walk Spoiled*. His patience in dealing with me through the years has been remarkable. After we had spent two hours together at the 2015 PGA Championship, he stood up and said, "Well, I guess this is just the first of many."

I doubt he had any idea *how* many, including me peppering him with last-second questions right through the copyediting of the book. He never once failed to respond.

I did *not* know Darren Clarke very well when I began my research, but I do now—probably much better than he dreamed when he first sat down with me. Like Davis, Darren was patient and honest and, as you can probably tell if you've just finished the book, he supplied me with stories that were poignant and funny and that gave me a wonderful inside look at his life, his preparation, and the week.

The vice captains of both sides were also helpful, especially Jim Furyk, Steve Stricker, Bubba Watson, and Tom Lehman on the American side and Ian Poulter, Padraig Harrington, and Sam Torrance on the European side. No, Tiger Woods didn't talk to me (surprise), but as you read the book I'm sure you will find that everyone else on the American side was willing to share stories about him that certainly surprised me and I suspect will surprise you.

The players also came through—big-time. On the European team, I'm especially grateful to Rory McIlroy, Justin Rose, Danny Willett, Martin Kaymer, Henrik Stenson, Sergio García, and Lee Westwood. Extra kudos to McIlroy for—like Love—answering repeated loop-back questions during the writing process, to Stenson for being so damn funny (cheeky), and to Willett for being willing to share his feelings about what had to have been the worst week of his professional career.

Among the Americans, I had lengthy sit-downs—most on more than one occasion—with Jordan Spieth, Patrick Reed—who is a *lot* more engaging than people give him credit for—Brandt Snedeker, Matt Kuchar, Phil Mickelson, Rickie Fowler, Brooks Koepka, Dustin Johnson, Zach Johnson, and Jimmy Walker. Mickelson was willing to answer sometimes tough questions about his dustup with Tom Watson at Gleneagles both before and after the U.S. victory at Hazeltine. Kuchar and Snedeker are natural storytellers. Spieth may have less ego than any truly great player I've ever met.

There were also a number of players who sat down with me knowing they might not play in 2016 but were willing, nevertheless, to share their past experiences and their hopes for the year. They included Keegan Bradley, Justin Thomas, Graeme McDowell, Luke Donald, Webb Simpson, Bill Haas, Jason Dufner, and Billy Horschel.

Thanks also to 2014 captains Paul McGinley and Tom Watson. I can assure you that reliving Gleneagles and all that came with it was not Watson's favorite thing to do, but, as usual, he did it, unblinking and as honest as ever. Thanks also to Paul Azinger, who provided me with a good deal of understanding about why his U.S. team was able to win in 2008 and why others failed.

I received remarkable aid from those who work for the PGA of America, including CEO Pete Bevacqua, former president Ted Bishop (whose book *Unfriended*—a brilliant title—gave me a good deal of information and insight on what led to his downfall), Bob Denny, Una Jones, John Dever, and, last but certainly not least, Julius Mason. I sincerely doubt Julius had *any* clue what he was getting into when I first told him I was writing this book. Yet because he is the grooviest guy in golf, he never once snapped *"Make it stop!"* as my questions and requests came in to him.

Richard Hills, Europe's Ryder Cup chairman, patiently answered questions throughout, and my pal—and occasional roomie—Ken Schofield was a guide throughout. So was NBC/Golf Channel's Mark Rolfing, who I believe knows more about the Ryder Cup than almost anyone alive.

I made some new friends and got reacquainted with some old ones in Minnesota. Chandler Withington, the pro at Hazeltine—in spite of his allegiance to the New York Rangers—could not possibly have been more helpful; same for superintendent Chris Tritabaugh. They were two of the unsung heroes of the week. Reed MacKenzie, past Hazeltine and USGA president, is an old friend, and he was, as always, extremely helpful. So too were the mayor of Chaska, Chris Windschitl, and the club's chairman of the event, Patrick Hunt. None of these people ever ducked a question or denied a request. Chandler even forgave me for showing up the Sunday before the week began in an Islanders sweatshirt. (It was really cold.)

It is fair to say that this book would not have been written if not for Jack Nicklaus. After all, it was Nicklaus who convinced both sides to include, beginning in 1979, all of Europe instead of just Great Britain and Ireland as the U.S. opponent. That idea and its execution probably saved the Ryder Cup and led to its becoming the massive event it is today. As always, I thank Jack for sitting down and patiently answering all my questions—and I'm also grateful that his memory is still as sharp as ever. Thanks also to his saintlike wife, Barbara, and his right-hand man Scott Tolley.

I don't often thank agents; I usually curse them. But in the case of this book, because there were some players who just didn't know me very well, I needed help in setting up first interviews with a number of them. I'm especially grateful to Chubby Chandler and his crew at ISM, who helped get me in contact with Darren Clarke, Danny Willett, and Lee Westwood. Chubby is very much a character in his own right, but my saviors on his staff were Martin Hardy and Graham Chase. They were both, as the English like to say, "brilliant."

David Winkle got Dustin Johnson, often a reluctant interview, to sit down with me at length. Jay Danzi, who was juggling more requests than anyone on earth in the summer of 2015—he's Jordan Spieth's agent—got the first interview set up and then let Jordan take it from there. I'm grateful. There were others: Carlos Rodriguez and Irek Myskow—both work with Sergio García. I actually *like* them. Never thought I'd say that about an agent. Brad Buffoni was great helping me hook up with Zach Johnson. The same goes for Sean O'Flaherty—I actually like him too—with Rory McIlroy. Colin Morrissey and I got off to a rocky start, but I credit him with coming straight to me when he got angry, which gave us a chance to iron things out.

This is my thirty-eighth book. Esther Newberg has negotiated every contract and played the bad guy—she loves it—whenever there have been issues each and every time. We've known each other for thirty-two years! And she still hasn't fired me. Amazing. Her recently promoted (richly deserved) assistant at ICM, Zoe Sandler, was always a joy to work with. So too are John Delaney, who lawyers every contract; Liz Farrell, who keeps coming up with audio deals for me; and Kari Stuart, who will be having twins right about the time this book is published.

At Doubleday: Jason Kaufman and Bill Thomas have provided constant support and ideas for three books now; Rob Bloom has also moved on to greener pastures; and Carolyn Williams is learning to put up with my sense of humor. Never easy.

And then there are my friends who are constants, listening to me whine and complain as I push through each book. If you have read me in the past, many of these names will be familiar:

Keith and Barbie Drum, Jackson Diehl and Jean Halperin, David and Linda Maraniss, Bob Woodward and Elsa Walsh, Sally Jenkins, Dan Jenkins, Lexie Verdon and Steve Barr, Terry and Patti Hanson, Doug and Beth Doughty, Andy Dolich, Wes Seeley, Pete Alfano, David Teel, Gary Cohen, Bethy Shumway-Brown, Beth Sherry-Downes, Pete Van Poppel, Frank DaVinney, Omar Nelson, Mike Werteen (still the best hoops line producer I ever worked with), Phil Hoffmann, Joe Speed, Andrew Thompson, Gordon Austin, Eddie Tapscott, Chris Knoche, Steve (Moose) Stirling, Tim Kelly, Dick Hall, Anthony and Kristen Noto, Derek Klein, Jim Cantelupe, Bob Sutton, Bob Zurfluh, Vivian Thompson-Goldstein, Tony and Karril Kornheiser, Mike Wilbon, Nancy Denlinger, Governor Harry Hughes, General Steve Sachs—and Sheila, Tim Maloney, Chris Ryan, Harry Kantarian, Jim Rome, Mike Purkey, Bob Edwards, Tom and Jane Goldman, Mik Gastineau, Dick and Joanie (Hoops) Weiss, Jim O'Connell, Holland and Jill Mickle, Jerry Tarde, Mike O'Malley, Larry Dorman (with special thanks for doing an early edit on this book), Marsha Edwards, Jay Edwards, Chris Edwards and John Cutcher, Len and Gwyn Edwards-Dieterle, Bill Leahey, Andy North, Paul Goydos, Steve Flesch, Olin Brown, John Cook, Billy Andrade, Gary "Grits" Crandall, Drew Miceli, Brian Henninger, and Tom and Hilary Watson. Special thanks to Tom Stathakes—again.

Thanks to my friends and colleagues at Golf Channel: Matt Hegarty, Kristi Setaro, Eric Rutledge, David Gross, Molly Solomon, Geoff Russell, Mike McCarley, Mark Summer, Adam Hertzog, Kory Kozak, Jon Steele, Tony Grbac (talk about unsung heroes), Courtney Holt, Kelly Tilghman, Andrew Bradley, Alan Robison, Brandel Chamblee, Rich Lerner, Ryan Burr, Whit Watson, Tim Rosaforte, Notah Begay, Lisa Cornwell, Gary Williams, Damon Hack, Tripp Isenhour, George Savaricas, Jay Coffin, Rex Hoggard, Randall Mell, Steve Burkowski, Justin Leonard, Billy Kratzert, David Duval, the one and only Todd Lewis, Don Cross, and a special shout-out to Frank Nobilo. I would tell one of Frank's jokes here, but that might delay the book's publication.

Thanks also to the many people it takes to get me on-camera (trust me, it's not easy): John Feyko, Julie Hoddy, Mike Davis, Brian Thorne, Tom Forrest, Robert (Swanny) Swanson, Tim Jungel, Jared Parfaite, and Rasheen Crawley.

At CBS Sports Radio: Andrew Bogusch, gone-(to-Canada)-but-*not*-forgotten Max Herman, Pete Bellotti, Dave Mayurnik, Mark Chernoff, Eric Spitz, Anthony Pierno, Billy Giacalone, and, in absentia, Mike Diaz.

At SiriusXM: Scott Greenstein, Steve Cohen, Chris Spatola, Tom Brennan, Jeremy Davis, Jon Albanese, Davis Williams, and (Minnesota) Tim Parochka.

At *The Washington Post*—in addition to those mentioned before: Matt Vita, Matt Rennie, Matt Bonesteel (seriously, the all-Matt team), David Larimer, Marty Weil, Mark Maske, Gene Wang, and Kathy Orton.

Others scattered across the sports world: David Fay, Mike Davis, Mary Lopuszynski, Pete Kowalski, Craig Smith. U.S. Open week isn't the same without Frank and Jaymie Bussey. Other golf people: Tim West (who has a hat); Marty Caffey, Henry Hughes and Sid Wilson (united forever), Joel Schuchmann, Todd Budnick, Dave Senko, Doug Milne, Chris Reimer, Colin Murray, John Bush, Laura Hill, Tracey Veale, James Carmer, Joe Chemyz, Phil Stambaugh, Dave Lancer, Ward

Clayton, and Guy Scheipers. No idea how I will manage going forward without Denise Taylor, whose retirement is more than well deserved.

The rules guys: Mark, Laura, and Alex Russell; and Slugger White. I hope you are forgiven your sins in the next life. Also: Steve Rintoul, Jon Brendle (emeritus), Robbie Ware, Dillard Pruitt, the great John Paramour, and Stephen Cox—go West, Brom!

More hoops people: Mike and Mickie Krzyzewski, Gary Williams, Roy Williams, David Stern (commish for life in my world, no offense to Adam Silver), Tim Frank, Brian McIntyre, Lefty and Joyce Driesell, Seth and Brad Greenberg, Jim Calhoun, Brad Stevens, Shaka Smart, Billy Donovan, Larry Shyatt, Dave Odom, Lynne Odom and Ryan Odom, Jim Larranaga, Mack McCarthy, Pat Flannery, Nathan Davis, Ralph Willard, Fran O'Hanlon (last man standing), Jim Crews, Zach Spiker, Pat Skerry, Emmett Davis, Ed DeChellis, Jimmy Allen, Billy Lange, and Tony Shaver. Frank Sullivan is still *the* best.

Others at Army and Navy: Boo Corrigan, Rich DeMarco, Dean Darling, John Minko, Joe Beckerle, Bob Beretta, Jeff Monken, Chet Gladchuk, Scott Strasemeier, Stacy Michaux, Justin Kishefski, and the most underrated coach in football, Ken Niamatulolo.

Docs—still a long list, even though, fortunately, most of our contact recently has been as friends: Eddie and Amy McDevitt, Dean and Ann Taylor, Bob Arciero, Gus Mazzocca, Murray Lieberman, Steve Boyce, and Joe Vassallo. As I write this, it is almost eight years to the day since the last two saved my life.

In a category all his own: Tom Konchalski, the only honest man in the gym—seriously.

The swimming knuckleheads, who, like me, keep getting older and slower—except for Jeff Roddin. The rest: Jason Crist, Clay F. Britt, Wally Dicks, Mark Pugliese, Paul Doremus, Danny Pick, Erik (Dr. Post) Osbourne, John Craig, Doug Chestnut, Peter Ward, Penny Bates, Carole Kammel, Mary Dowling, Margot Pettijohn, Tom Denes, A. J. Block, Peter Lawler, and Mike (three-timer) Fell.

The China Doll/Shanghai Village gang: Aubre Jones, Jack Kvanz, Stanley Copeland, Reid Collins, Harry Huang, George Solomon, Geoff Kaplan, Joe McKeown, Pete Dowling, Bob Campbell, Joe Greenberg, Morgan Wootten, Jack Kvancz, Jeff Gemunder and Lou Flashenberg. Gone but certainly not forgotten—*ever*—Red, Zang, Hymie, Rob, and Arnie.

The Rio Gang, where we have agreed *not* to talk politics: Tate Armstrong (who is bearable), Mark Alarie, Clay Buckley, and Terry Chili—not bearable.

The Feinstein advisory board: Dave Kindred, Keith Drum, Frank Mastrandrea, and, of course, Bill Brill.

As you get older, the list of those you miss gets longer. Since *The Legends Club,* I have lost too many close friends: Bud Collins, whose death was so difficult I couldn't face the media room at the U.S. Open tennis last fall; Jack Hecker, who played such an important role in making the fall of '95 enjoyable at Army and remained a close friend; the one and only Howard Garfinkel, the most Runyonesque character I've ever known. *If* he gets to heaven, I hope God will grant him a winning horse or two—unlike when he was on earth.

And, finally, Joan Walsh, who lived ninety-four amazing years. She was Bruce Edwards's aunt and one of the most wonderful people I ever met. I *loved* the way she went after her brother Jay—Bruce's dad—when he started spouting his completely ridiculous political opinions.

Almost last, certainly not least, my family: Bobby, Jennifer, Matthew, and Brian; Margaret, David, Ethan, and Ben; Marylnn, Cheryl, and Marcia.

And most of all—as always—the four people I cherish every day: Danny, without whom I could not have written this book; Brigid, of whom I am so proud as she goes on to college; Jane, who gets cuter and funnier and smarter every day; and Christine, who somehow puts up with me, a fact for which I am grateful every single moment.